DARK SHADOWS™

VAMPIRELLA®

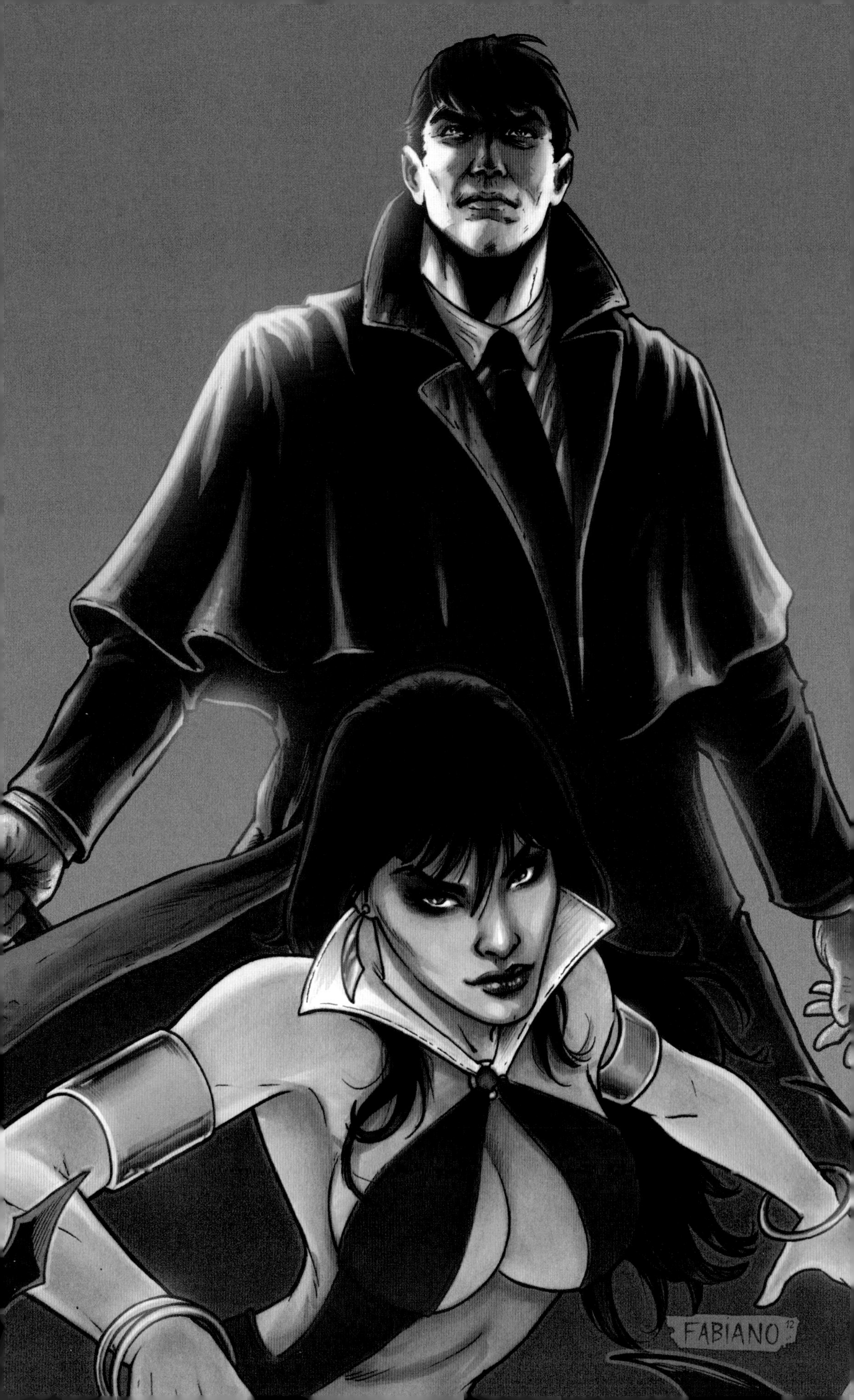

FABIANO '12

DARK SHADOWS™

VAMPIRELLA®

Written by:
MARC ANDREYKO

Illustrated by:
PATRICK BERKENKOTTER (issues 1-2)
& JOSE MALAGA (issues 3-5)

Colored by:
THIAGO DAL BELLO

Lettered by:
TROY PETERI

Covers by:
FABIANO NEVES

Special thanks to JIM PIERSON

DYNAMITE®

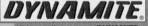

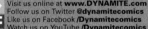

Visit us online at **www.DYNAMITE.com**
Follow us on Twitter **@dynamitecomics**
Like us on Facebook **/Dynamitecomics**
Watch us on YouTube **/Dynamitecomics**

Nick Barrucci, CEO / Publisher
Juan Collado, President / COO
Joe Rybandt, Senior Editor
Josh Johnson, Art Director
Rich Young, Director Business Development
Jason Ullmeyer, Senior Graphic Designer
Josh Green, Traffic Coordinator
Chris Caniano, Production Assistant

COMIC SHOP LOCATOR SERVICE
888-COMIC-BOOK
comicshoplocator.com

First Printing
ISBN-10: 1-60690-395-0
ISBN-13: 978-1-60690-395-7
10 9 8 7 6 5 4 3 2 1

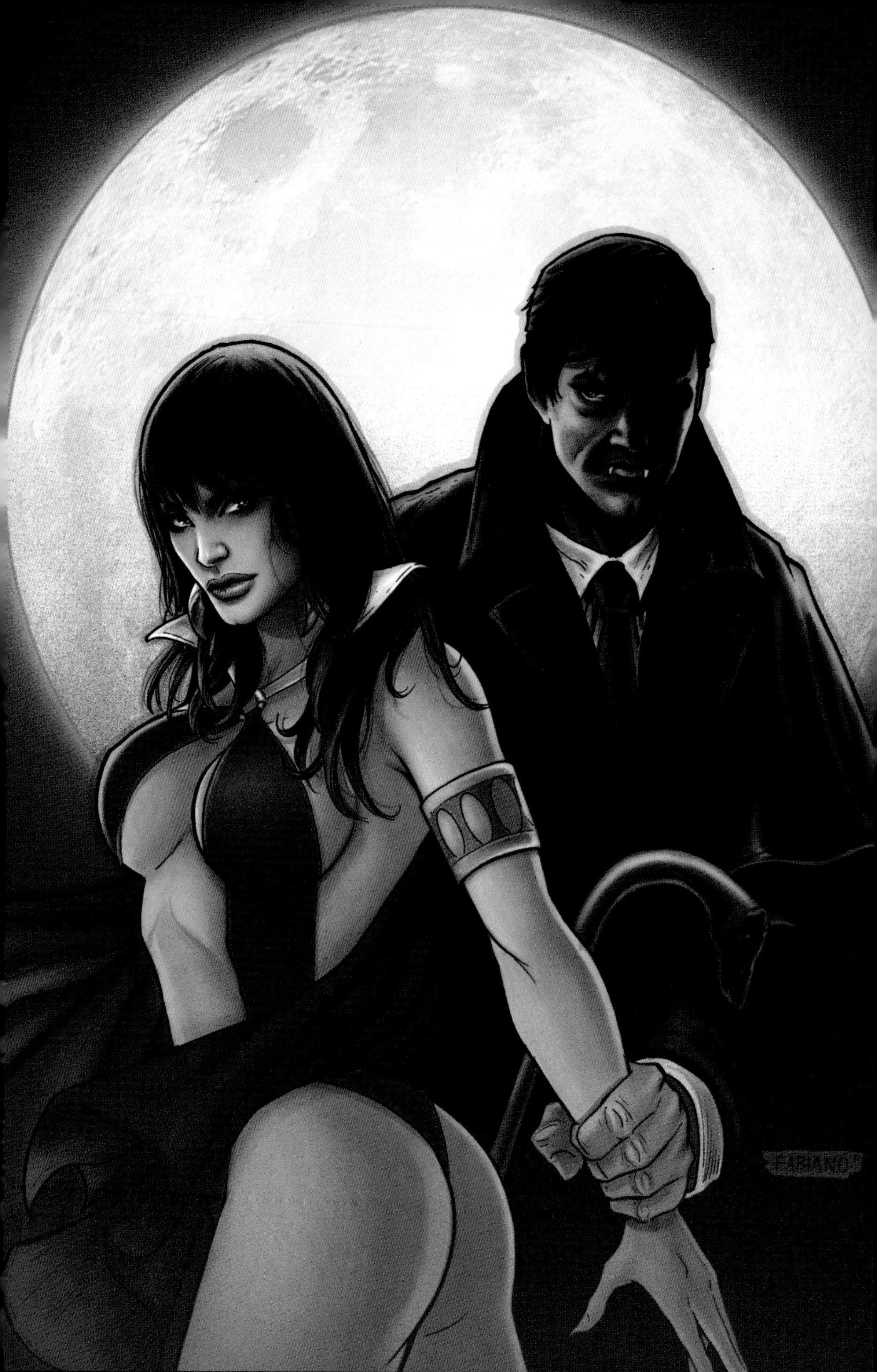
FABIANO

ISSUE #1 COVER BY FABIANO NEVES

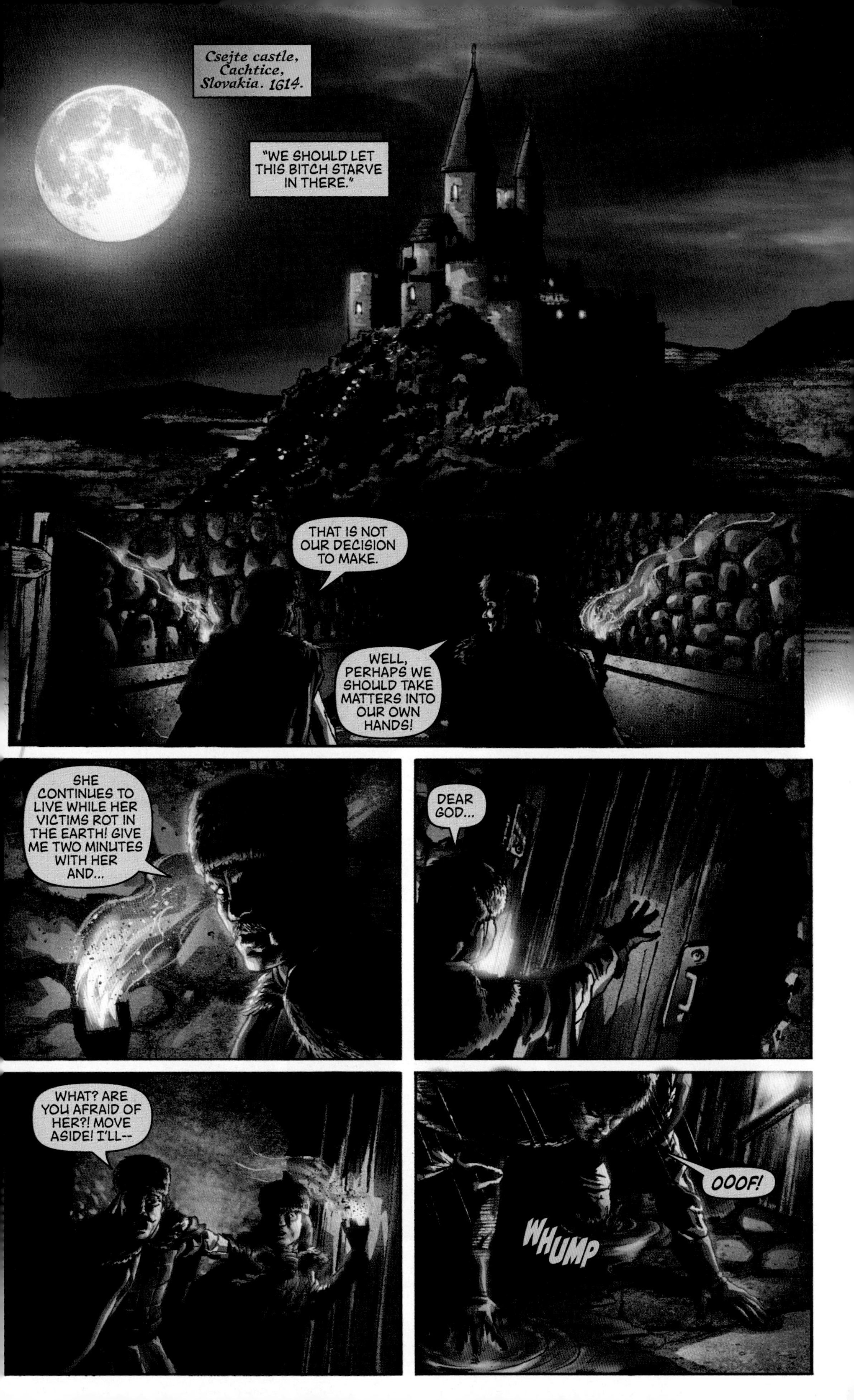
Csejte castle, Cachtice, Slovakia. 1614.
"WE SHOULD LET THIS BITCH STARVE IN THERE."
THAT IS NOT OUR DECISION TO MAKE.
WELL, PERHAPS WE SHOULD TAKE MATTERS INTO OUR OWN HANDS!
SHE CONTINUES TO LIVE WHILE HER VICTIMS ROT IN THE EARTH! GIVE ME TWO MINUTES WITH HER AND...
DEAR GOD...
WHAT? ARE YOU AFRAID OF HER?! MOVE ASIDE! I'LL--
OOOF!
WHUMP

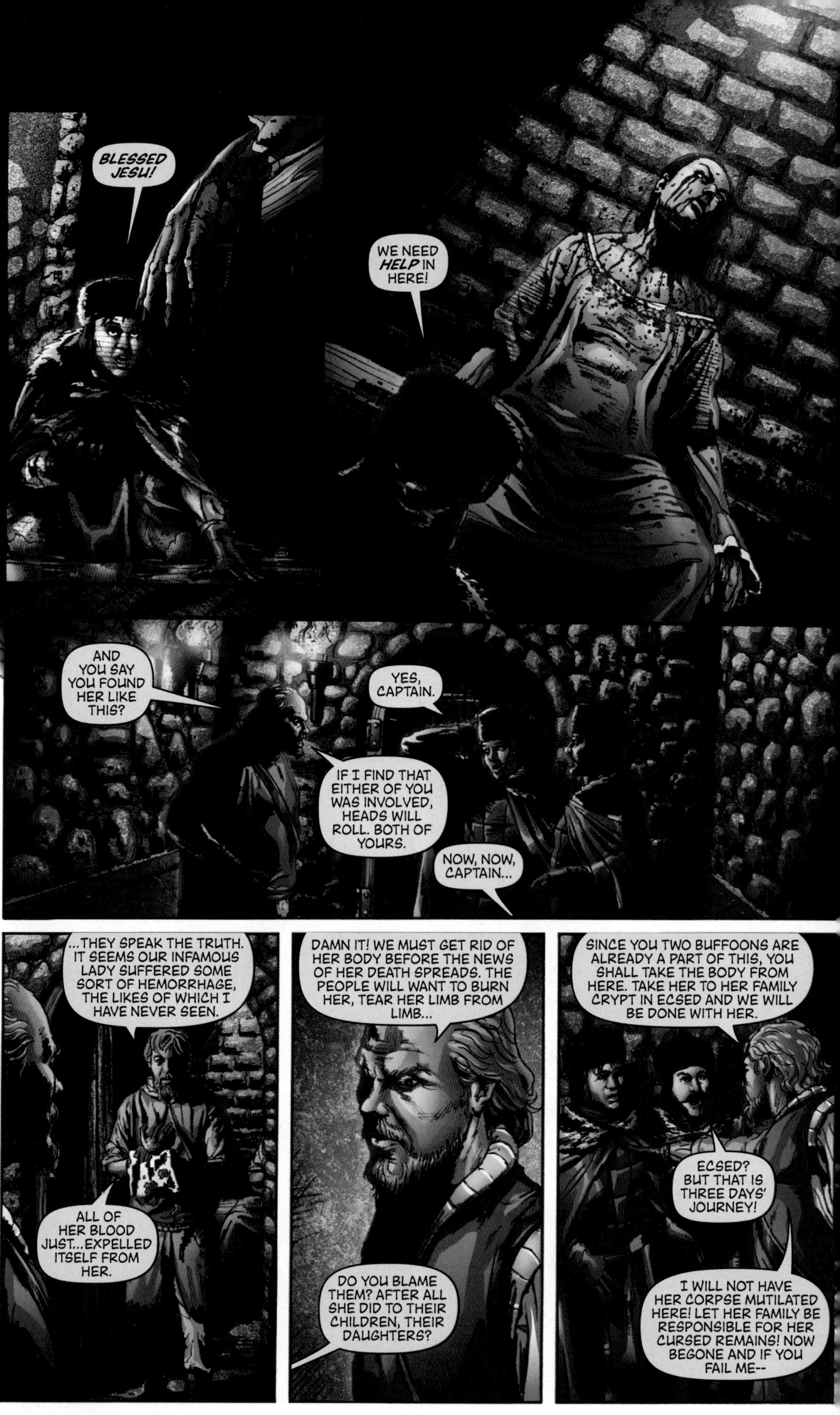
BLESSED JESU!
WE NEED HELP IN HERE!
AND YOU SAY YOU FOUND HER LIKE THIS?
YES, CAPTAIN.
IF I FIND THAT EITHER OF YOU WAS INVOLVED, HEADS WILL ROLL. BOTH OF YOURS.
NOW, NOW, CAPTAIN...
...THEY SPEAK THE TRUTH. IT SEEMS OUR INFAMOUS LADY SUFFERED SOME SORT OF HEMORRHAGE, THE LIKES OF WHICH I HAVE NEVER SEEN.
ALL OF HER BLOOD JUST...EXPELLED ITSELF FROM HER.
DAMN IT! WE MUST GET RID OF HER BODY BEFORE THE NEWS OF HER DEATH SPREADS. THE PEOPLE WILL WANT TO BURN HER, TEAR HER LIMB FROM LIMB...
DO YOU BLAME THEM? AFTER ALL SHE DID TO THEIR CHILDREN, THEIR DAUGHTERS?
SINCE YOU TWO BUFFOONS ARE ALREADY A PART OF THIS, YOU SHALL TAKE THE BODY FROM HERE. TAKE HER TO HER FAMILY CRYPT IN ECSED AND WE WILL BE DONE WITH HER.
ECSED? BUT THAT IS THREE DAYS' JOURNEY!
I WILL NOT HAVE HER CORPSE MUTILATED HERE! LET HER FAMILY BE RESPONSIBLE FOR HER CURSED REMAINS! NOW BEGONE AND IF YOU FAIL ME--

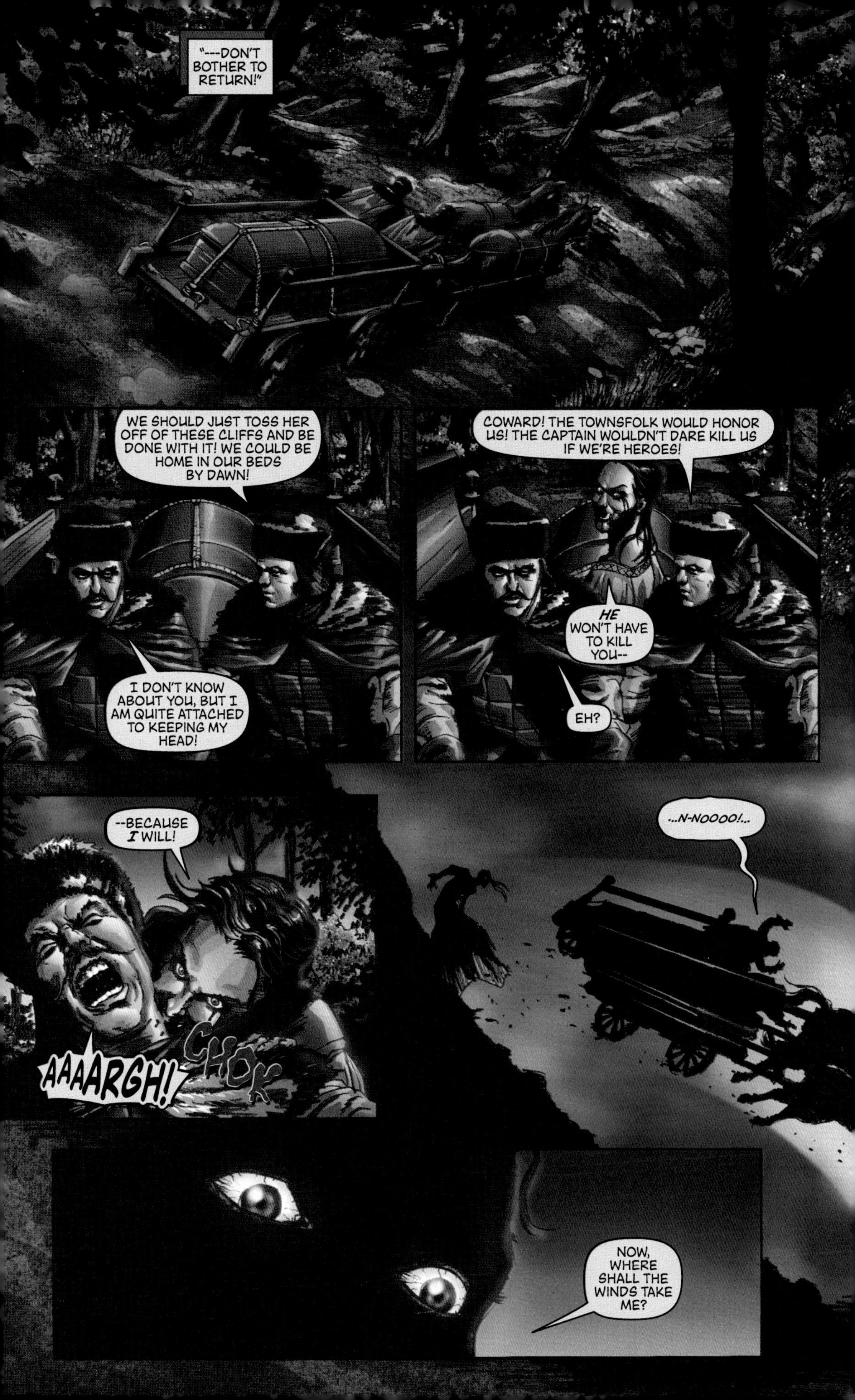
"---DON'T BOTHER TO RETURN!"
WE SHOULD JUST TOSS HER OFF OF THESE CLIFFS AND BE DONE WITH IT! WE COULD BE HOME IN OUR BEDS BY DAWN!
I DON'T KNOW ABOUT YOU, BUT I AM QUITE ATTACHED TO KEEPING MY HEAD!
COWARD! THE TOWNSFOLK WOULD HONOR US! THE CAPTAIN WOULDN'T DARE KILL US IF WE'RE HEROES!
HE WON'T HAVE TO KILL YOU--
EH?
--BECAUSE I WILL!
AAAARGH!
CHOK
...N-NOOOO!...
NOW, WHERE SHALL THE WINDS TAKE ME?

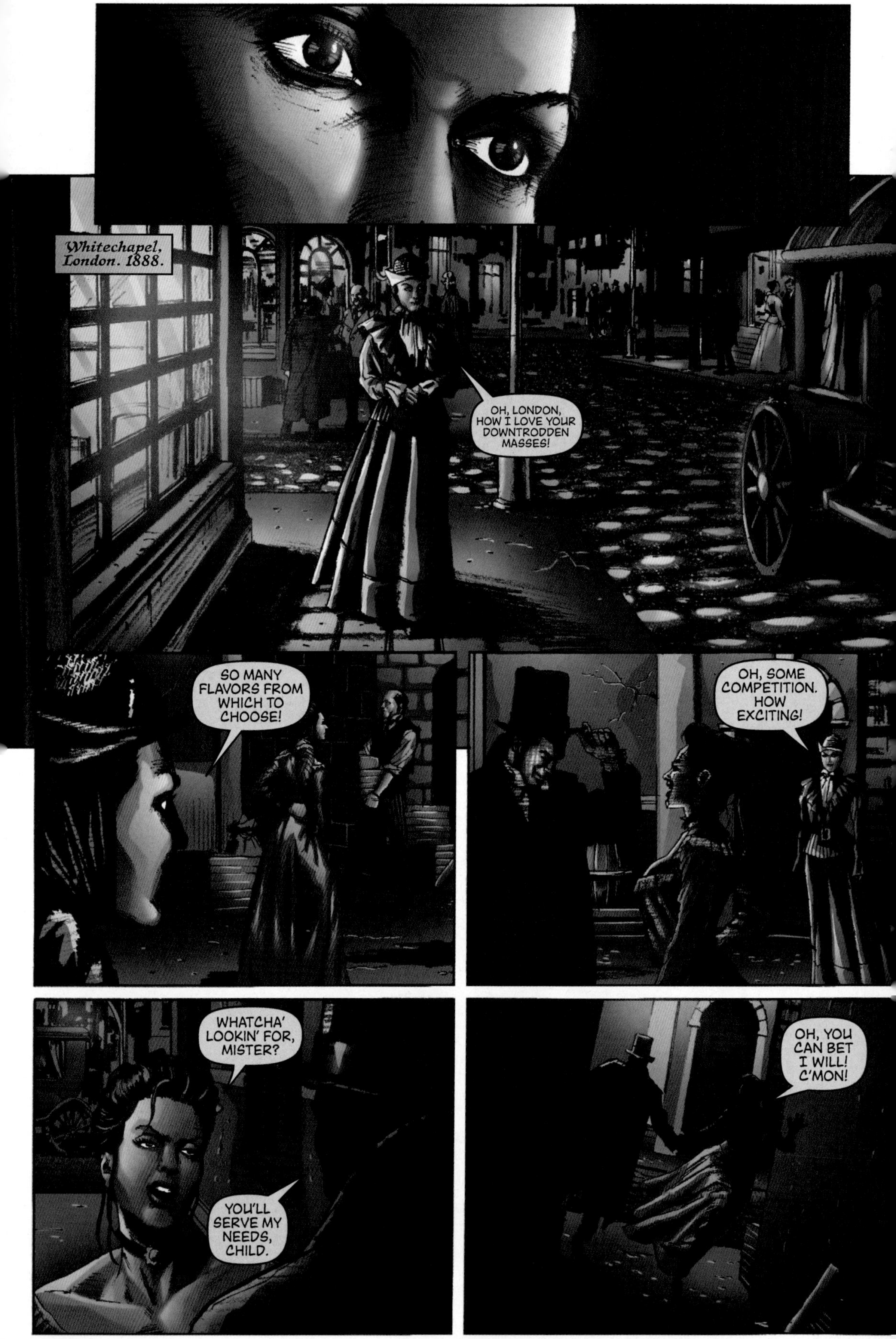
Whitechapel, London. 1888.
OH, LONDON, HOW I LOVE YOUR DOWNTRODDEN MASSES!
SO MANY FLAVORS FROM WHICH TO CHOOSE!
OH, SOME COMPETITION. HOW EXCITING!
WHATCHA' LOOKIN' FOR, MISTER?
YOU'LL SERVE MY NEEDS, CHILD.
OH, YOU CAN BET I WILL! C'MON!

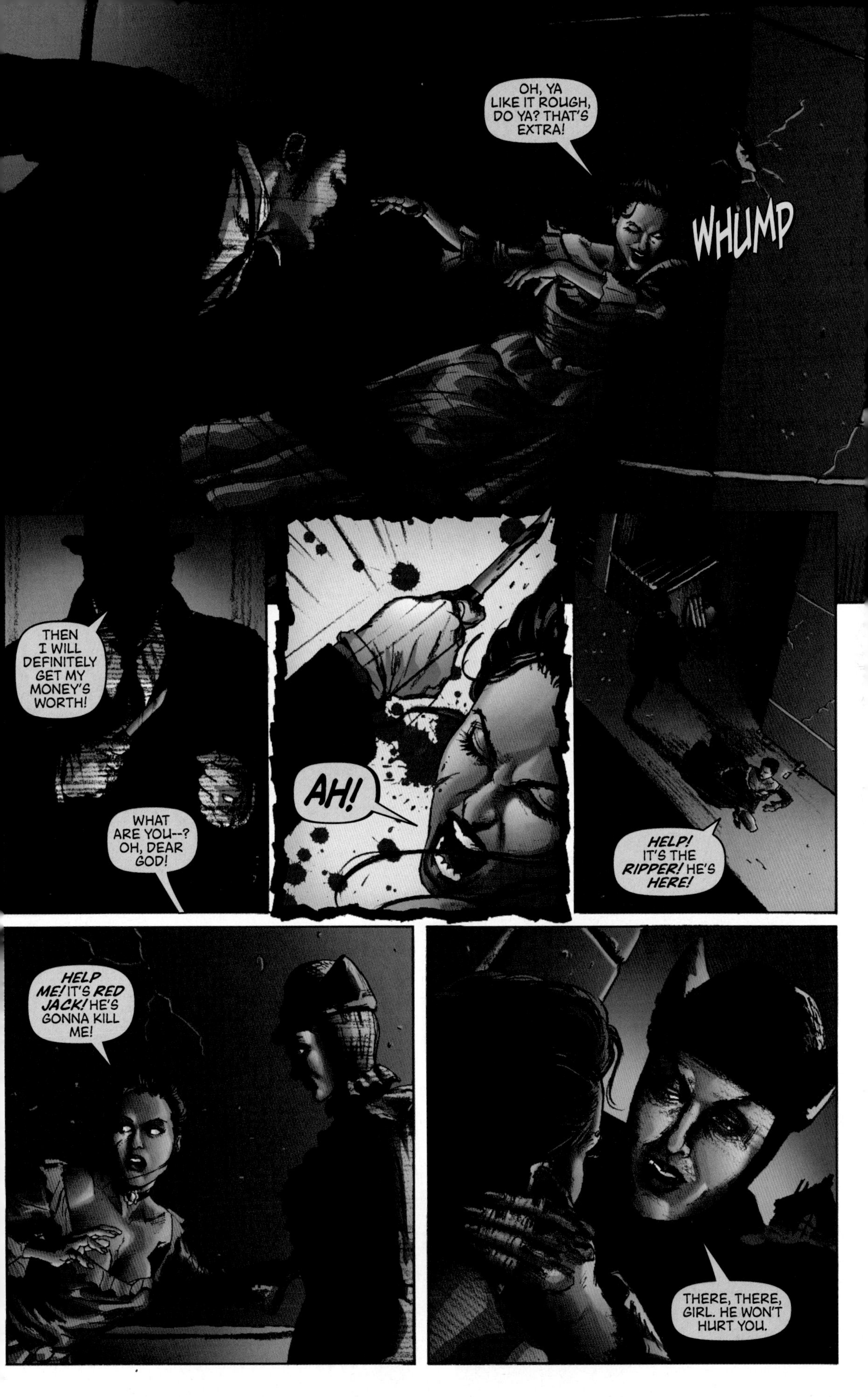
OH, YA LIKE IT ROUGH, DO YA? THAT'S EXTRA!
WHUMP
THEN I WILL DEFINITELY GET MY MONEY'S WORTH!
WHAT ARE YOU--? OH, DEAR GOD!
AH!
HELP! IT'S THE RIPPER! HE'S HERE!
HELP ME! IT'S RED JACK! HE'S GONNA KILL ME!
THERE, THERE, GIRL. HE WON'T HURT YOU.

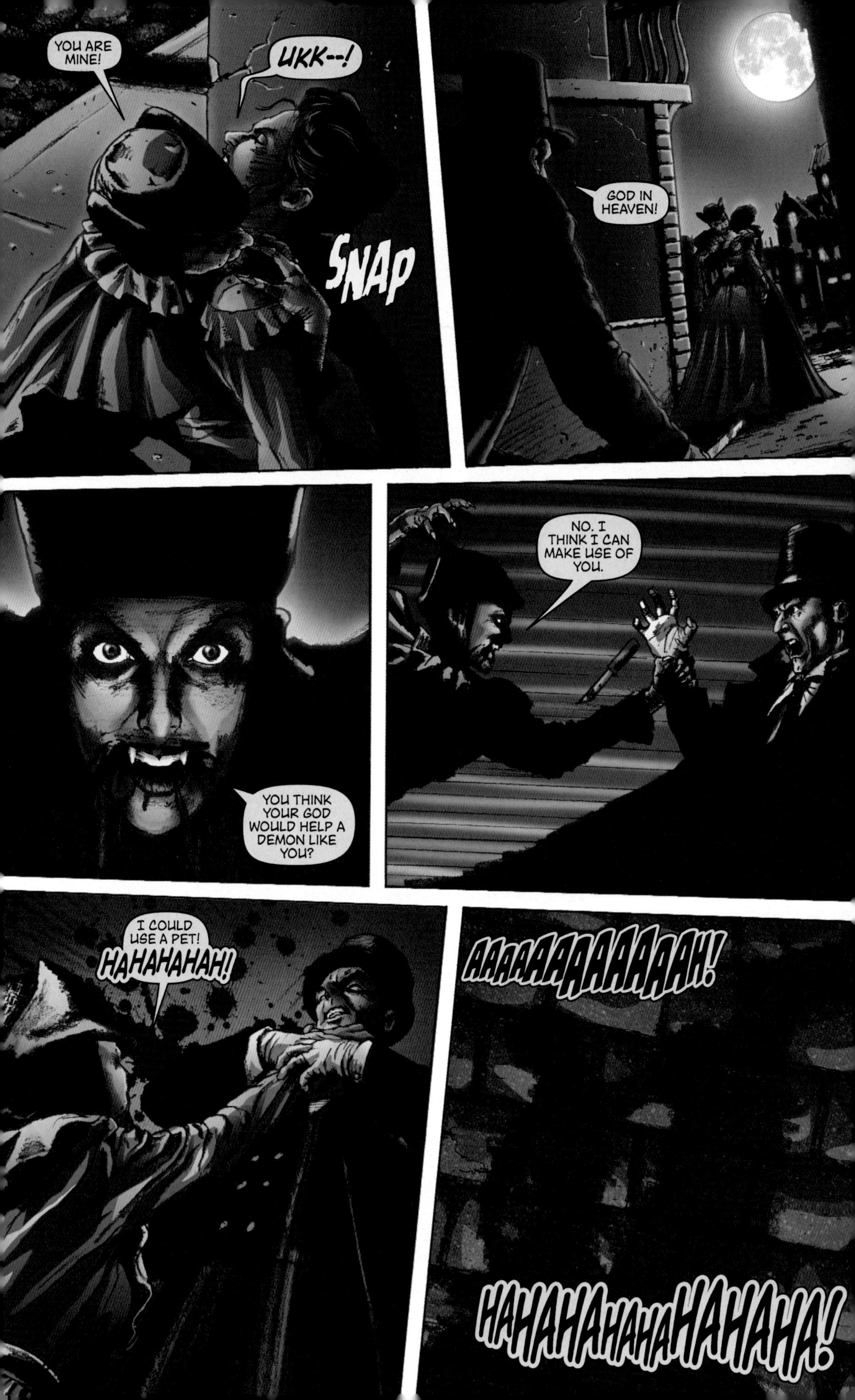
YOU ARE MINE!
UKK--!
SNAP
GOD IN HEAVEN!
YOU THINK YOUR GOD WOULD HELP A DEMON LIKE YOU?
NO. I THINK I CAN MAKE USE OF YOU.
I COULD USE A PET! HAHAHAHAH!
AAAAAAAAAAAAAH!
HAHAHAHAHAHAHAHAHA!

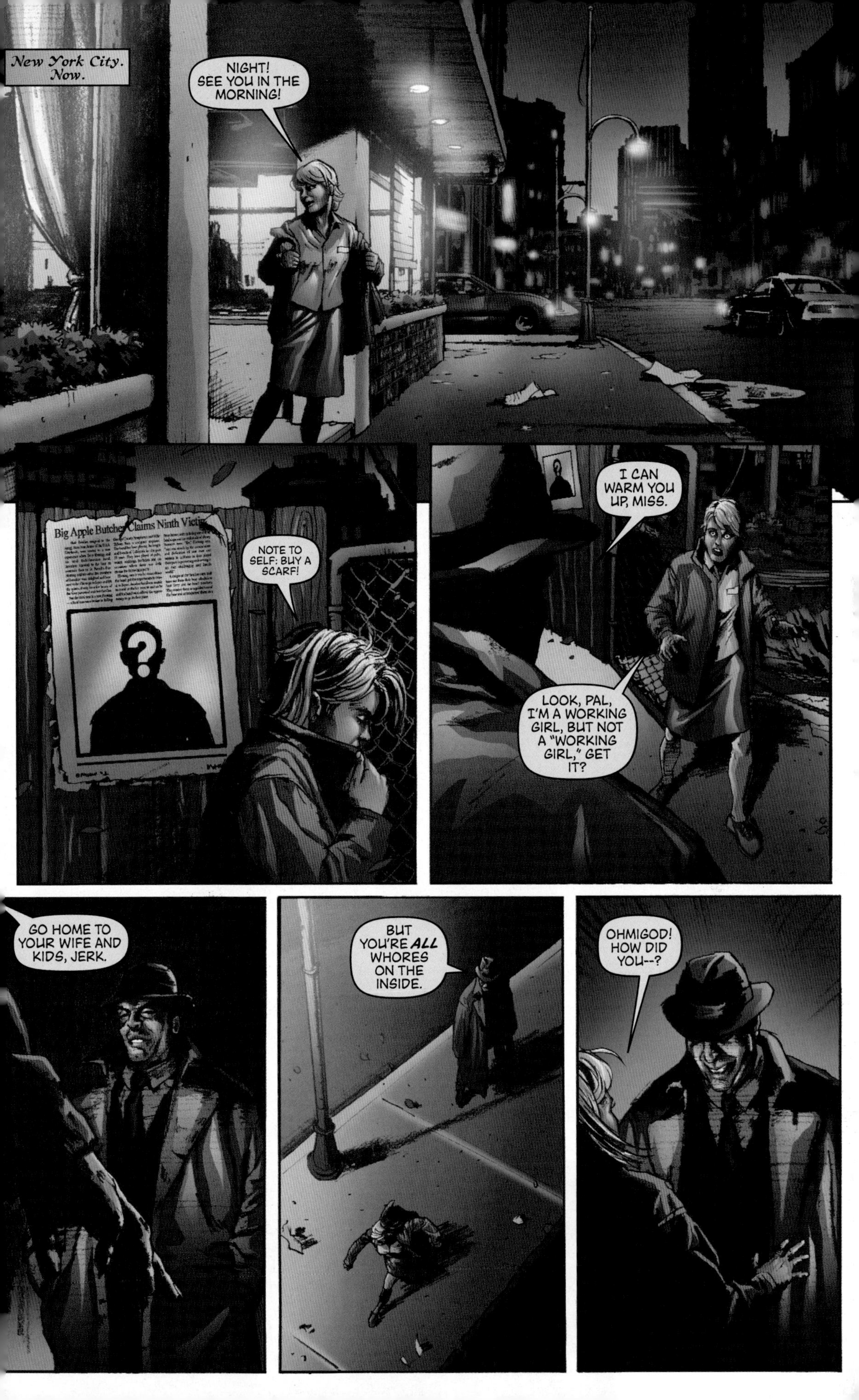

New York City. Now.
NIGHT! SEE YOU IN THE MORNING!
Big Apple Butcher Claims Ninth Victi
NOTE TO SELF: BUY A SCARF!
I CAN WARM YOU UP, MISS.
LOOK, PAL, I'M A WORKING GIRL, BUT NOT A "WORKING GIRL," GET IT?
GO HOME TO YOUR WIFE AND KIDS, JERK.
BUT YOU'RE *ALL* WHORES ON THE INSIDE.
OHMIGOD! HOW DID YOU--?

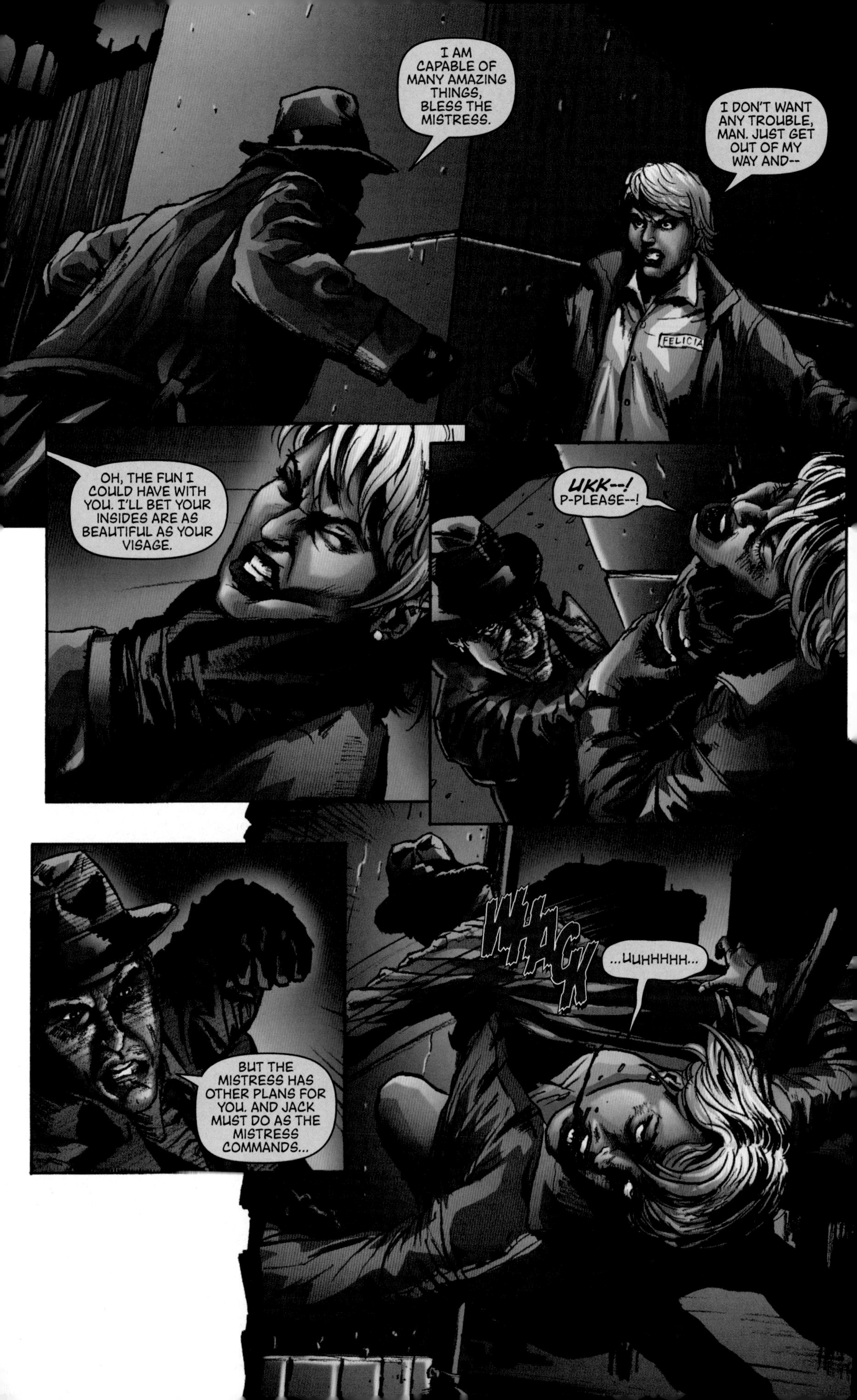
I AM CAPABLE OF MANY AMAZING THINGS, BLESS THE MISTRESS.
I DON'T WANT ANY TROUBLE, MAN. JUST GET OUT OF MY WAY AND--
FELICIA
OH, THE FUN I COULD HAVE WITH YOU. I'LL BET YOUR INSIDES ARE AS BEAUTIFUL AS YOUR VISAGE.
UKK--! P-PLEASE--!
BUT THE MISTRESS HAS OTHER PLANS FOR YOU. AND JACK MUST DO AS THE MISTRESS COMMANDS...
WHACK
...UUHHHHH...

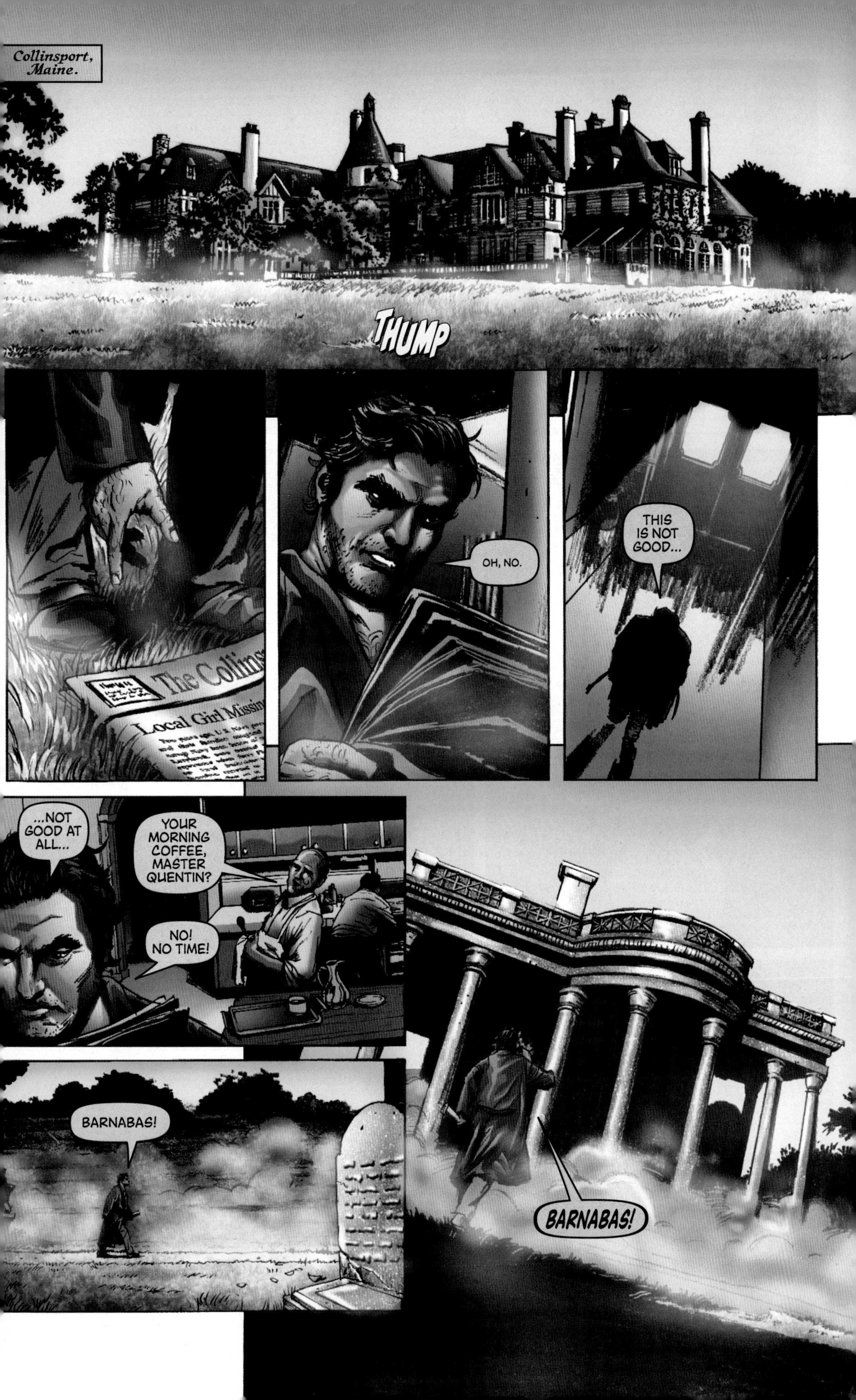
Collinsport, Maine.
THUMP
The Collins
Local Girl Missing
OH, NO.
THIS IS NOT GOOD...
...NOT GOOD AT ALL...
YOUR MORNING COFFEE, MASTER QUENTIN?
NO! NO TIME!
BARNABAS!
BARNABAS!

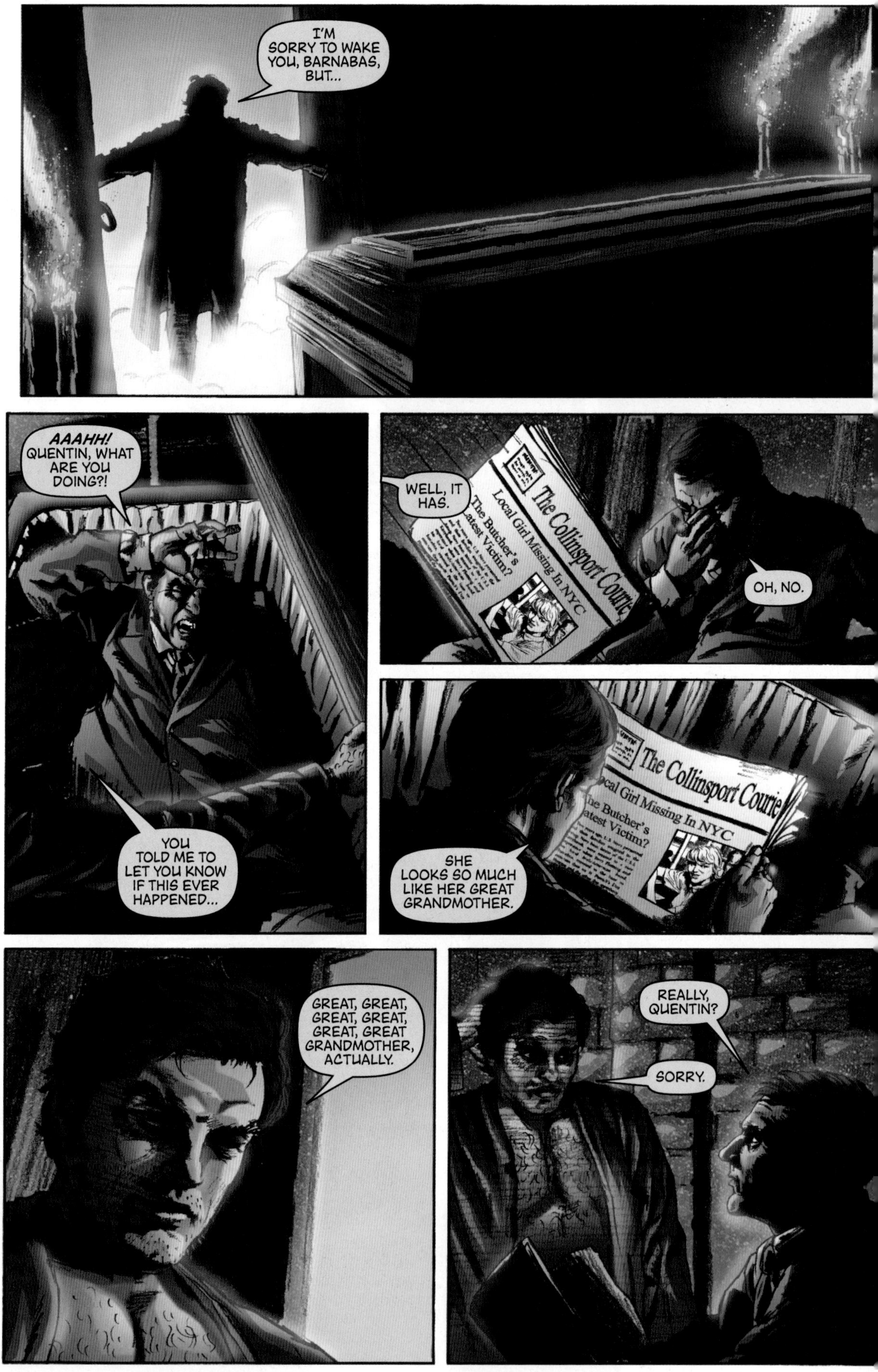
I'M SORRY TO WAKE YOU, BARNABAS, BUT...
AAAHH! QUENTIN, WHAT ARE YOU DOING?!
YOU TOLD ME TO LET YOU KNOW IF THIS EVER HAPPENED...
WELL, IT HAS.
The Collinsport Courie
Local Girl Missing In NYC
The Butcher's Latest Victim?
OH, NO.
SHE LOOKS SO MUCH LIKE HER GREAT GRANDMOTHER.
GREAT, GREAT, GREAT, GREAT, GREAT, GREAT GRANDMOTHER, ACTUALLY.
REALLY, QUENTIN?
SORRY.

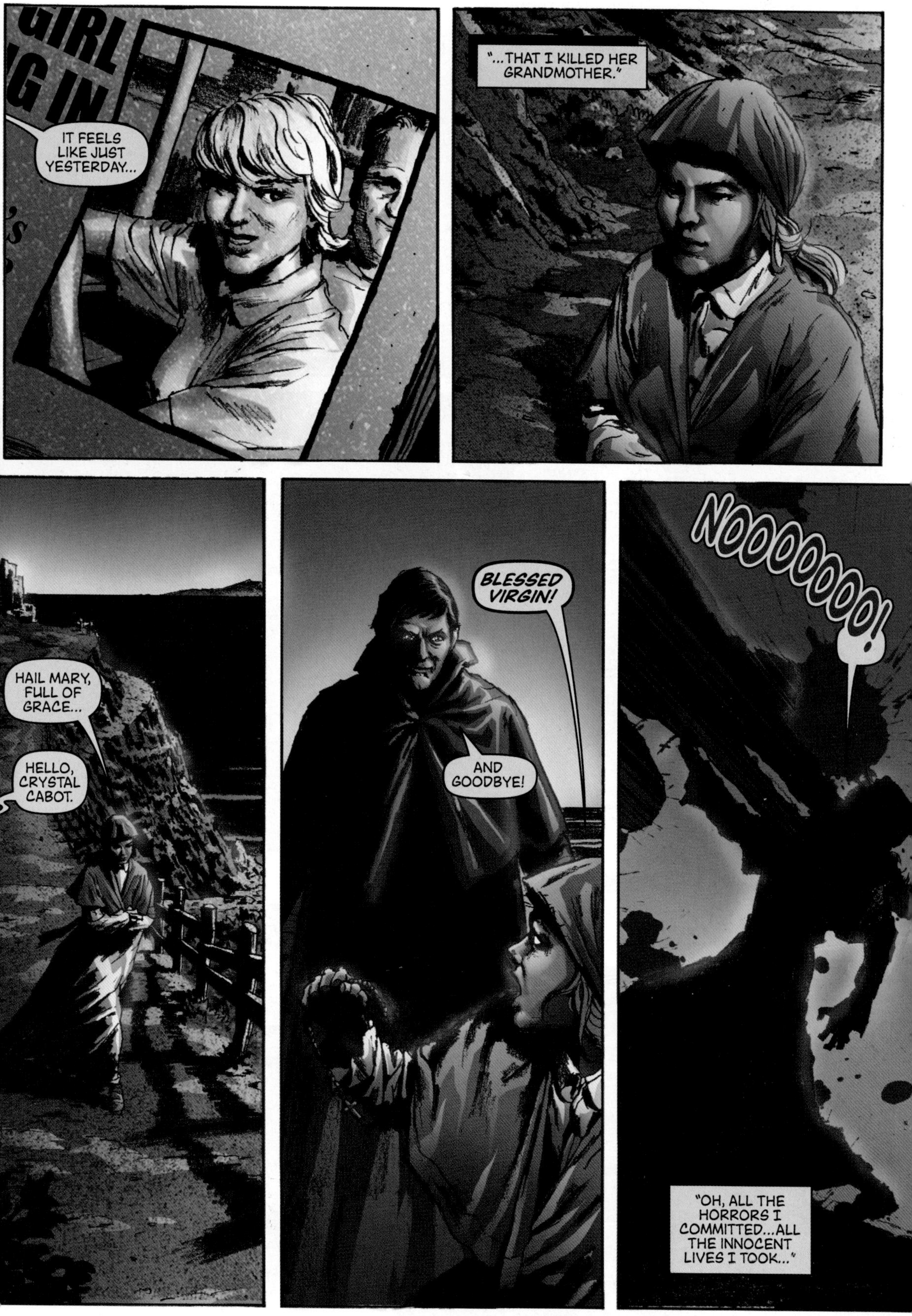
GIRL
IT FEELS LIKE JUST YESTERDAY...
"...THAT I KILLED HER GRANDMOTHER."
HAIL MARY, FULL OF GRACE...
HELLO, CRYSTAL CABOT.
BLESSED VIRGIN!
AND GOODBYE!
NOOOOOOO!
"OH, ALL THE HORRORS I COMMITTED...ALL THE INNOCENT LIVES I TOOK..."

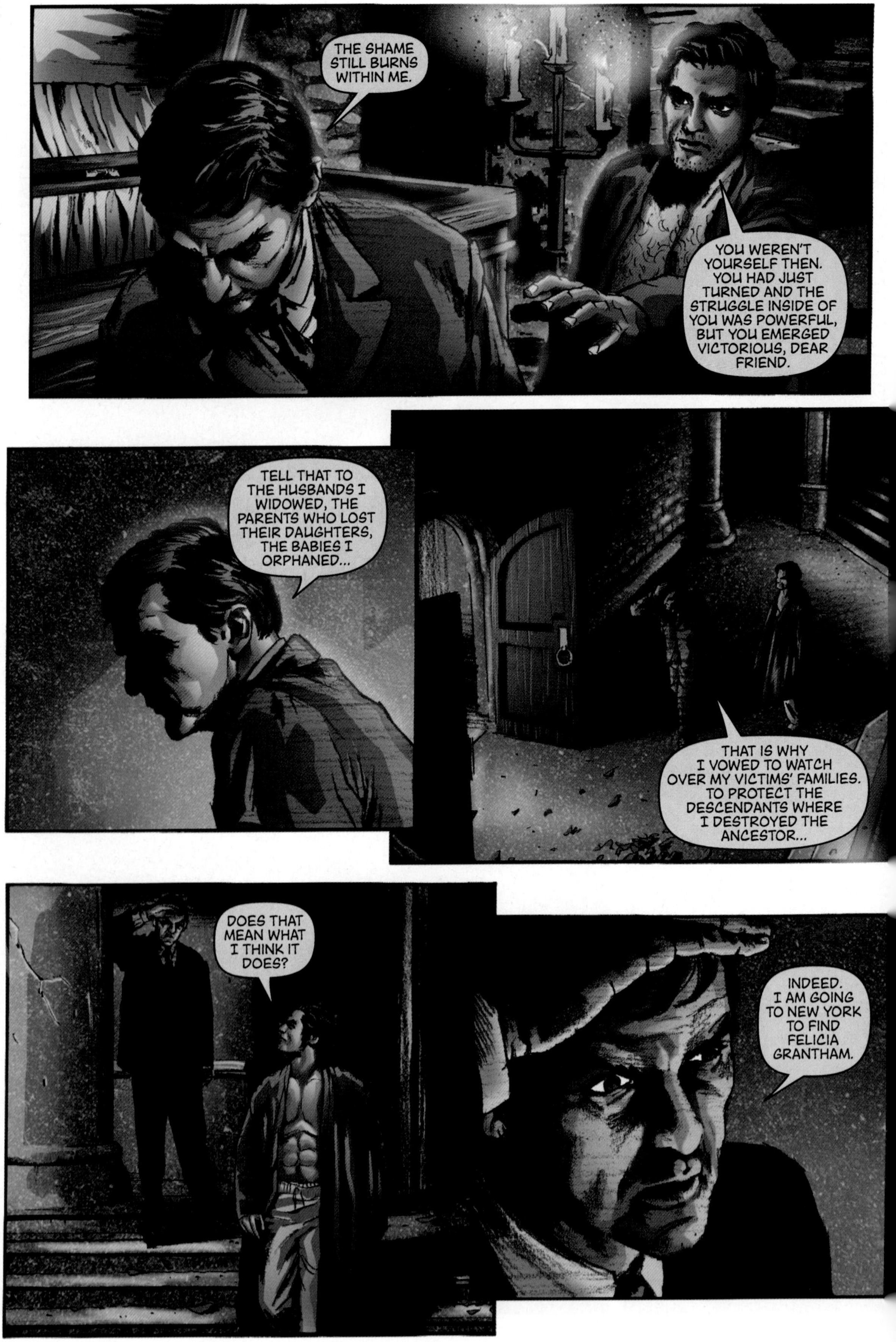
THE SHAME STILL BURNS WITHIN ME.
YOU WEREN'T YOURSELF THEN. YOU HAD JUST TURNED AND THE STRUGGLE INSIDE OF YOU WAS POWERFUL, BUT YOU EMERGED VICTORIOUS, DEAR FRIEND.
TELL THAT TO THE HUSBANDS I WIDOWED, THE PARENTS WHO LOST THEIR DAUGHTERS, THE BABIES I ORPHANED...
THAT IS WHY I VOWED TO WATCH OVER MY VICTIMS' FAMILIES. TO PROTECT THE DESCENDANTS WHERE I DESTROYED THE ANCESTOR...
DOES THAT MEAN WHAT I THINK IT DOES?
INDEED. I AM GOING TO NEW YORK TO FIND FELICIA GRANTHAM.

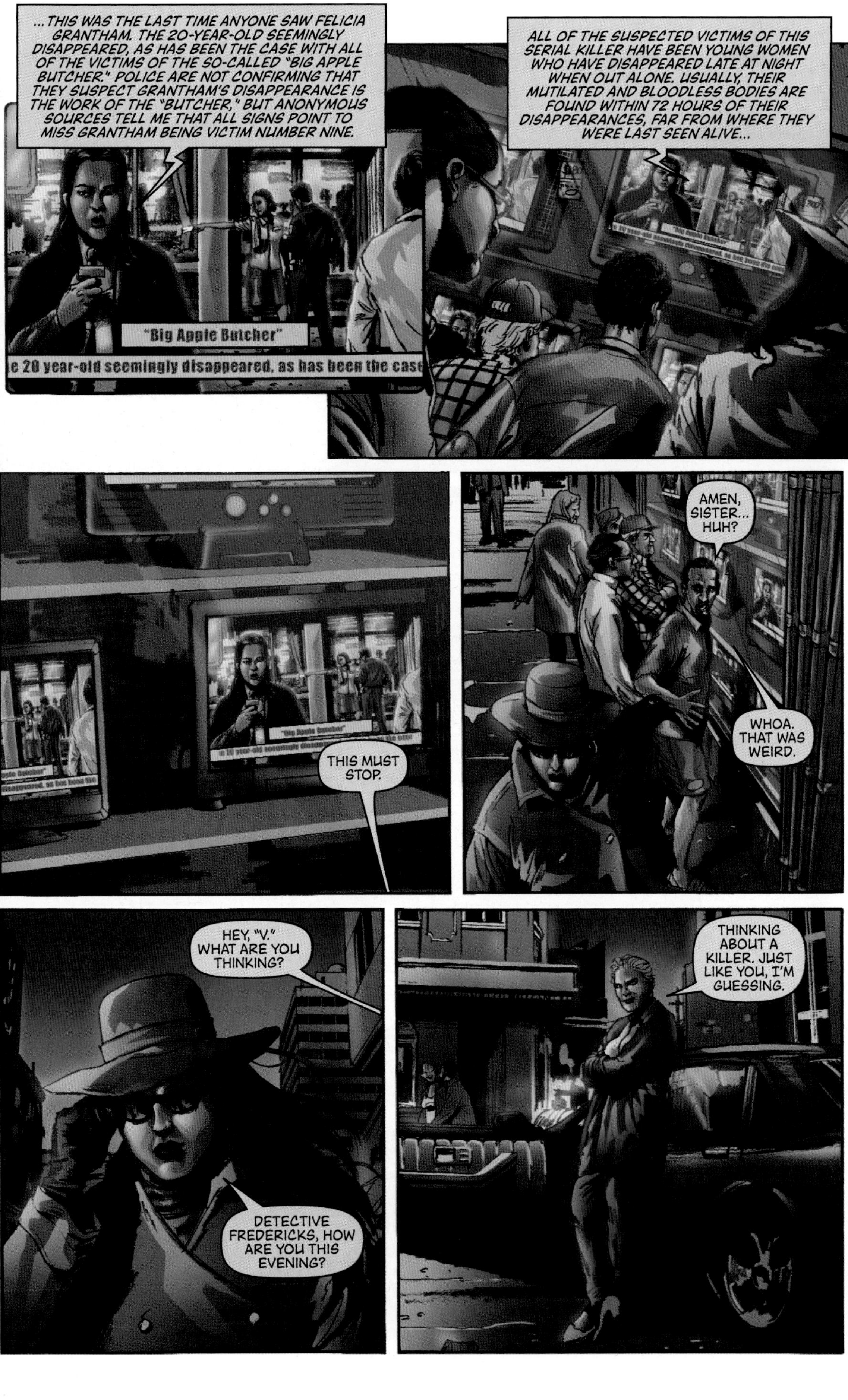
...THIS WAS THE LAST TIME ANYONE SAW FELICIA GRANTHAM. THE 20-YEAR-OLD SEEMINGLY DISAPPEARED, AS HAS BEEN THE CASE WITH ALL OF THE VICTIMS OF THE SO-CALLED "BIG APPLE BUTCHER." POLICE ARE NOT CONFIRMING THAT THEY SUSPECT GRANTHAM'S DISAPPEARANCE IS THE WORK OF THE "BUTCHER," BUT ANONYMOUS SOURCES TELL ME THAT ALL SIGNS POINT TO MISS GRANTHAM BEING VICTIM NUMBER NINE.
"Big Apple Butcher"
e 20 year-old seemingly disappeared, as has been the case
ALL OF THE SUSPECTED VICTIMS OF THIS SERIAL KILLER HAVE BEEN YOUNG WOMEN WHO HAVE DISAPPEARED LATE AT NIGHT WHEN OUT ALONE. USUALLY, THEIR MUTILATED AND BLOODLESS BODIES ARE FOUND WITHIN 72 HOURS OF THEIR DISAPPEARANCES, FAR FROM WHERE THEY WERE LAST SEEN ALIVE...
THIS MUST STOP.
AMEN, SISTER... HUH?
WHOA. THAT WAS WEIRD.
HEY, "V." WHAT ARE YOU THINKING?
DETECTIVE FREDERICKS, HOW ARE YOU THIS EVENING?
THINKING ABOUT A KILLER. JUST LIKE YOU, I'M GUESSING.

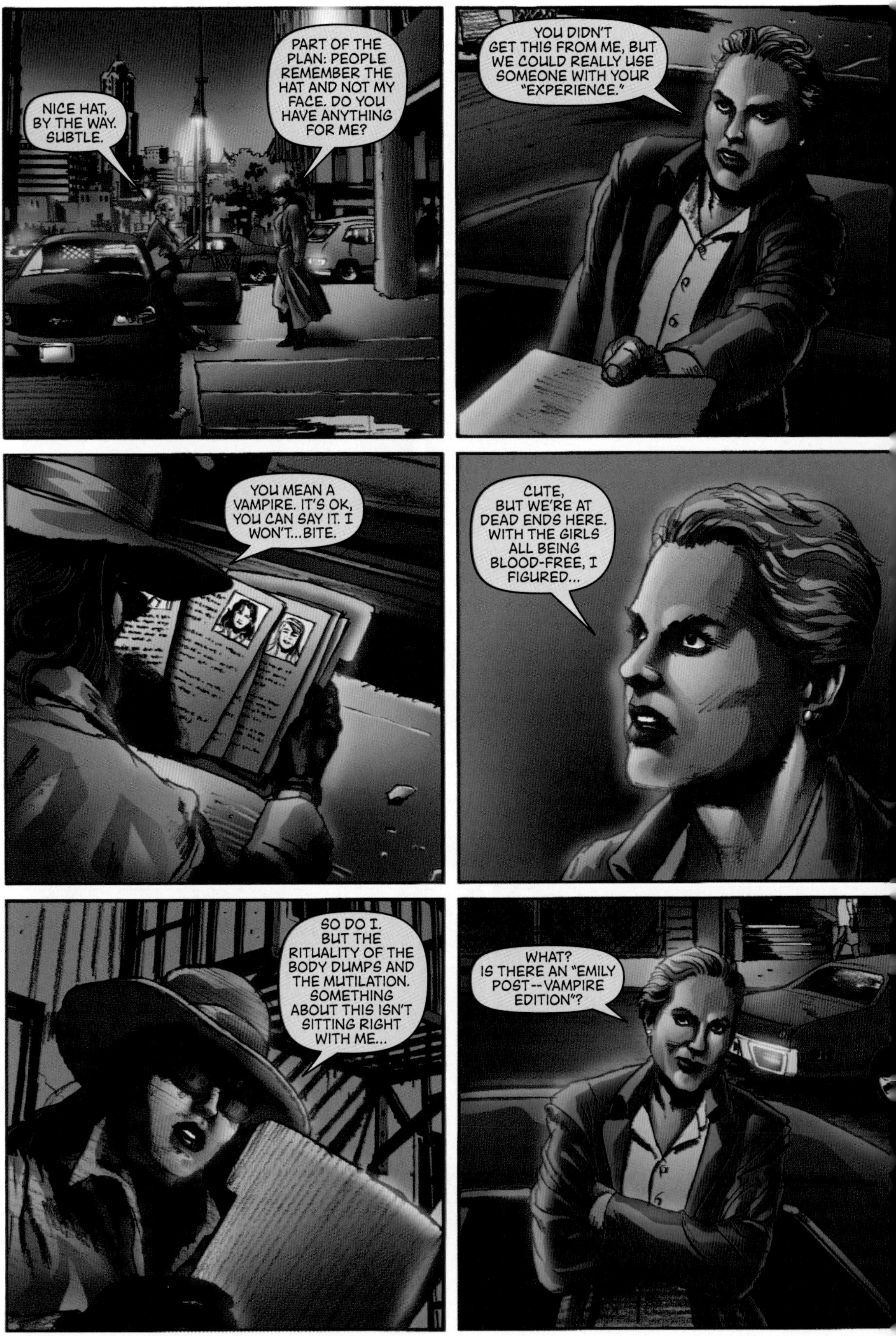
NICE HAT, BY THE WAY. SUBTLE.
PART OF THE PLAN: PEOPLE REMEMBER THE HAT AND NOT MY FACE. DO YOU HAVE ANYTHING FOR ME?
YOU DIDN'T GET THIS FROM ME, BUT WE COULD REALLY USE SOMEONE WITH YOUR "EXPERIENCE."
YOU MEAN A VAMPIRE. IT'S OK, YOU CAN SAY IT. I WON'T...BITE.
CUTE, BUT WE'RE AT DEAD ENDS HERE. WITH THE GIRLS ALL BEING BLOOD-FREE, I FIGURED...
SO DO I. BUT THE RITUALITY OF THE BODY DUMPS AND THE MUTILATION. SOMETHING ABOUT THIS ISN'T SITTING RIGHT WITH ME...
WHAT? IS THERE AN "EMILY POST--VAMPIRE EDITION"?

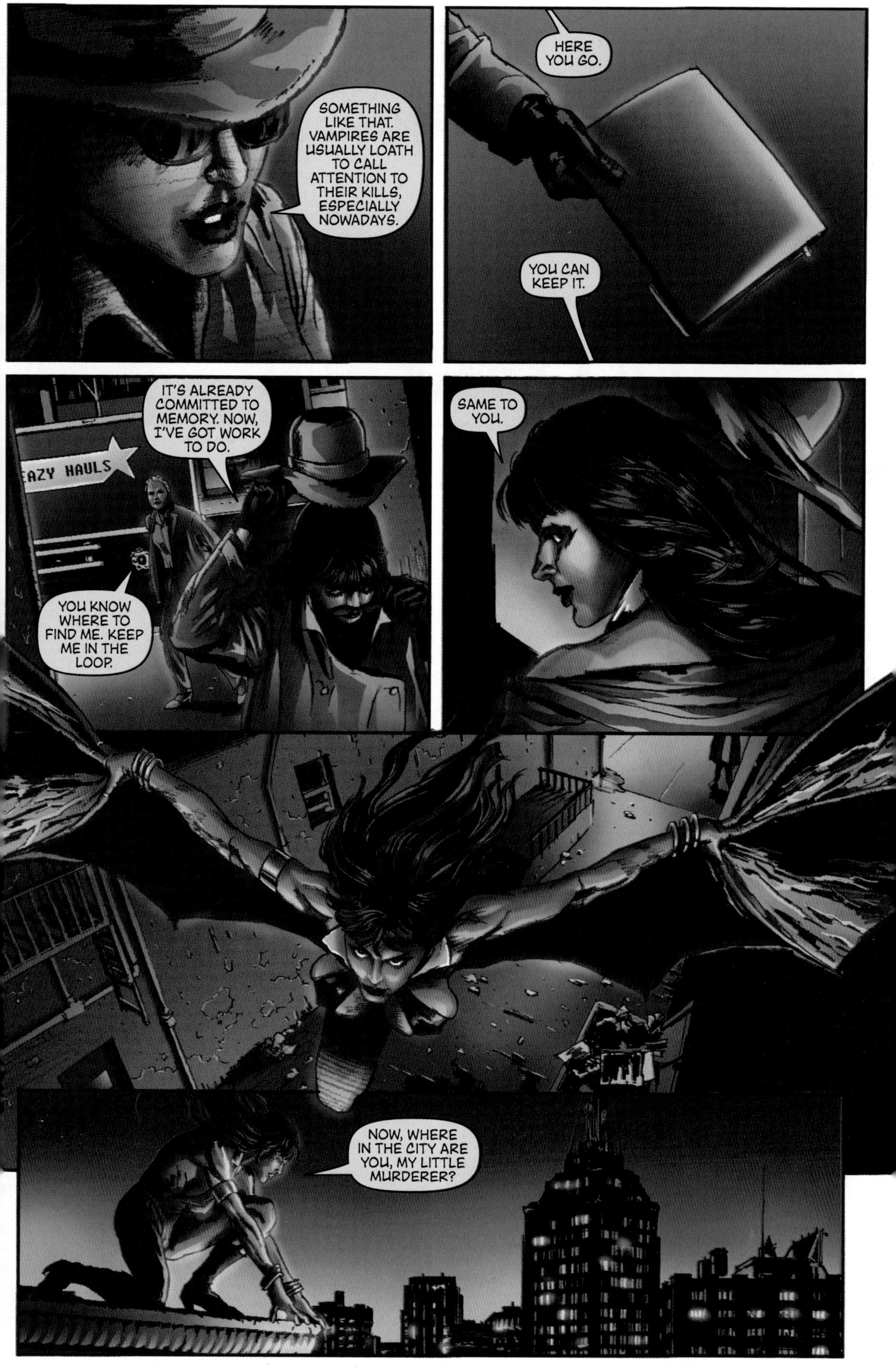
SOMETHING LIKE THAT. VAMPIRES ARE USUALLY LOATH TO CALL ATTENTION TO THEIR KILLS, ESPECIALLY NOWADAYS.
HERE YOU GO.
YOU CAN KEEP IT.
IT'S ALREADY COMMITTED TO MEMORY. NOW, I'VE GOT WORK TO DO.
EAZY HAULS
YOU KNOW WHERE TO FIND ME. KEEP ME IN THE LOOP.
SAME TO YOU.
NOW, WHERE IN THE CITY ARE YOU, MY LITTLE MURDERER?

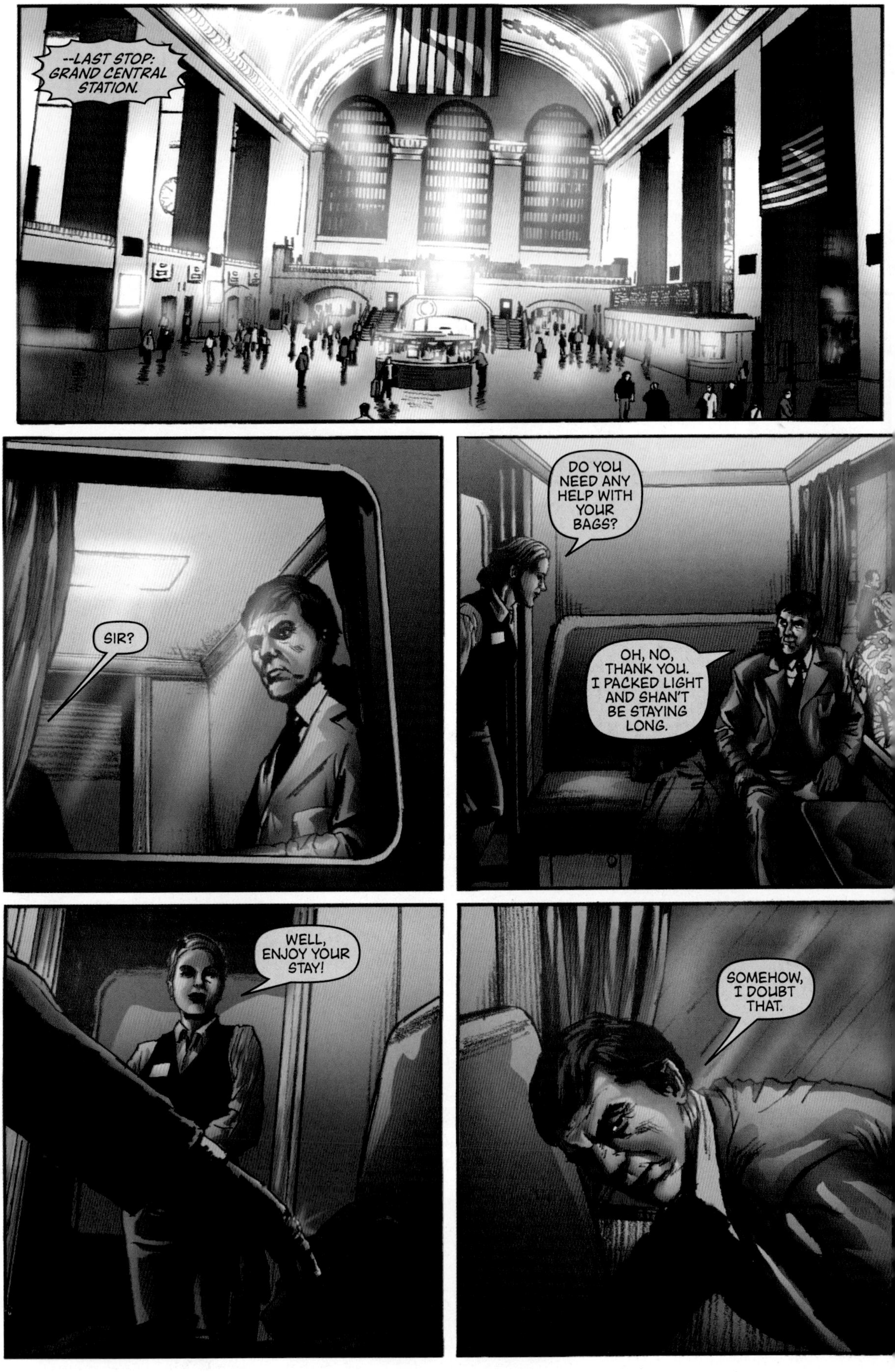
--LAST STOP: GRAND CENTRAL STATION.
SIR?
DO YOU NEED ANY HELP WITH YOUR BAGS?
OH, NO, THANK YOU. I PACKED LIGHT AND SHAN'T BE STAYING LONG.
WELL, ENJOY YOUR STAY!
SOMEHOW, I DOUBT THAT.

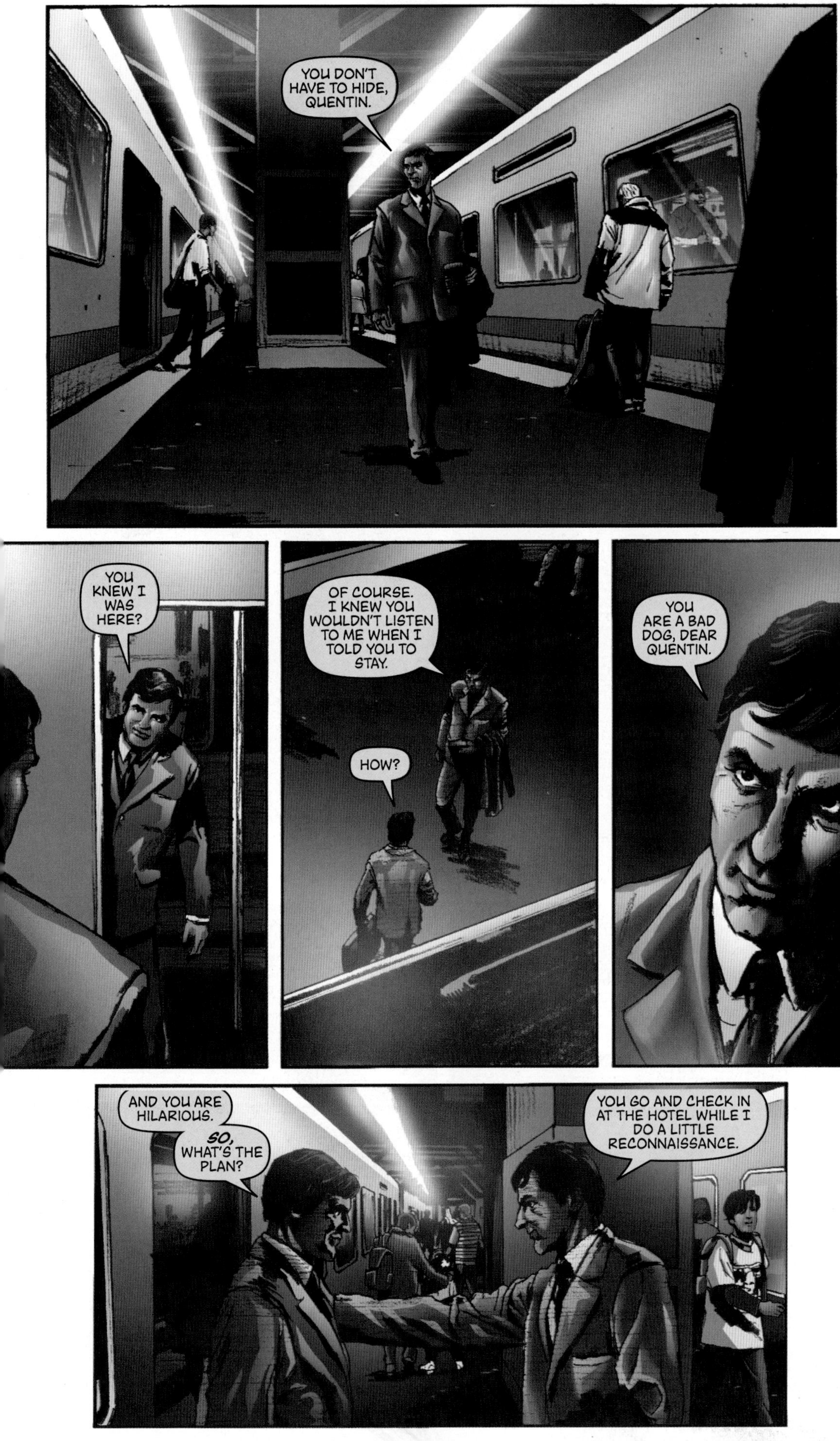

YOU DON'T HAVE TO HIDE, QUENTIN.
YOU KNEW I WAS HERE?
OF COURSE. I KNEW YOU WOULDN'T LISTEN TO ME WHEN I TOLD YOU TO STAY.
HOW?
YOU ARE A BAD DOG, DEAR QUENTIN.
AND YOU ARE HILARIOUS.
SO, WHAT'S THE PLAN?
YOU GO AND CHECK IN AT THE HOTEL WHILE I DO A LITTLE RECONNAISSANCE.

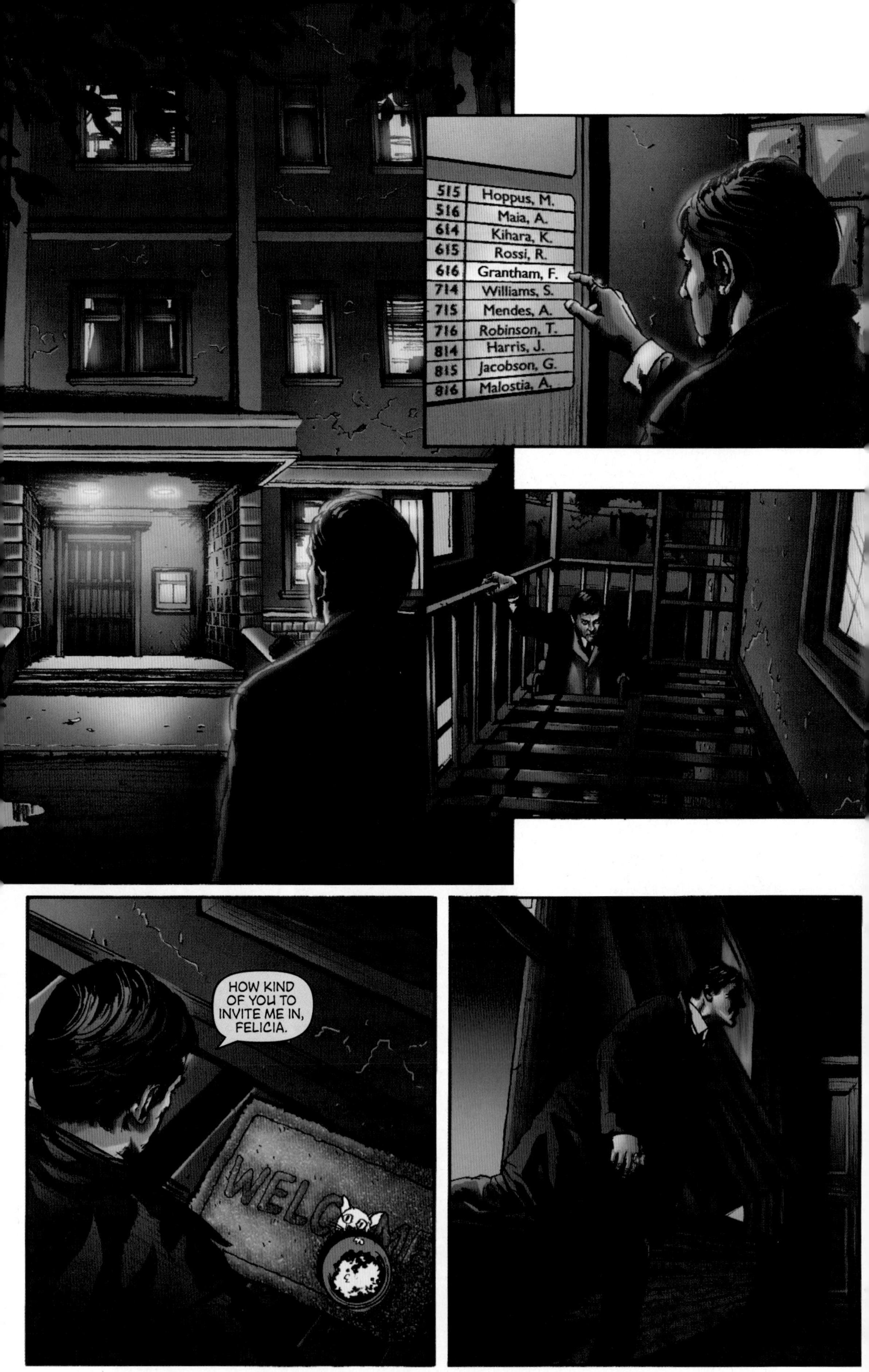
515 Hoppus, M.
516 Maia, A.
614 Kihara, K.
615 Rossi, R.
616 Grantham, F.
714 Williams, S.
715 Mendes, A.
716 Robinson, T.
814 Harris, J.
815 Jacobson, G.
816 Malostia, A.
HOW KIND OF YOU TO INVITE ME IN, FELICIA.
WELC

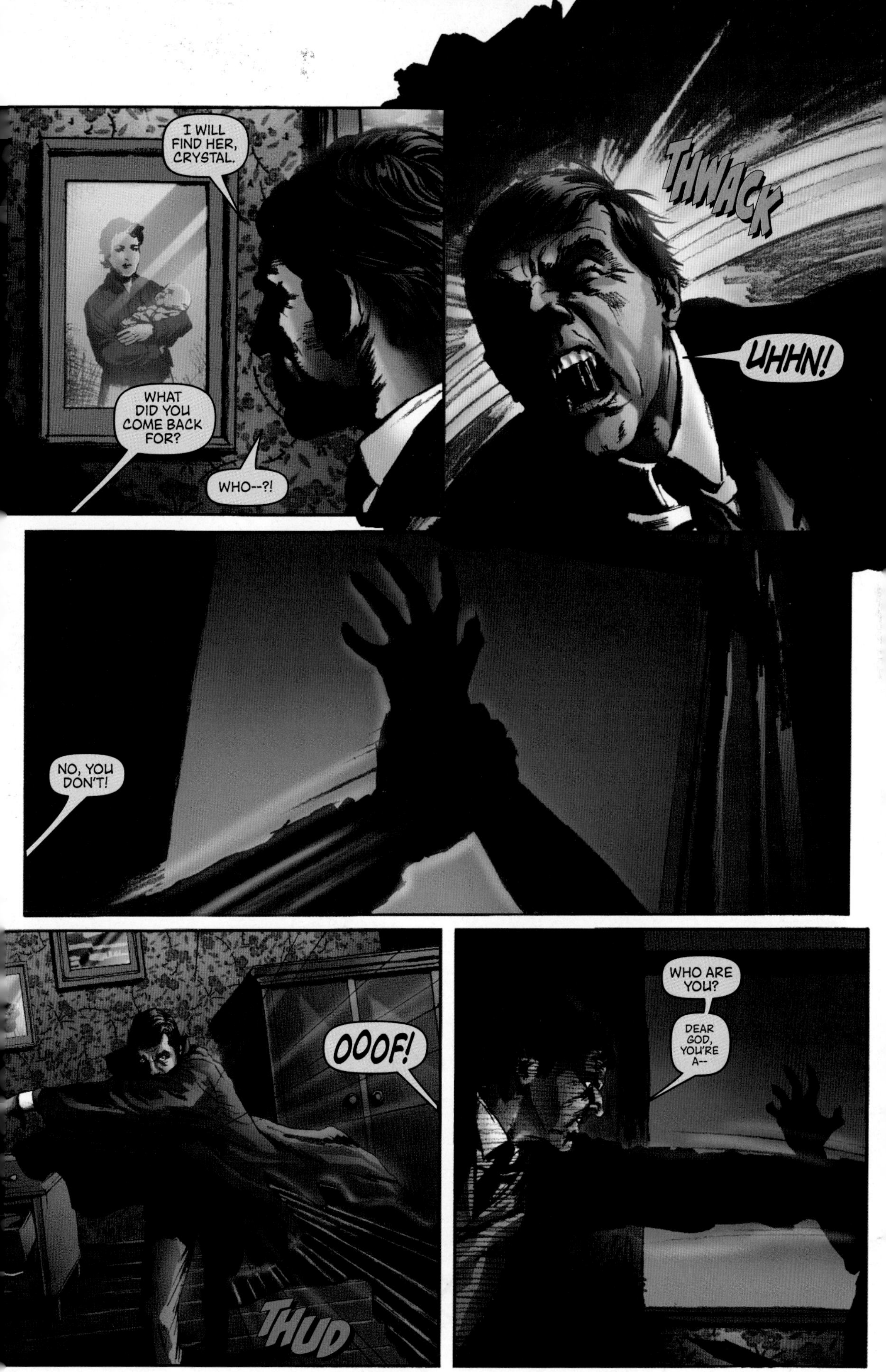
I WILL FIND HER, CRYSTAL.
WHAT DID YOU COME BACK FOR?
WHO--?!
THWACK
UHHN!
NO, YOU DON'T!
OOOF!
THUD
WHO ARE YOU?
DEAR GOD, YOU'RE A--

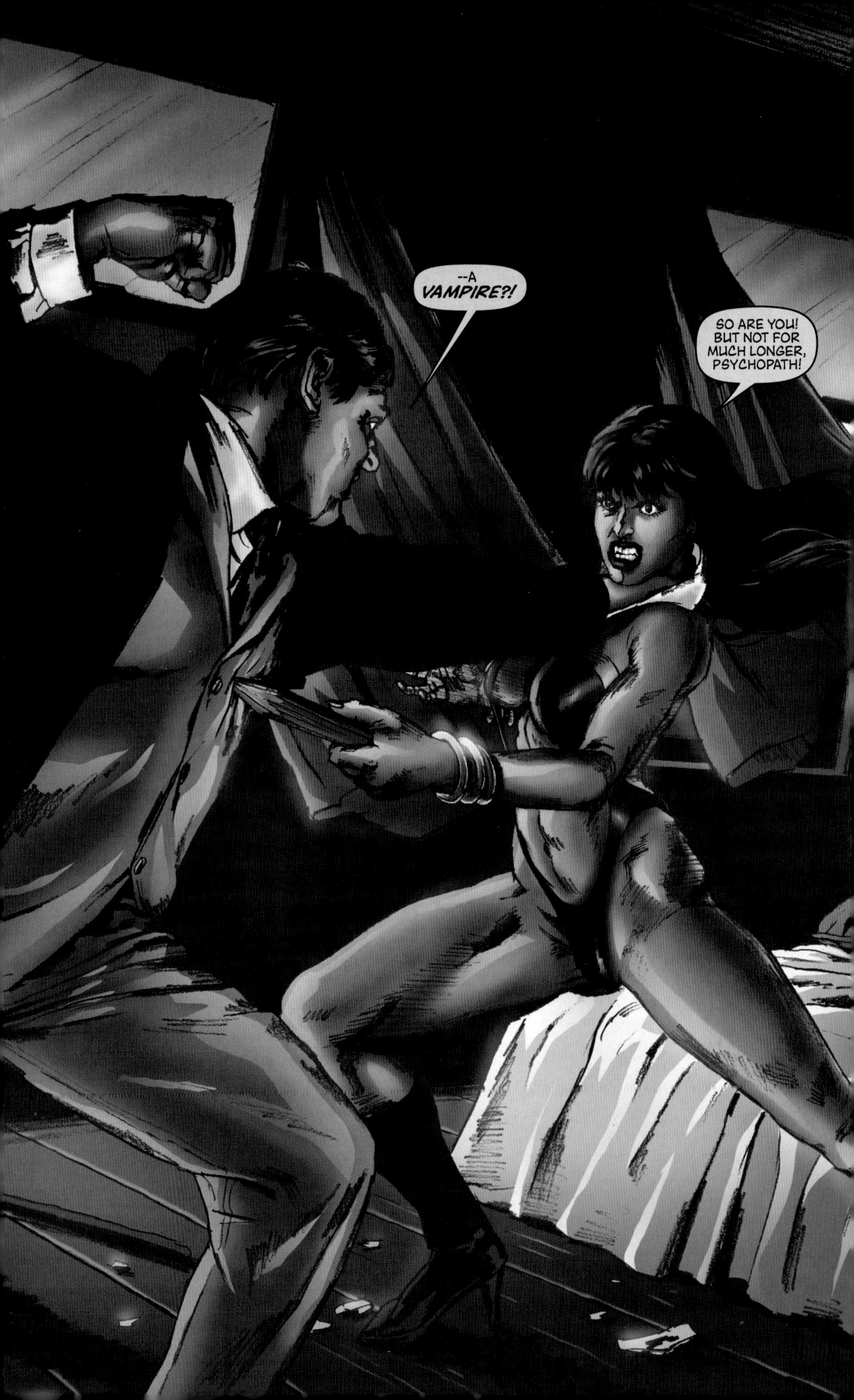
--A VAMPIRE?!
SO ARE YOU! BUT NOT FOR MUCH LONGER, PSYCHOPATH!

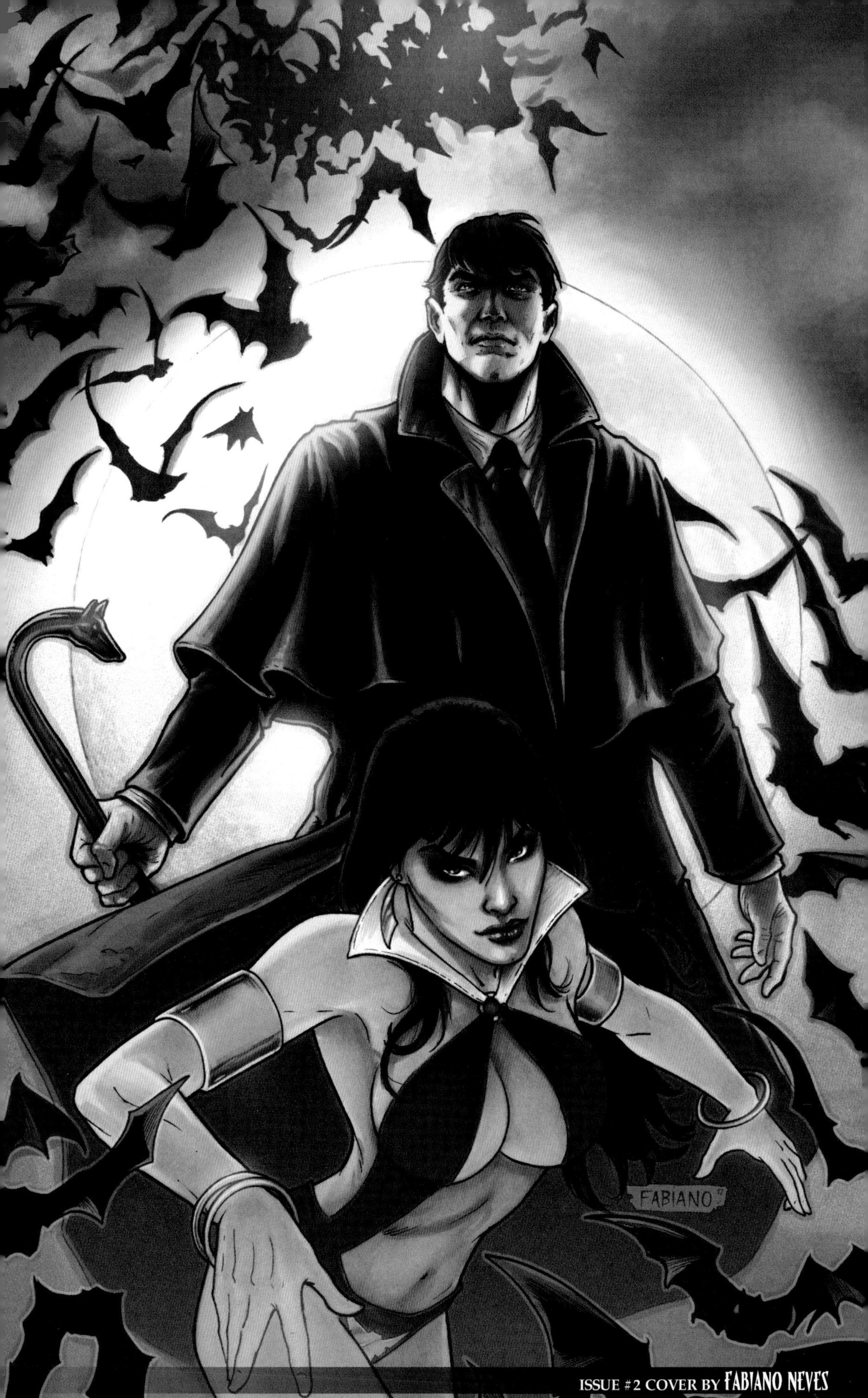
FABIANO '07
ISSUE #2 COVER BY FABIANO NEVES

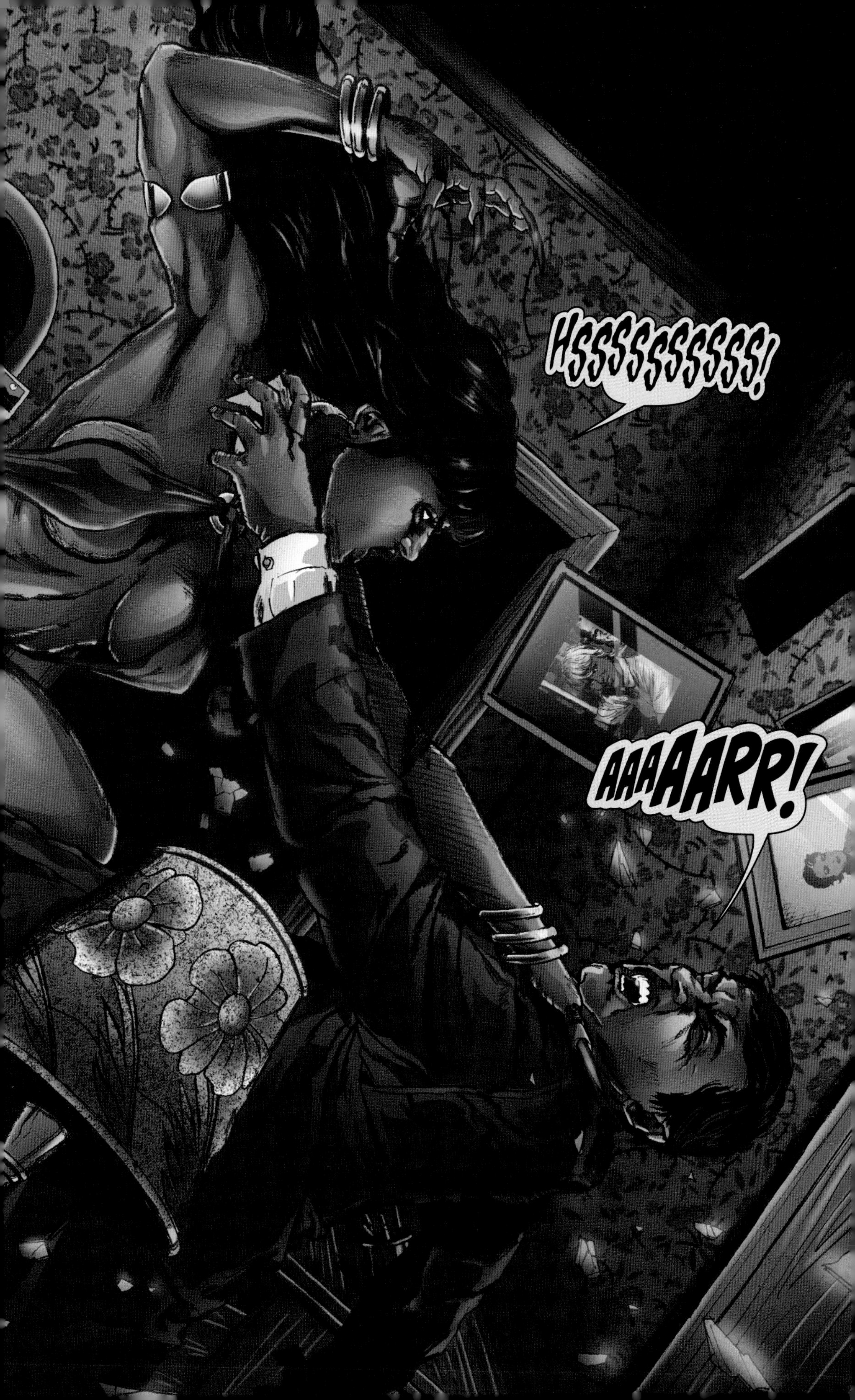
HSSSSSSSSSS!
AAAAARR!

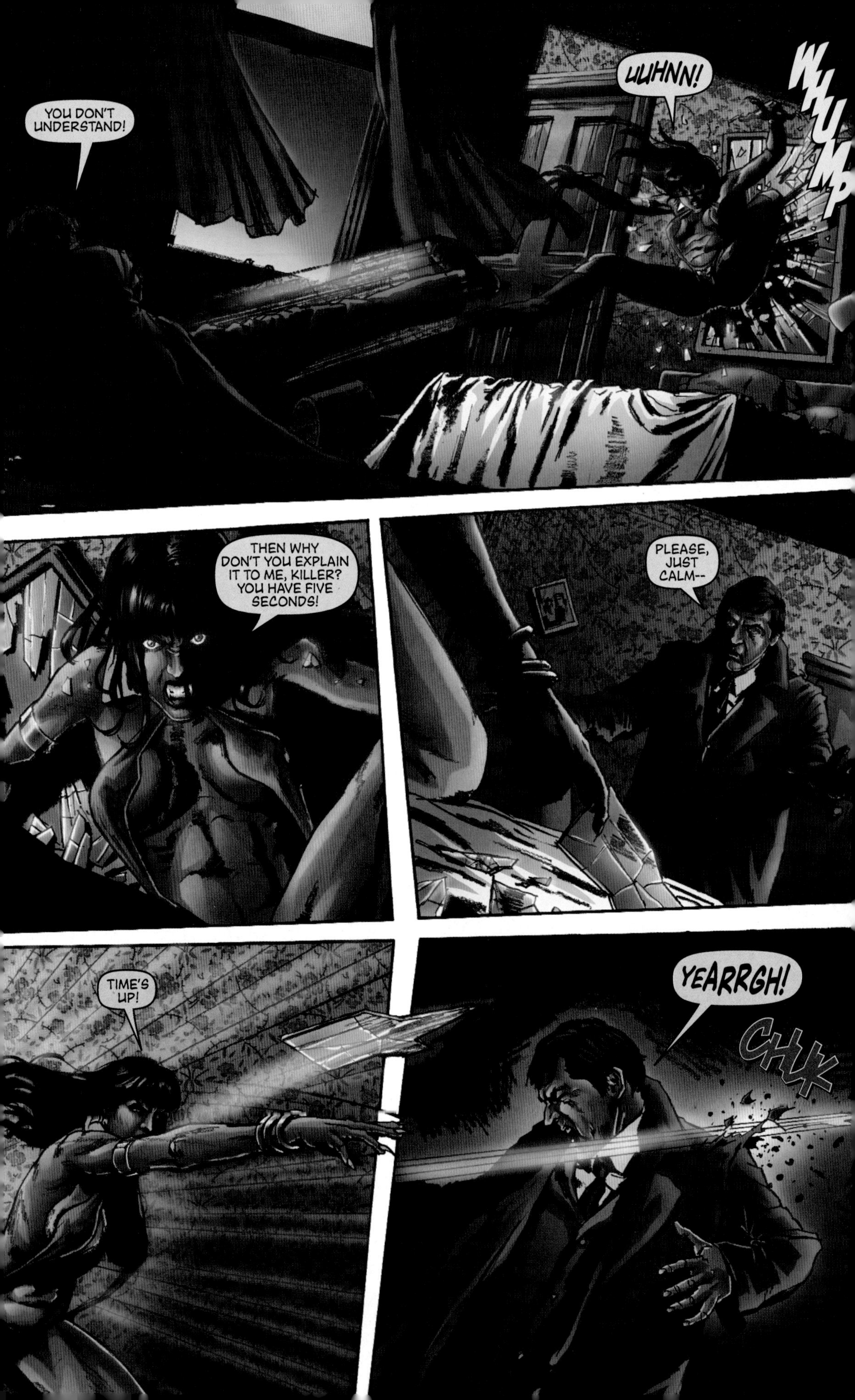
YOU DON'T UNDERSTAND!
UUHNN!
WHUMP
THEN WHY DON'T YOU EXPLAIN IT TO ME, KILLER? YOU HAVE FIVE SECONDS!
PLEASE, JUST CALM--
TIME'S UP!
YEARRGH!
CHUK

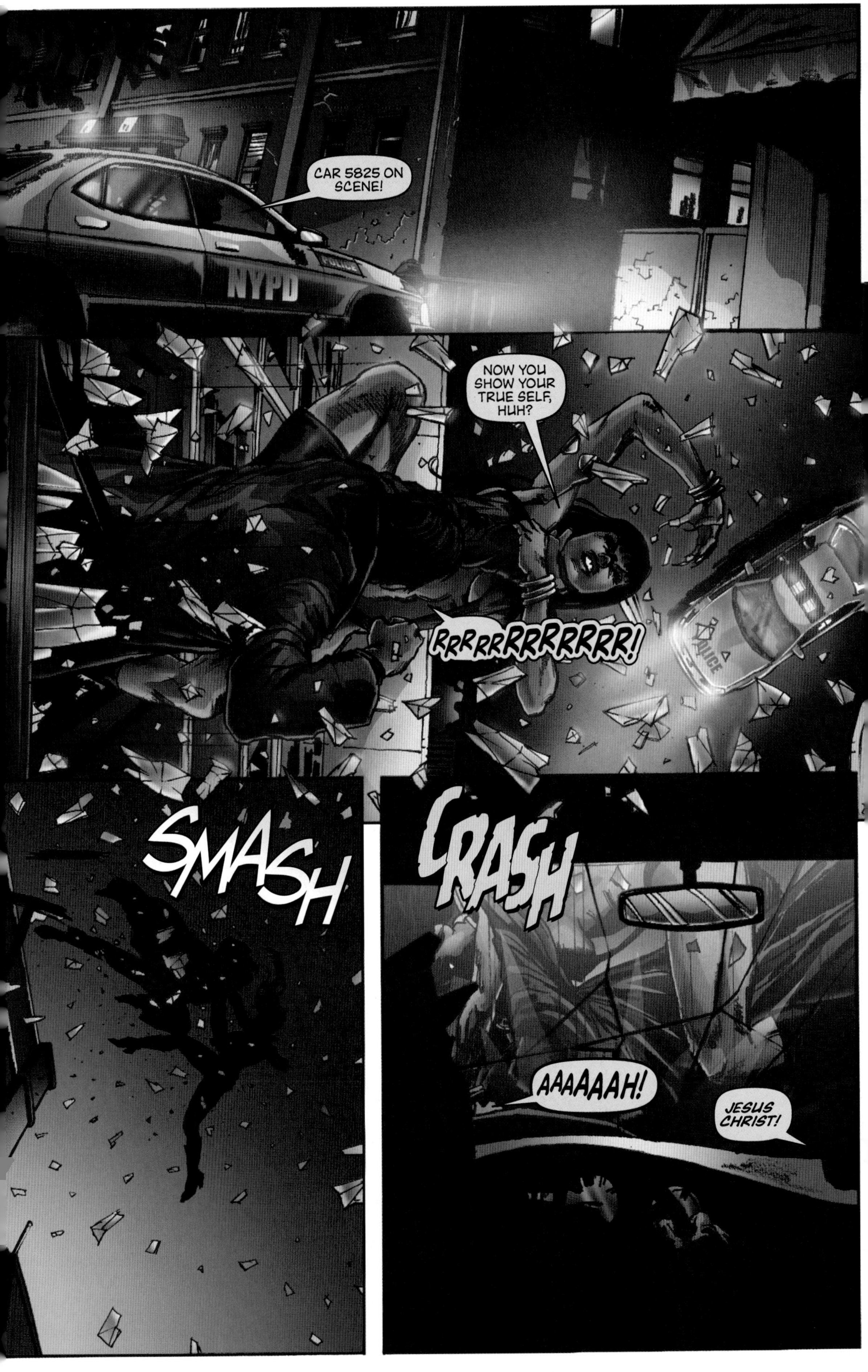
CAR 5825 ON SCENE!
NOW YOU SHOW YOUR TRUE SELF, HUH?
RRRRRRRRRRRR!
SMASH
CRASH
AAAAAAH!
JESUS CHRIST!

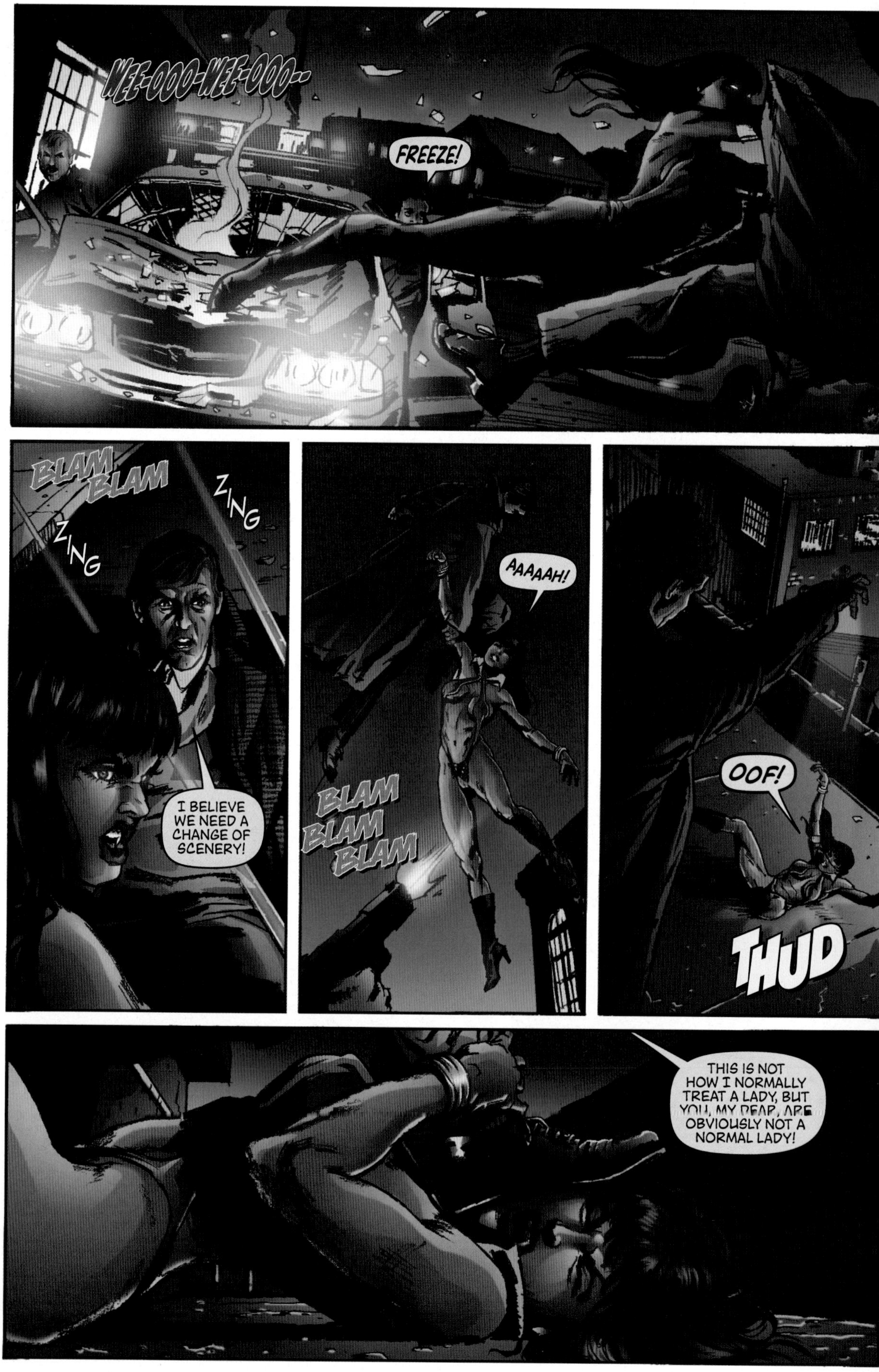
WEE-OOO-WEE-OOO..
FREEZE!
BLAM BLAM
ZING
ZING
I BELIEVE WE NEED A CHANGE OF SCENERY!
AAAAAH!
BLAM BLAM BLAM
OOF!
THUD
THIS IS NOT HOW I NORMALLY TREAT A LADY, BUT YOU, MY DEAR, ARE OBVIOUSLY NOT A NORMAL LADY!

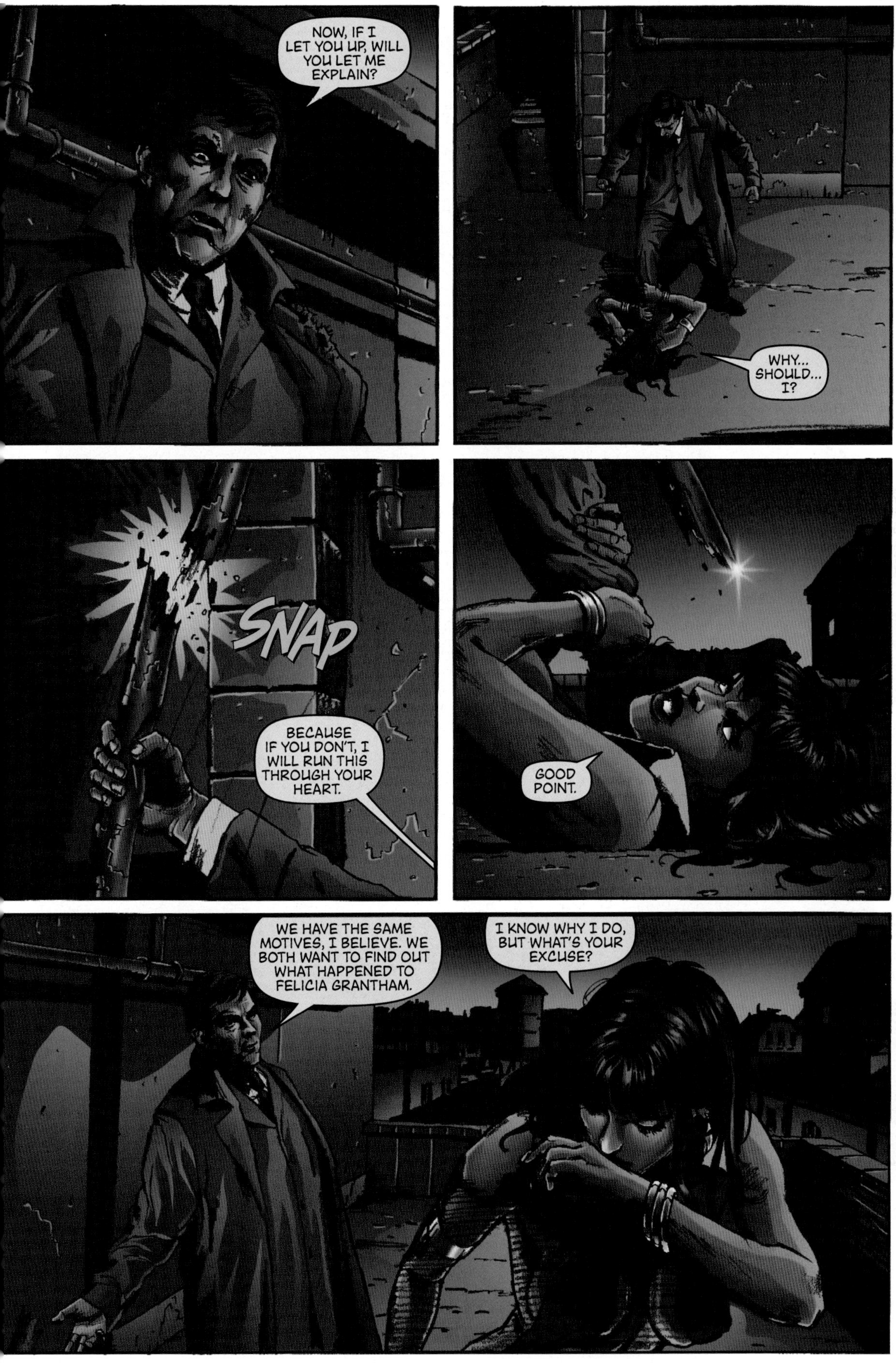
NOW, IF I LET YOU UP, WILL YOU LET ME EXPLAIN?
WHY... SHOULD... I?
SNAP
BECAUSE IF YOU DON'T, I WILL RUN THIS THROUGH YOUR HEART.
GOOD POINT.
WE HAVE THE SAME MOTIVES, I BELIEVE. WE BOTH WANT TO FIND OUT WHAT HAPPENED TO FELICIA GRANTHAM.
I KNOW WHY I DO, BUT WHAT'S YOUR EXCUSE?

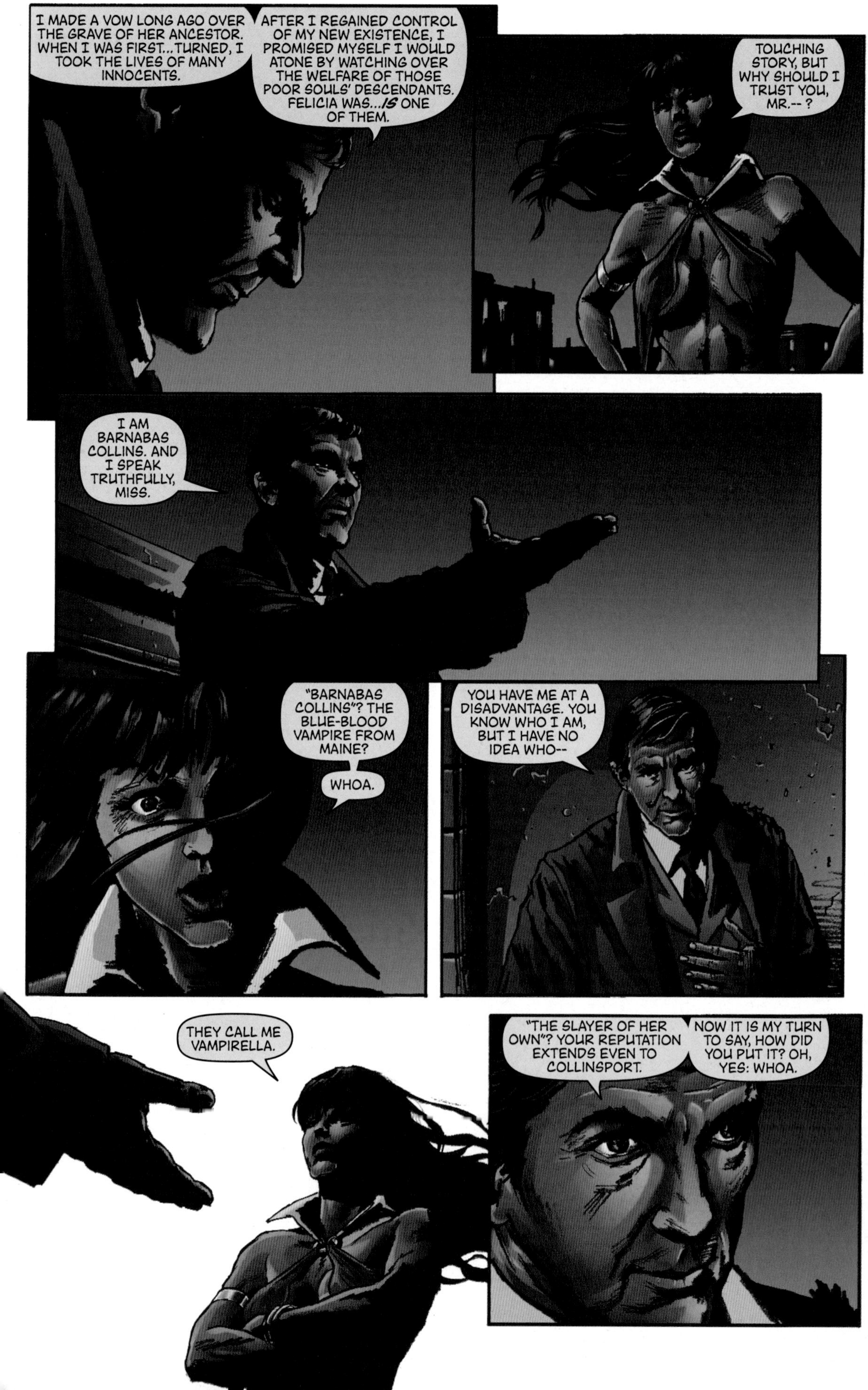
I MADE A VOW LONG AGO OVER THE GRAVE OF HER ANCESTOR. WHEN I WAS FIRST...TURNED, I TOOK THE LIVES OF MANY INNOCENTS.
AFTER I REGAINED CONTROL OF MY NEW EXISTENCE, I PROMISED MYSELF I WOULD ATONE BY WATCHING OVER THE WELFARE OF THOSE POOR SOULS' DESCENDANTS. FELICIA WAS...*IS* ONE OF THEM.
TOUCHING STORY, BUT WHY SHOULD I TRUST YOU, MR.-- ?
I AM BARNABAS COLLINS. AND I SPEAK TRUTHFULLY, MISS.
"BARNABAS COLLINS"? THE BLUE-BLOOD VAMPIRE FROM MAINE?
WHOA.
YOU HAVE ME AT A DISADVANTAGE. YOU KNOW WHO I AM, BUT I HAVE NO IDEA WHO--
THEY CALL ME VAMPIRELLA.
"THE SLAYER OF HER OWN"? YOUR REPUTATION EXTENDS EVEN TO COLLINSPORT.
NOW IT IS MY TURN TO SAY, HOW DID YOU PUT IT? OH, YES: WHOA.

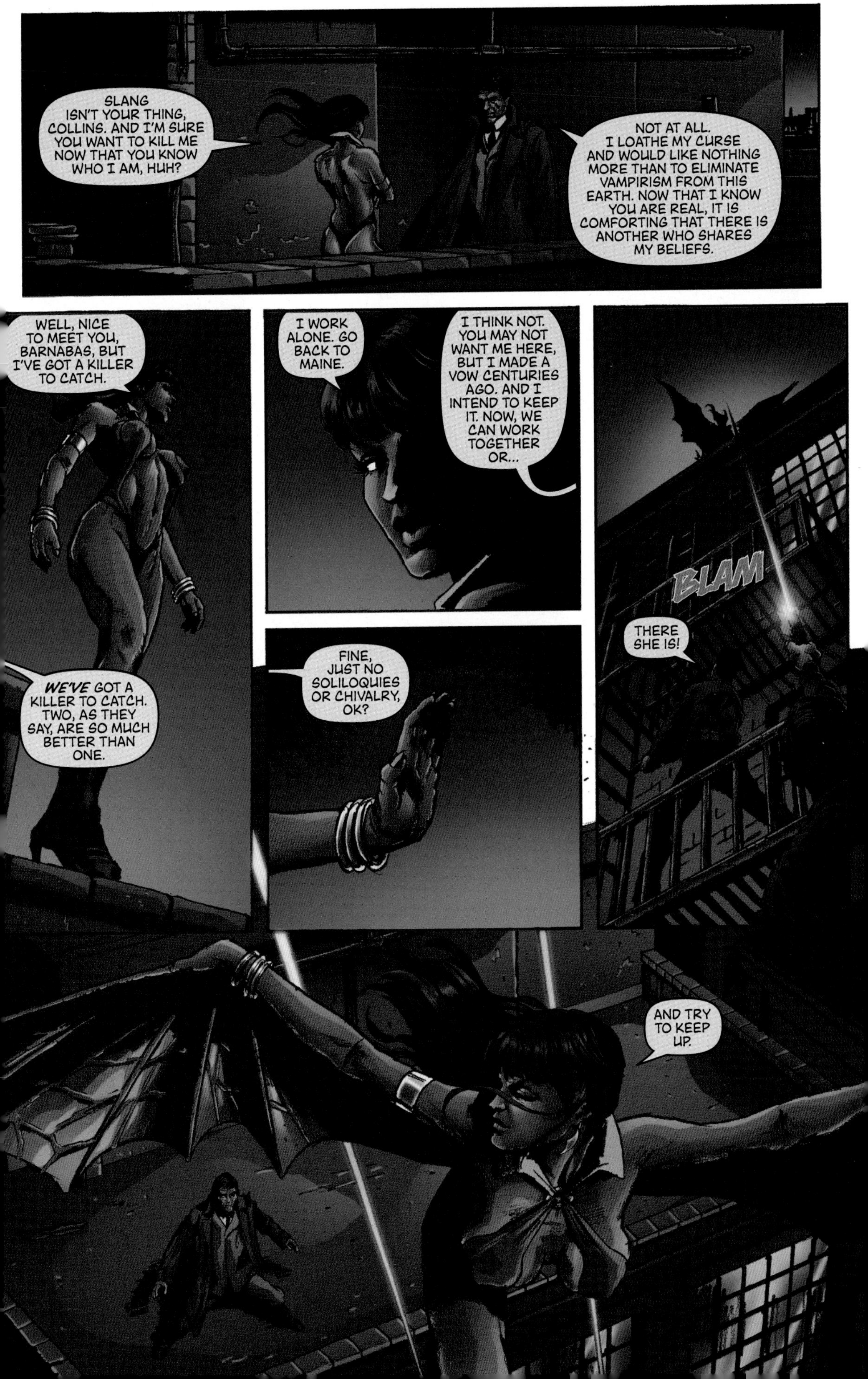
SLANG ISN'T YOUR THING, COLLINS. AND I'M SURE YOU WANT TO KILL ME NOW THAT YOU KNOW WHO I AM, HUH?
NOT AT ALL. I LOATHE MY CURSE AND WOULD LIKE NOTHING MORE THAN TO ELIMINATE VAMPIRISM FROM THIS EARTH. NOW THAT I KNOW YOU ARE REAL, IT IS COMFORTING THAT THERE IS ANOTHER WHO SHARES MY BELIEFS.
WELL, NICE TO MEET YOU, BARNABAS, BUT I'VE GOT A KILLER TO CATCH.
WE'VE GOT A KILLER TO CATCH. TWO, AS THEY SAY, ARE SO MUCH BETTER THAN ONE.
I WORK ALONE. GO BACK TO MAINE.
I THINK NOT. YOU MAY NOT WANT ME HERE, BUT I MADE A VOW CENTURIES AGO. AND I INTEND TO KEEP IT. NOW, WE CAN WORK TOGETHER OR...
FINE, JUST NO SOLILOQUIES OR CHIVALRY, OK?
BLAM
THERE SHE IS!
AND TRY TO KEEP UP.

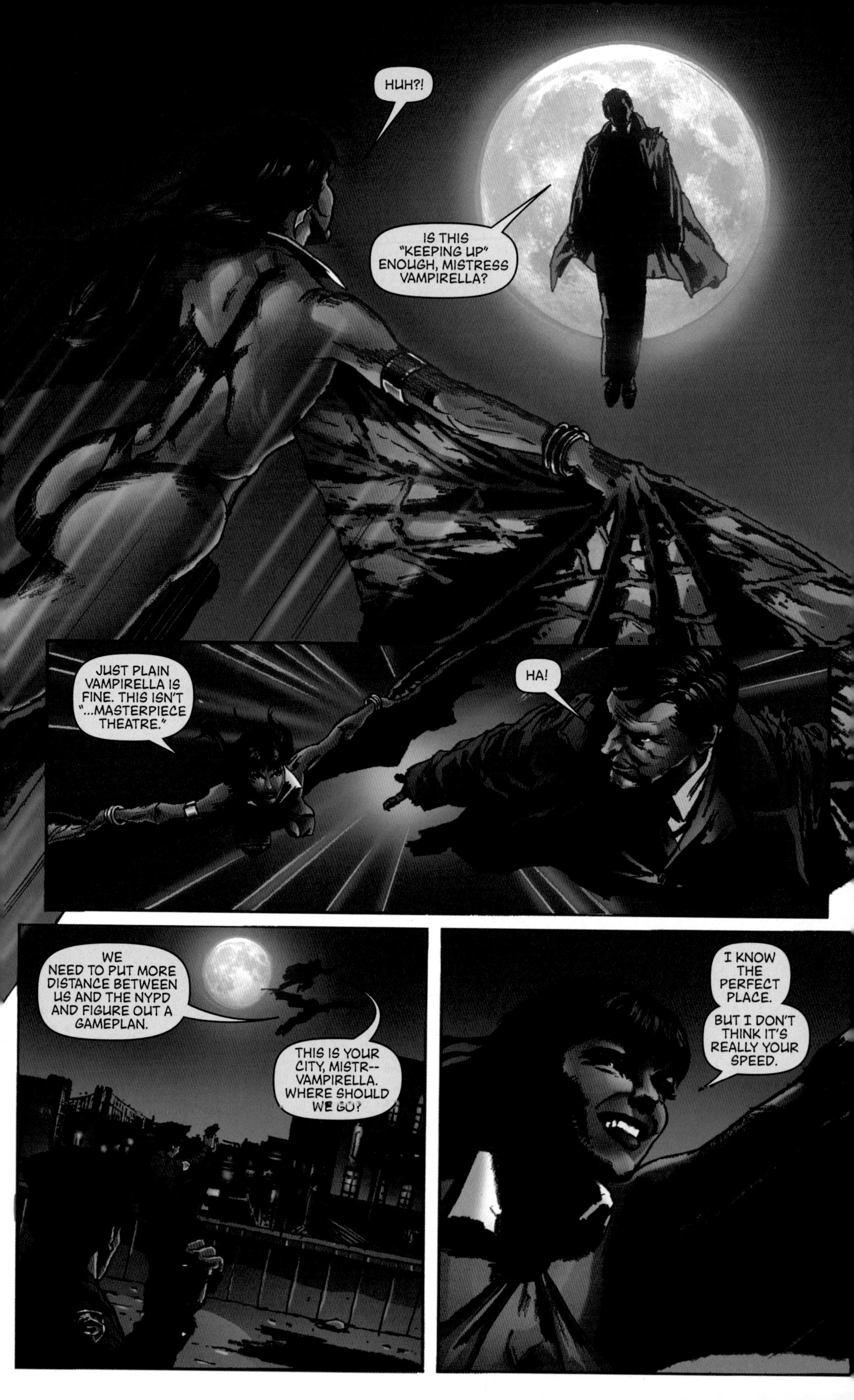
HUH?!
IS THIS "KEEPING UP" ENOUGH, MISTRESS VAMPIRELLA?
JUST PLAIN VAMPIRELLA IS FINE. THIS ISN'T "...MASTERPIECE THEATRE."
HA!
WE NEED TO PUT MORE DISTANCE BETWEEN US AND THE NYPD AND FIGURE OUT A GAMEPLAN.
THIS IS YOUR CITY, MISTR-- VAMPIRELLA. WHERE SHOULD WE GO?
I KNOW THE PERFECT PLACE.
BUT I DON'T THINK IT'S REALLY YOUR SPEED.

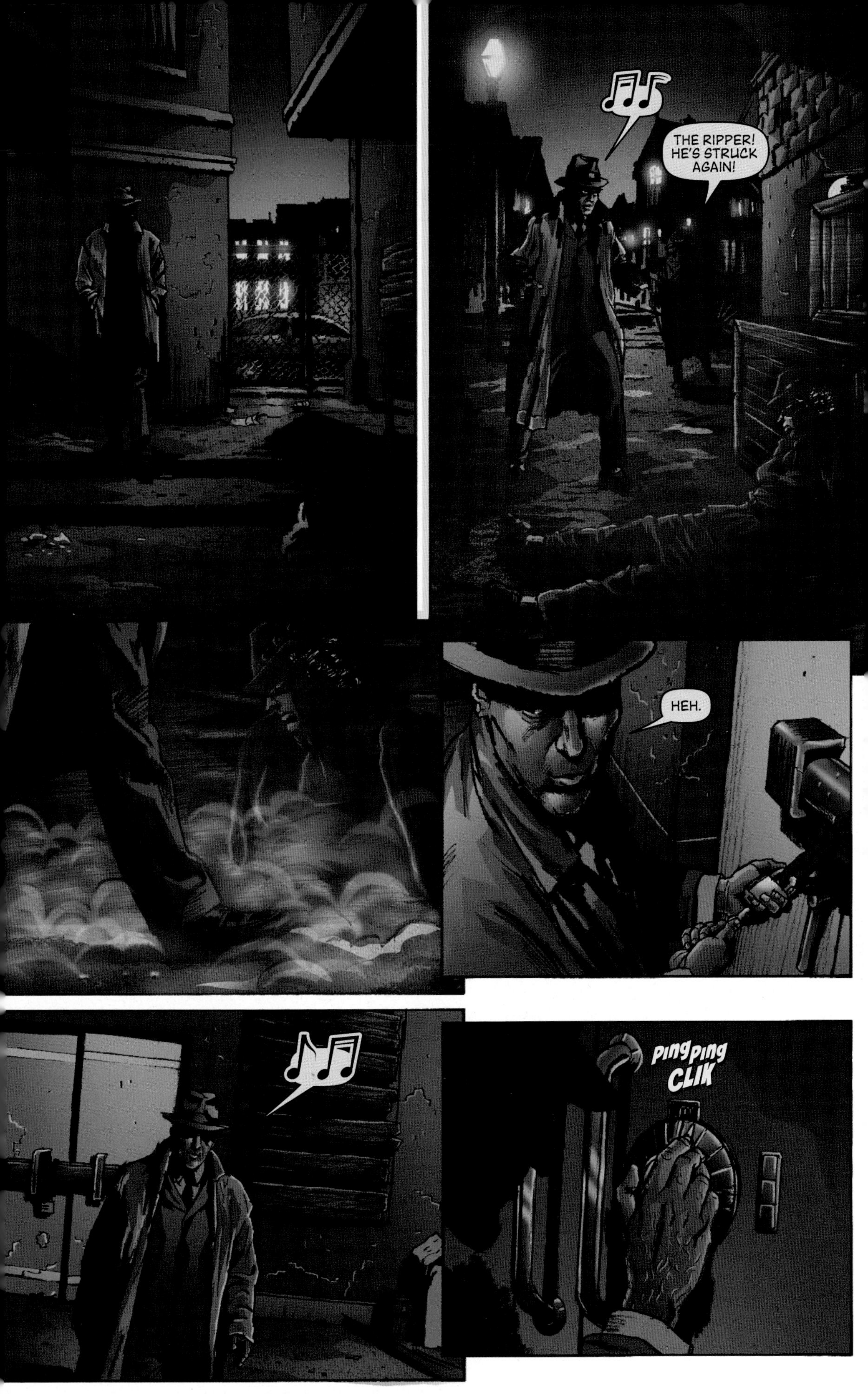

THE RIPPER! HE'S STRUCK AGAIN!
HEH.
PING PING
CLIK

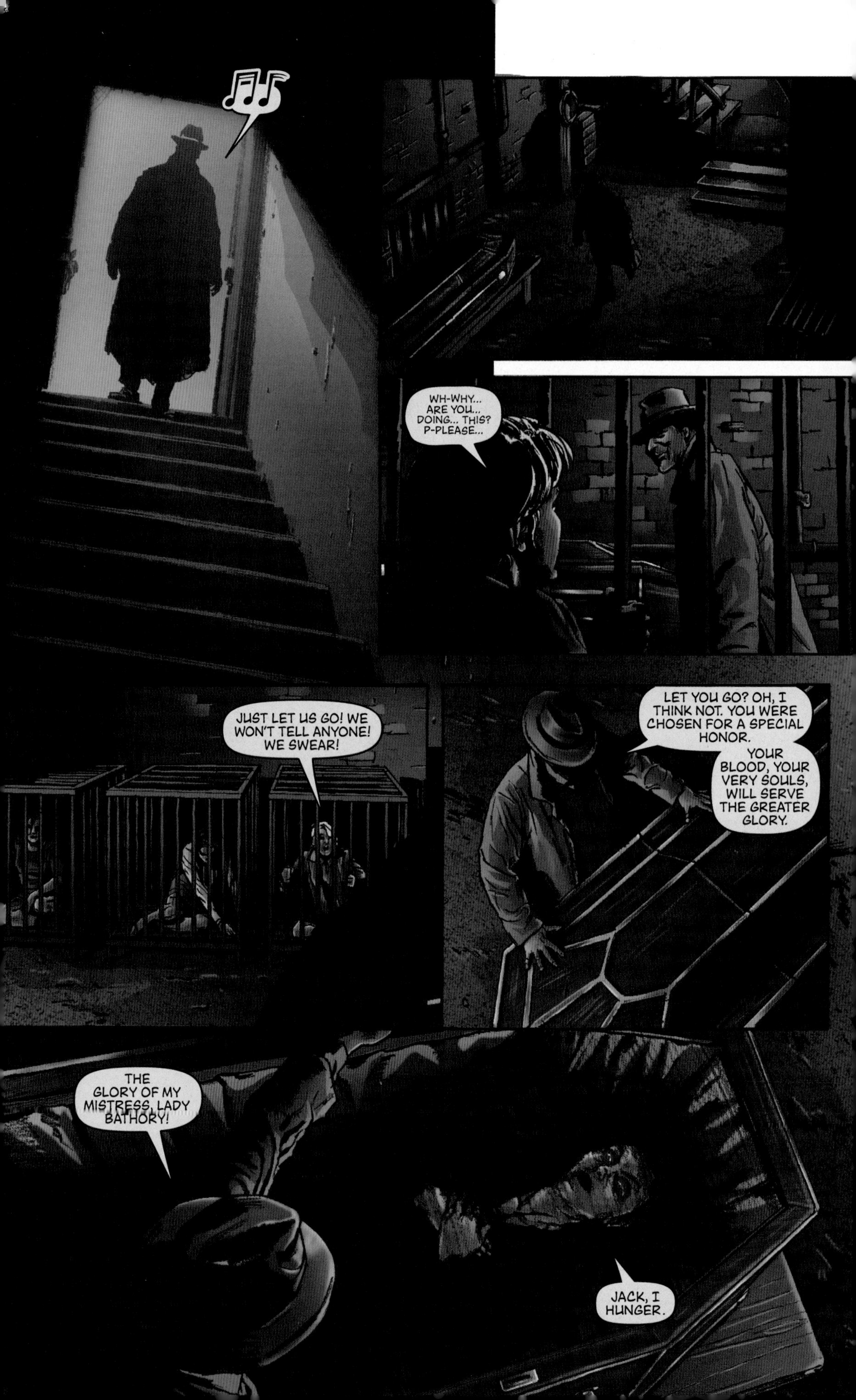
WH-WHY... ARE YOU... DOING... THIS? P-PLEASE...
JUST LET US GO! WE WON'T TELL ANYONE! WE SWEAR!
LET YOU GO? OH, I THINK NOT. YOU WERE CHOSEN FOR A SPECIAL HONOR.
YOUR BLOOD, YOUR VERY SOULS, WILL SERVE THE GREATER GLORY.
THE GLORY OF MY MISTRESS, LADY BATHORY!
JACK, I HUNGER.

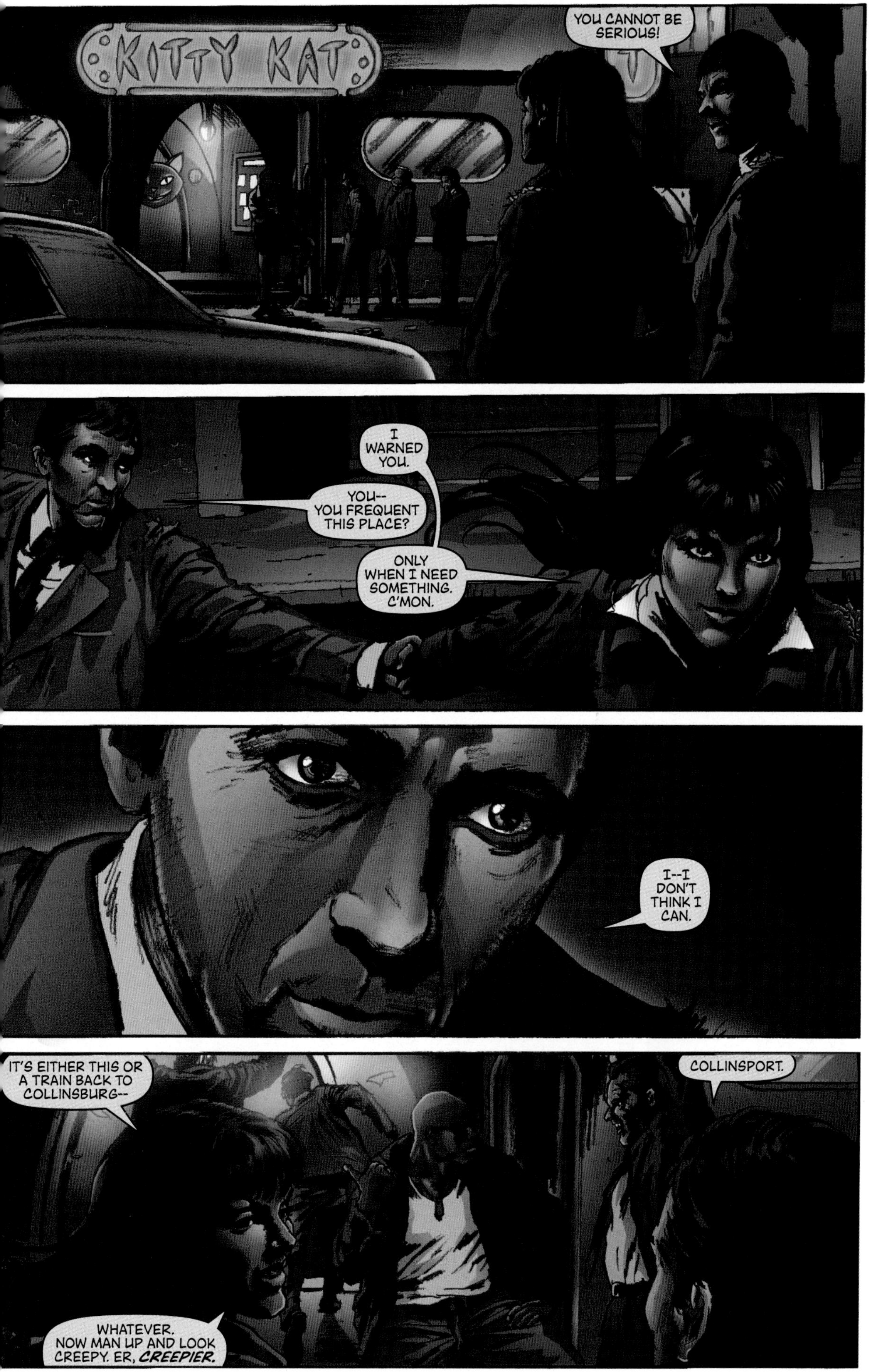
KITTY KAT
YOU CANNOT BE SERIOUS!
I WARNED YOU.
YOU-- YOU FREQUENT THIS PLACE?
ONLY WHEN I NEED SOMETHING. C'MON.
I--I DON'T THINK I CAN.
IT'S EITHER THIS OR A TRAIN BACK TO COLLINSBURG--
COLLINSPORT.
WHATEVER. NOW MAN UP AND LOOK CREEPY. ER, *CREEPIER.*

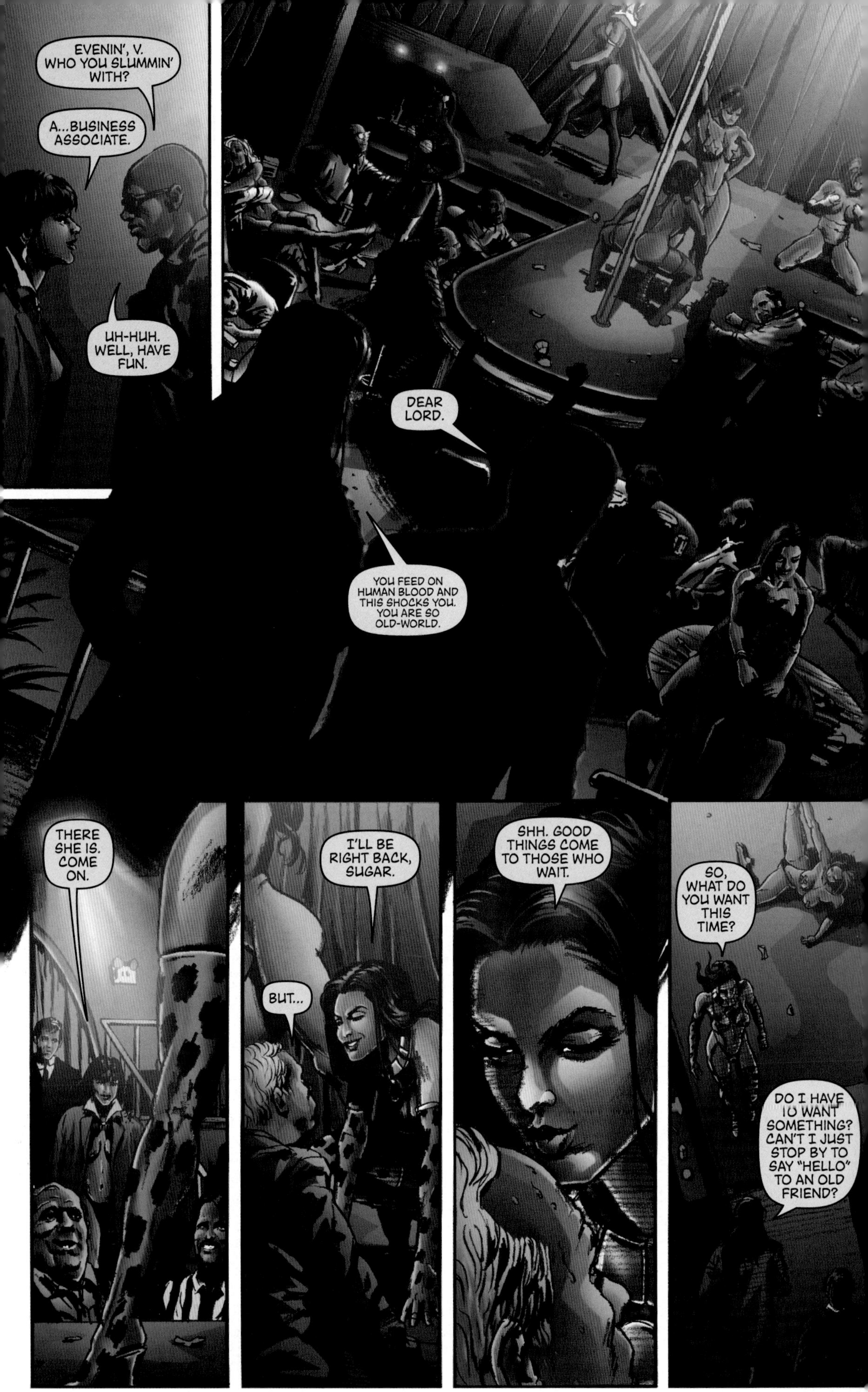
EVENIN', V. WHO YOU SLUMMIN' WITH?
A...BUSINESS ASSOCIATE.
UH-HUH. WELL, HAVE FUN.
DEAR LORD.
YOU FEED ON HUMAN BLOOD AND THIS SHOCKS YOU. YOU ARE SO OLD-WORLD.
THERE SHE IS. COME ON.
I'LL BE RIGHT BACK, SUGAR.
BUT...
SHH. GOOD THINGS COME TO THOSE WHO WAIT.
SO, WHAT DO YOU WANT THIS TIME?
DO I HAVE TO WANT SOMETHING? CAN'T I JUST STOP BY TO SAY "HELLO" TO AN OLD FRIEND?

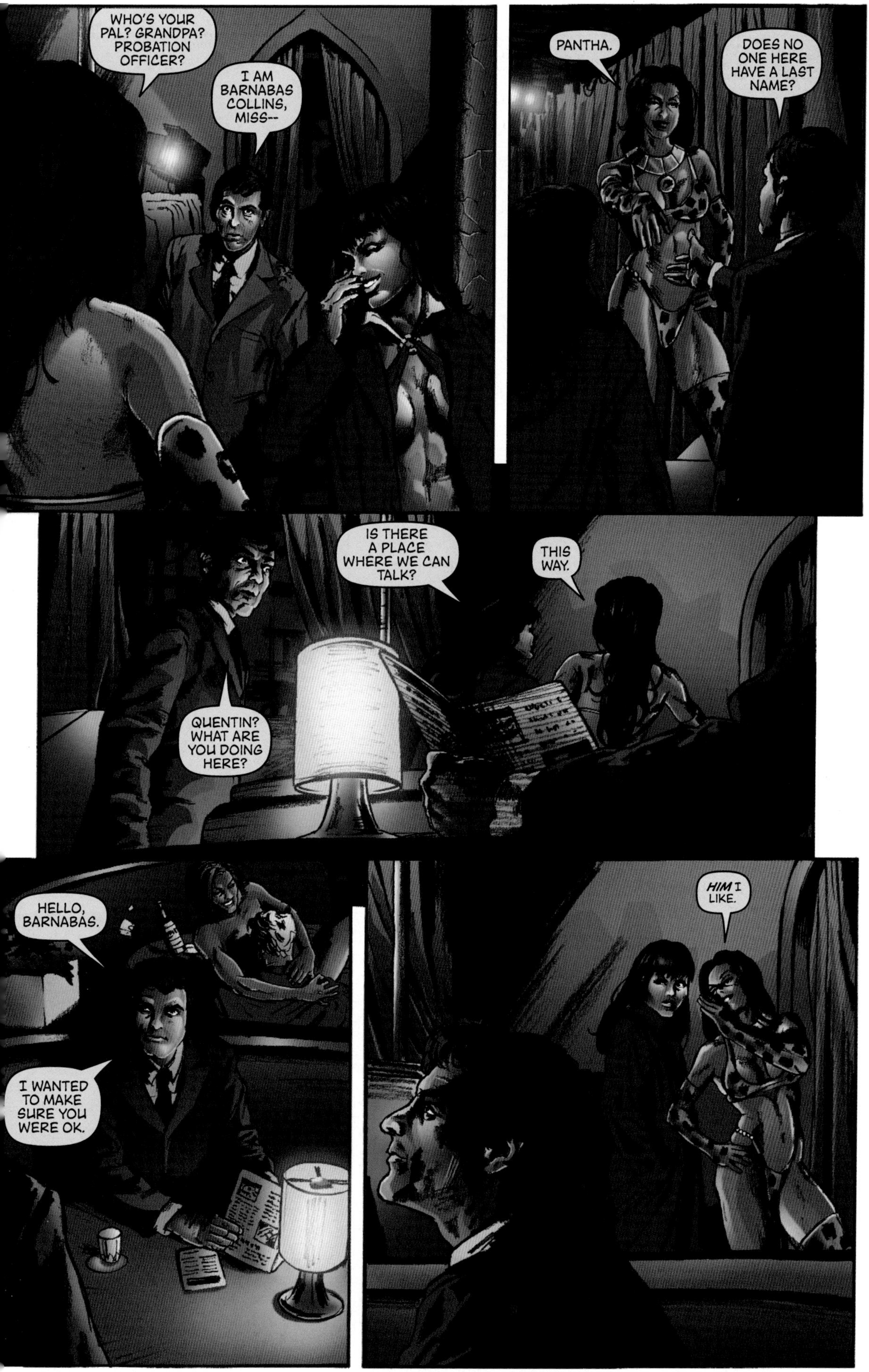

WHO'S YOUR PAL? GRANDPA? PROBATION OFFICER?
I AM BARNABAS COLLINS, MISS--
PANTHA.
DOES NO ONE HERE HAVE A LAST NAME?
IS THERE A PLACE WHERE WE CAN TALK?
THIS WAY.
QUENTIN? WHAT ARE YOU DOING HERE?
HELLO, BARNABAS.
I WANTED TO MAKE SURE YOU WERE OK.
HIM I LIKE.

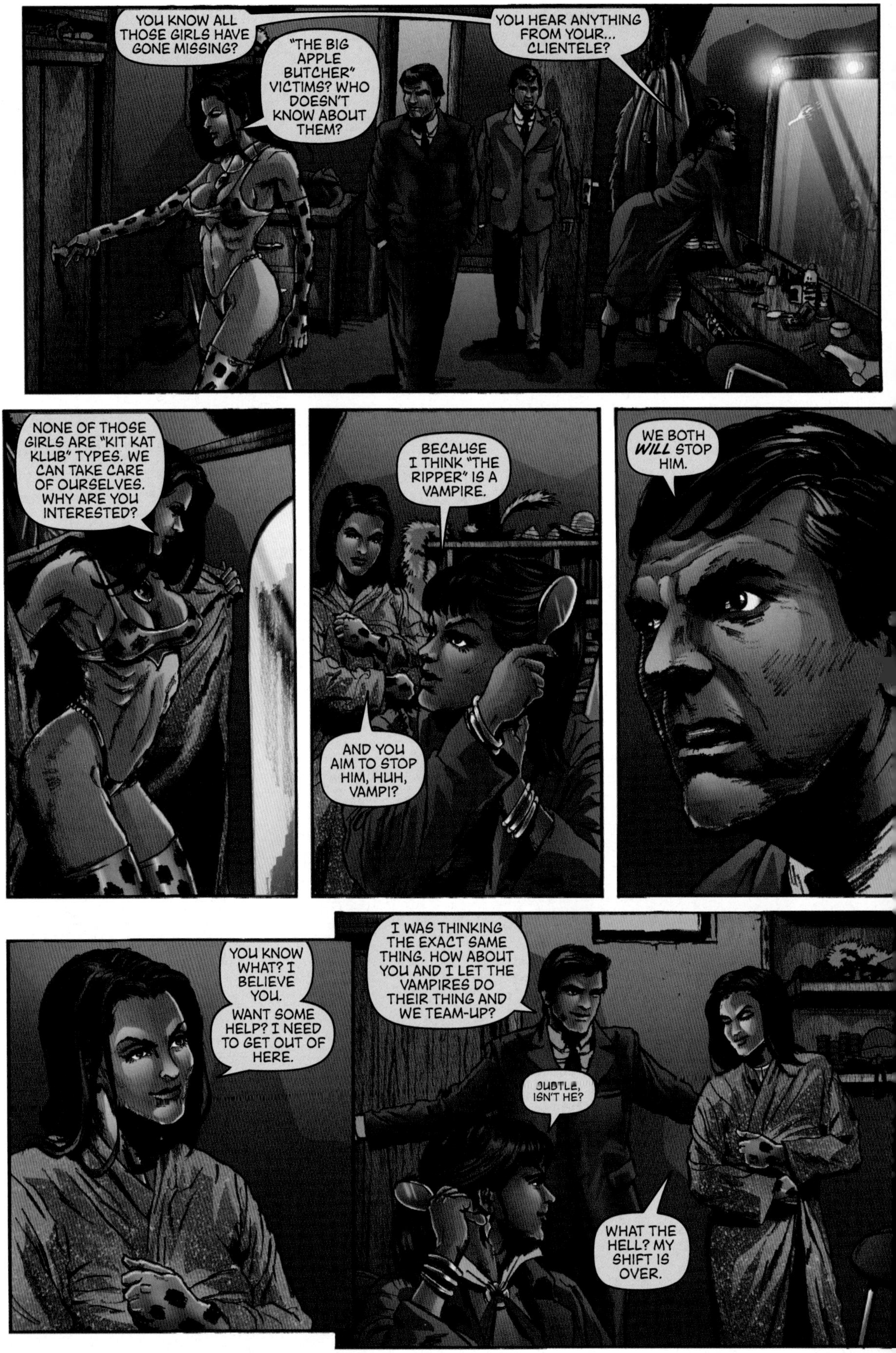
YOU KNOW ALL THOSE GIRLS HAVE GONE MISSING?
"THE BIG APPLE BUTCHER" VICTIMS? WHO DOESN'T KNOW ABOUT THEM?
YOU HEAR ANYTHING FROM YOUR... CLIENTELE?
NONE OF THOSE GIRLS ARE "KIT KAT KLUB" TYPES. WE CAN TAKE CARE OF OURSELVES. WHY ARE YOU INTERESTED?
BECAUSE I THINK "THE RIPPER" IS A VAMPIRE.
AND YOU AIM TO STOP HIM, HUH, VAMPI?
WE BOTH *WILL* STOP HIM.
YOU KNOW WHAT? I BELIEVE YOU.
WANT SOME HELP? I NEED TO GET OUT OF HERE.
I WAS THINKING THE EXACT SAME THING. HOW ABOUT YOU AND I LET THE VAMPIRES DO THEIR THING AND WE TEAM-UP?
SUBTLE, ISN'T HE?
WHAT THE HELL? MY SHIFT IS OVER.

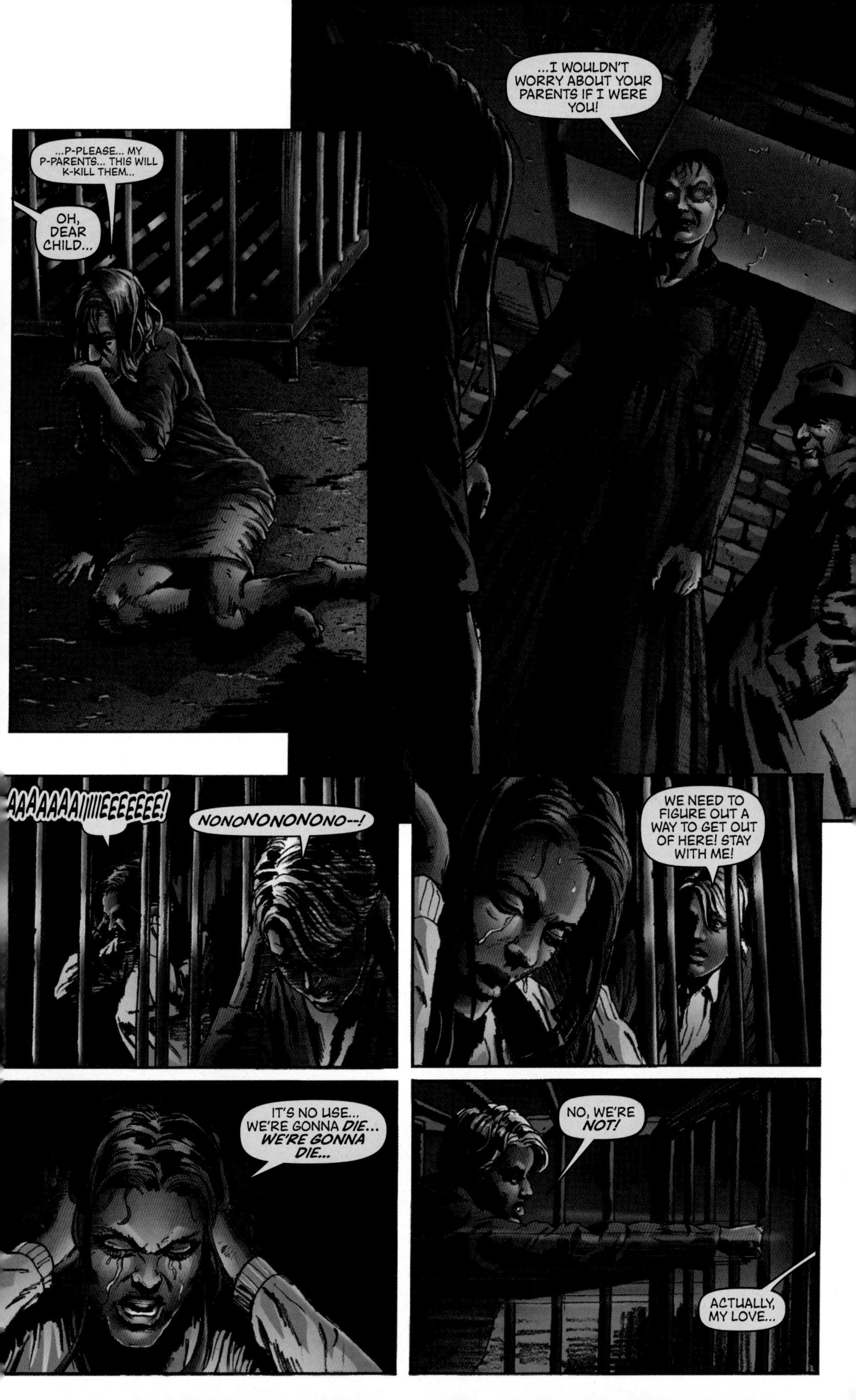
...P-PLEASE... MY P-PARENTS... THIS WILL K-KILL THEM...
OH, DEAR CHILD...
...I WOULDN'T WORRY ABOUT YOUR PARENTS IF I WERE YOU!
AAAAAAAIIIIIEEEEEEE!
NONONONONONO--!
WE NEED TO FIGURE OUT A WAY TO GET OUT OF HERE! STAY WITH ME!
IT'S NO USE... WE'RE GONNA *DIE*... ***WE'RE GONNA DIE***...
NO, WE'RE ***NOT!***
ACTUALLY, MY LOVE...

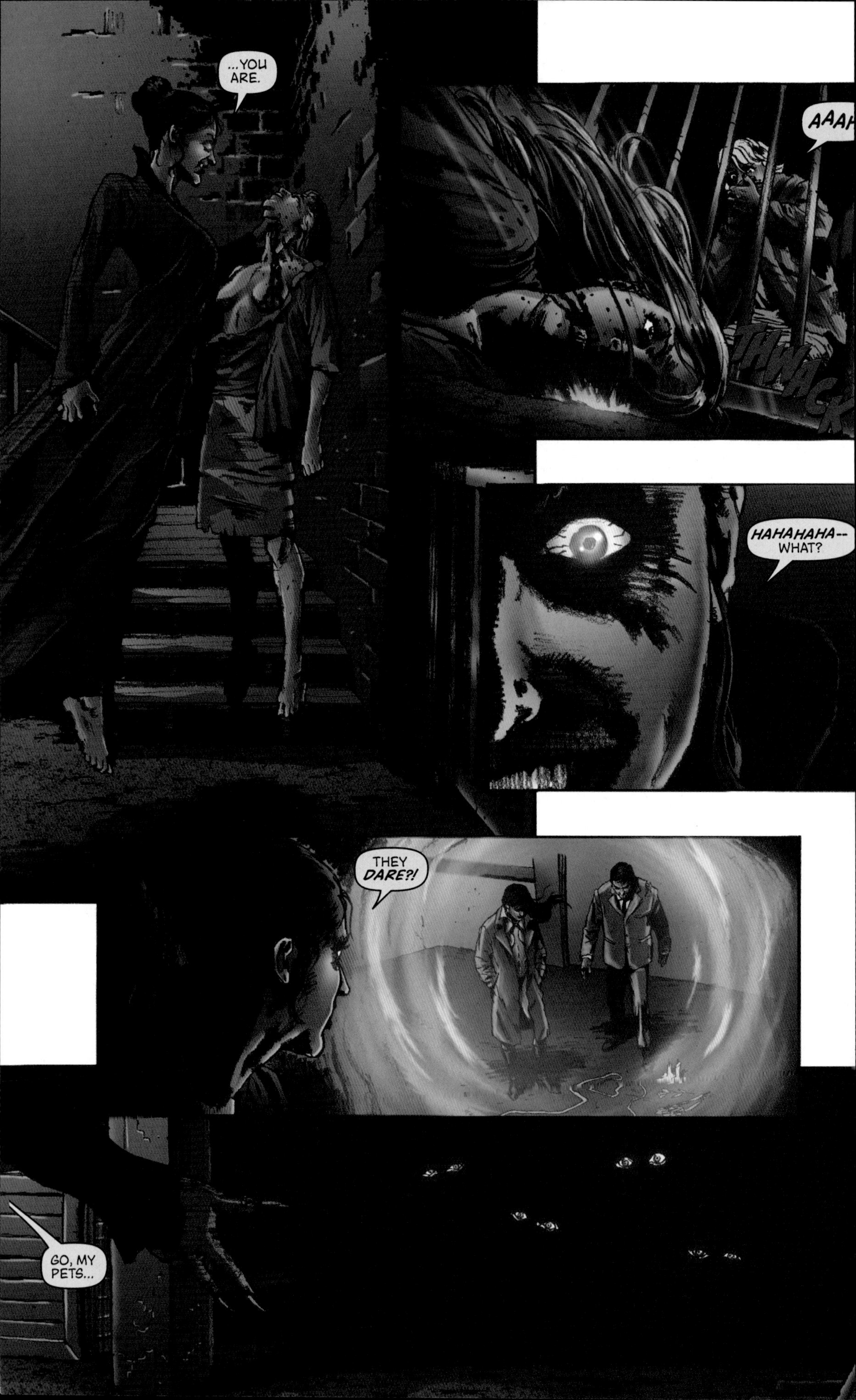
...YOU ARE.
AAAH
THWACK
HAHAHAHA-- WHAT?
THEY DARE?!
GO, MY PETS...

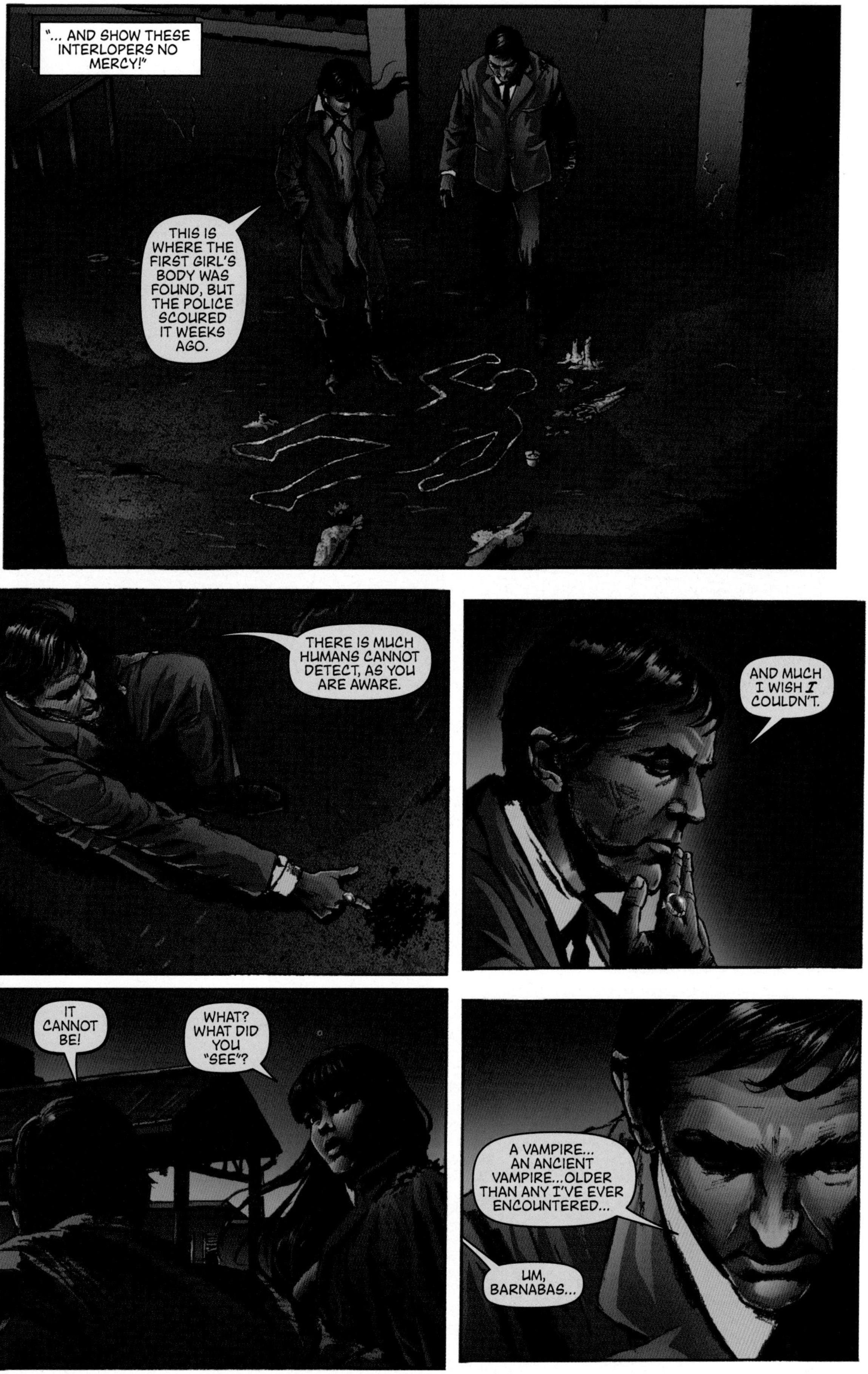
"... AND SHOW THESE INTERLOPERS NO MERCY!"
THIS IS WHERE THE FIRST GIRL'S BODY WAS FOUND, BUT THE POLICE SCOURED IT WEEKS AGO.
THERE IS MUCH HUMANS CANNOT DETECT, AS YOU ARE AWARE.
AND MUCH I WISH *I* COULDN'T.
IT CANNOT BE!
WHAT? WHAT DID YOU "SEE"?
A VAMPIRE... AN ANCIENT VAMPIRE...OLDER THAN ANY I'VE EVER ENCOUNTERED...
UM, BARNABAS...

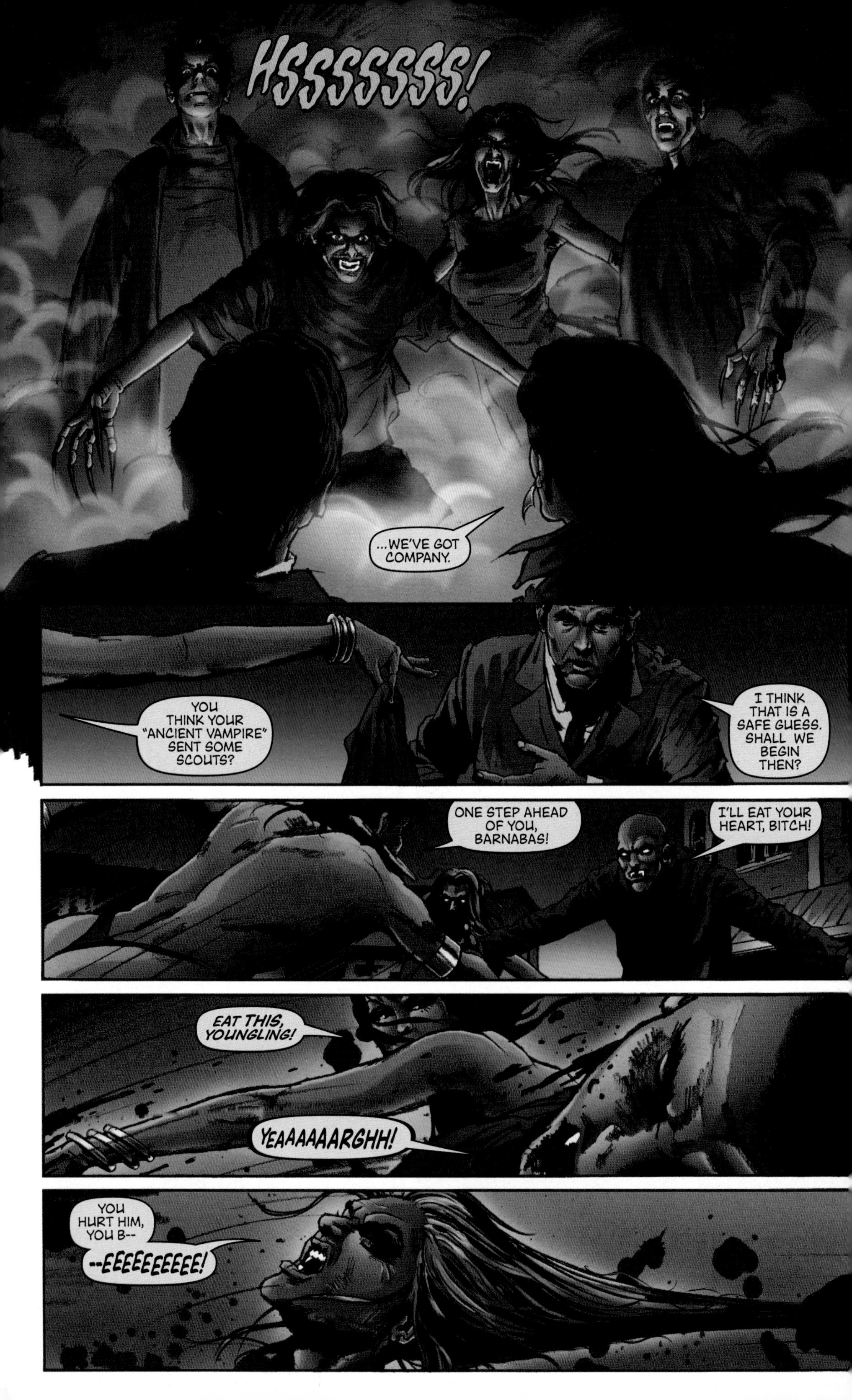
HSSSSSSS!
...WE'VE GOT COMPANY.
YOU THINK YOUR "ANCIENT VAMPIRE" SENT SOME SCOUTS?
I THINK THAT IS A SAFE GUESS. SHALL WE BEGIN THEN?
ONE STEP AHEAD OF YOU, BARNABAS!
I'LL EAT YOUR HEART, BITCH!
EAT THIS, YOUNGLING!
YEAAAAAARGHH!
YOU HURT HIM, YOU B--
--EEEEEEEEEE!

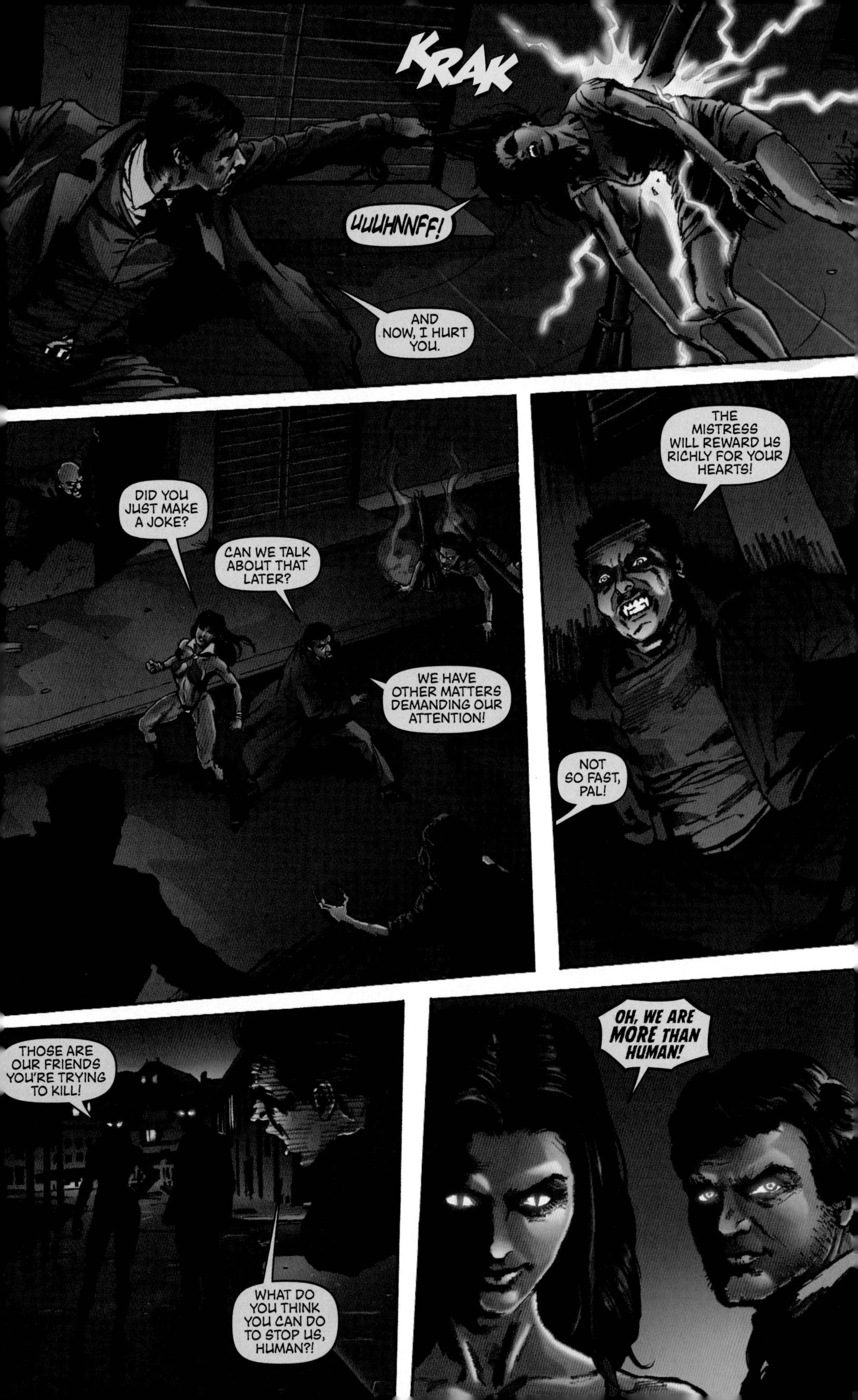
KRAK
UUUHNNFF!
AND NOW, I HURT YOU.
DID YOU JUST MAKE A JOKE?
CAN WE TALK ABOUT THAT LATER?
WE HAVE OTHER MATTERS DEMANDING OUR ATTENTION!
THE MISTRESS WILL REWARD US RICHLY FOR YOUR HEARTS!
NOT SO FAST, PAL!
THOSE ARE OUR FRIENDS YOU'RE TRYING TO KILL!
WHAT DO YOU THINK YOU CAN DO TO STOP US, HUMAN?!
OH, WE ARE MORE THAN HUMAN!

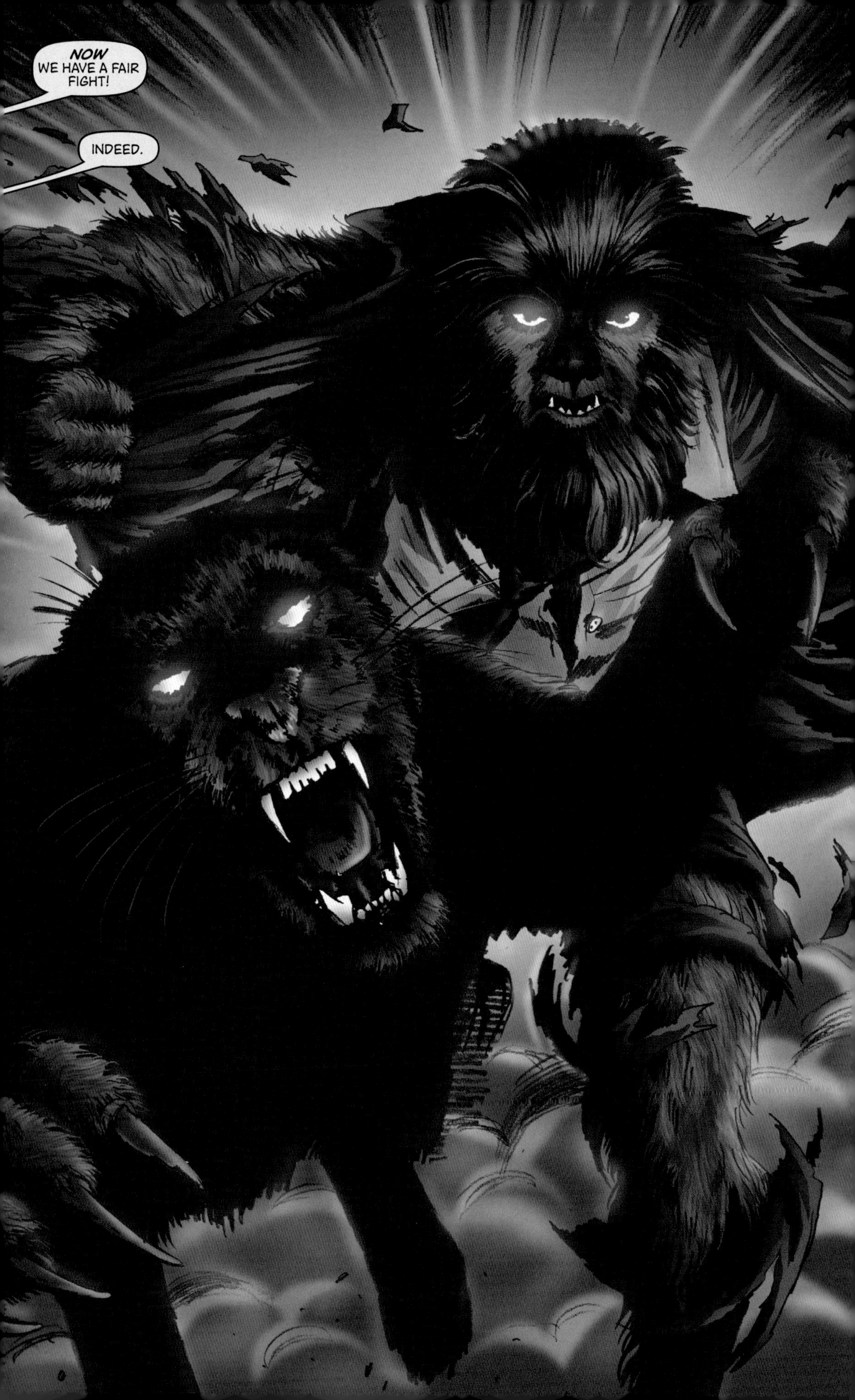
NOW WE HAVE A FAIR FIGHT!
INDEED.

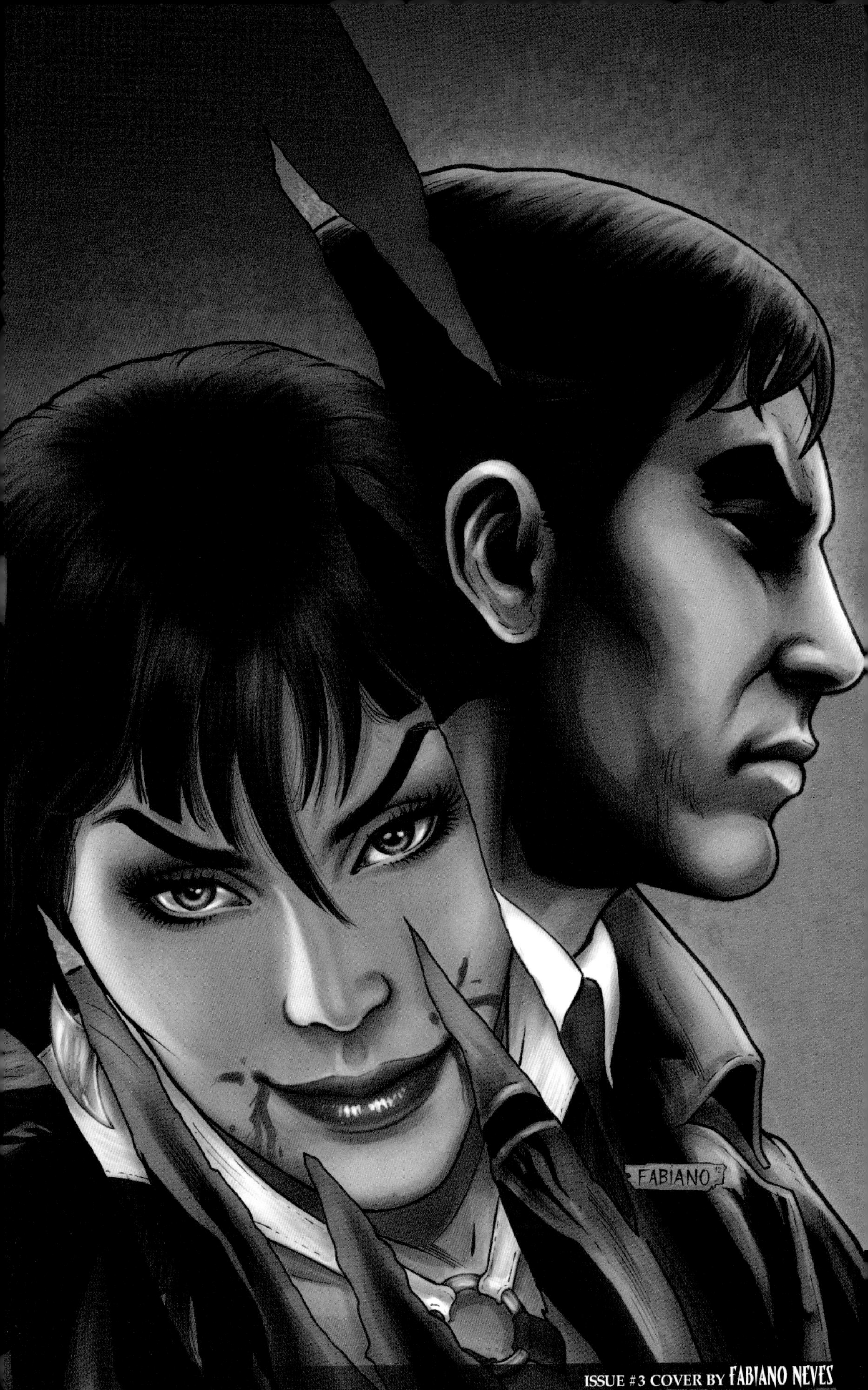
FABIANO

ISSUE #3 COVER BY FABIANO NEVES

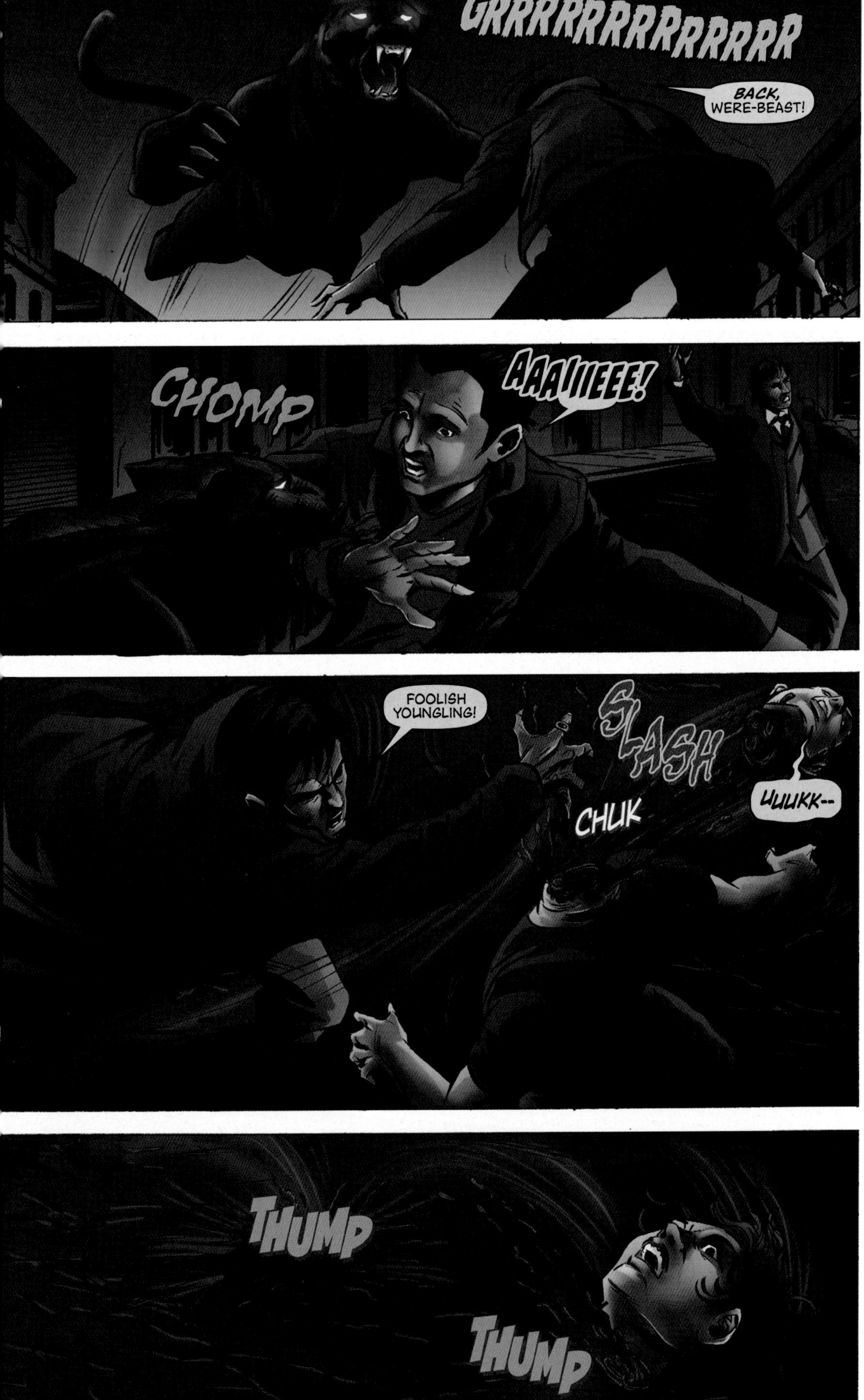
GRRRRRRRRRRRRR
BACK, WERE-BEAST!
CHOMP
AAAIIIEEE!
FOOLISH YOUNGLING!
SLASH
CHUK
UUUKK--
THUMP
THUMP

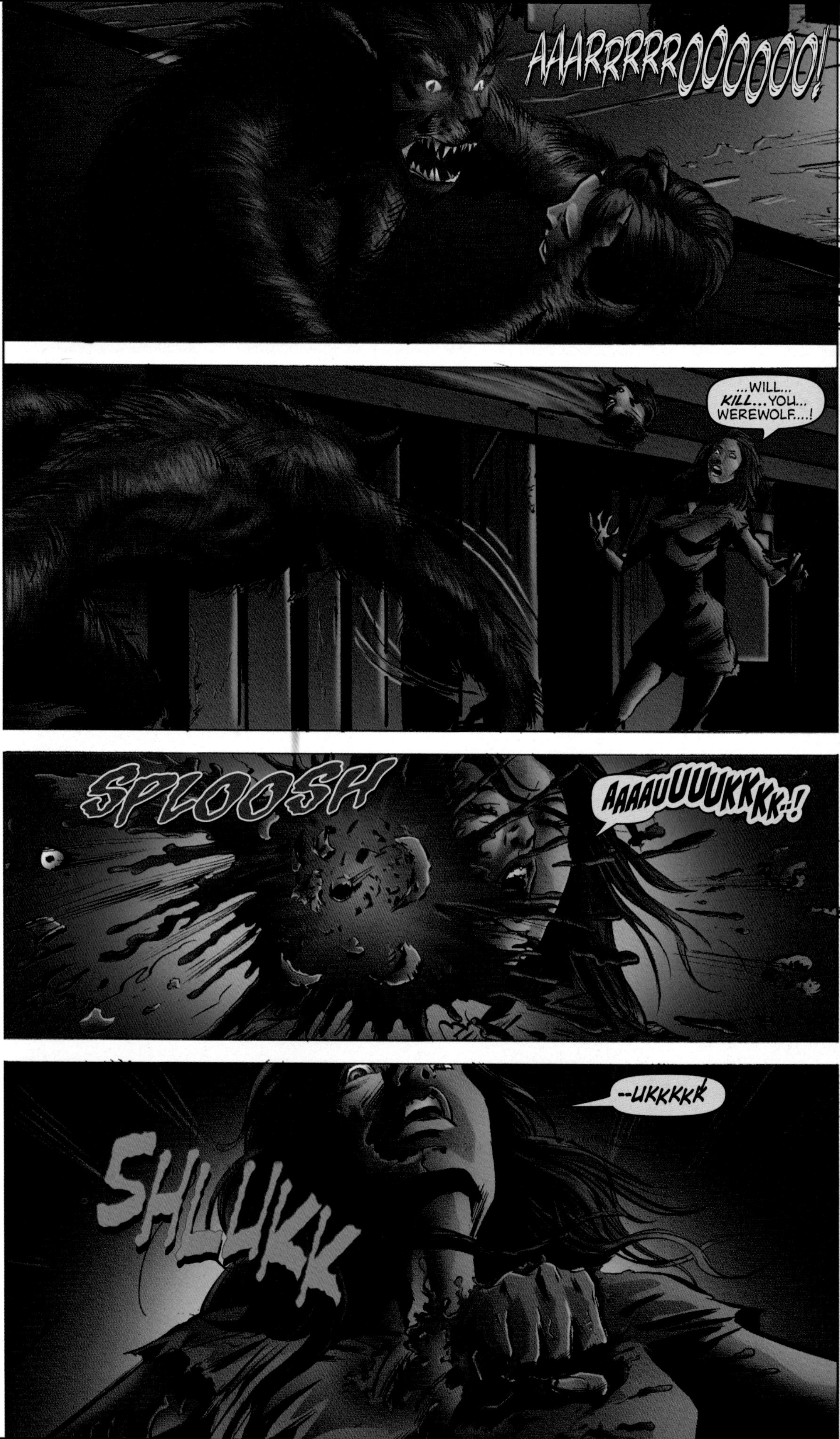
AAARRRRROOOOOO!
...WILL...
KILL...YOU...
WEREWOLF....!
SPLOOSH
AAAAUUUUKKKK-!
SHLUKK
--UKKKKK

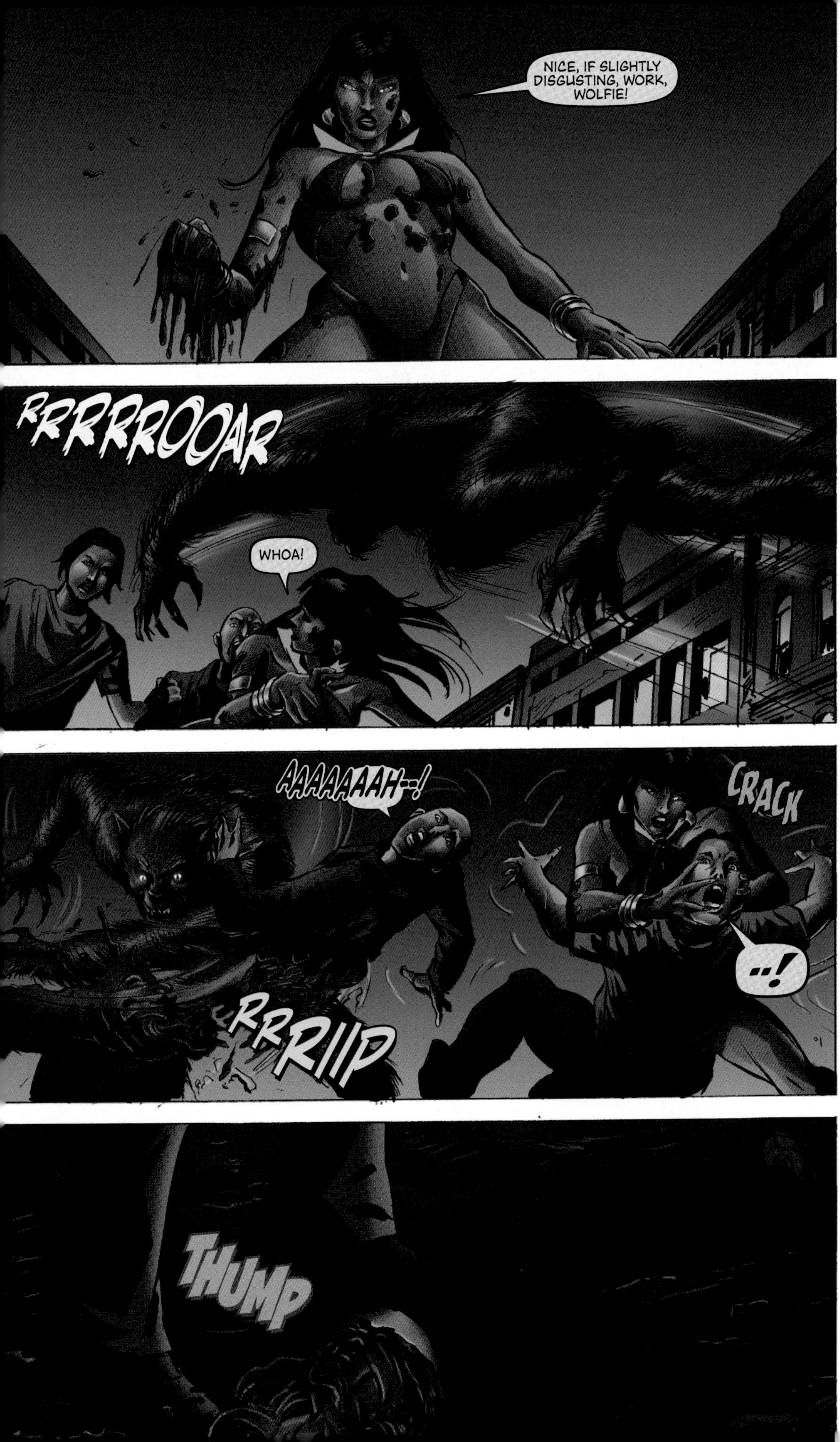
NICE, IF SLIGHTLY DISGUSTING, WORK, WOLFIE!
RRRRRROOAR
WHOA!
AAAAAAAH--!
CRACK
--!
RRRIIP
THUMP

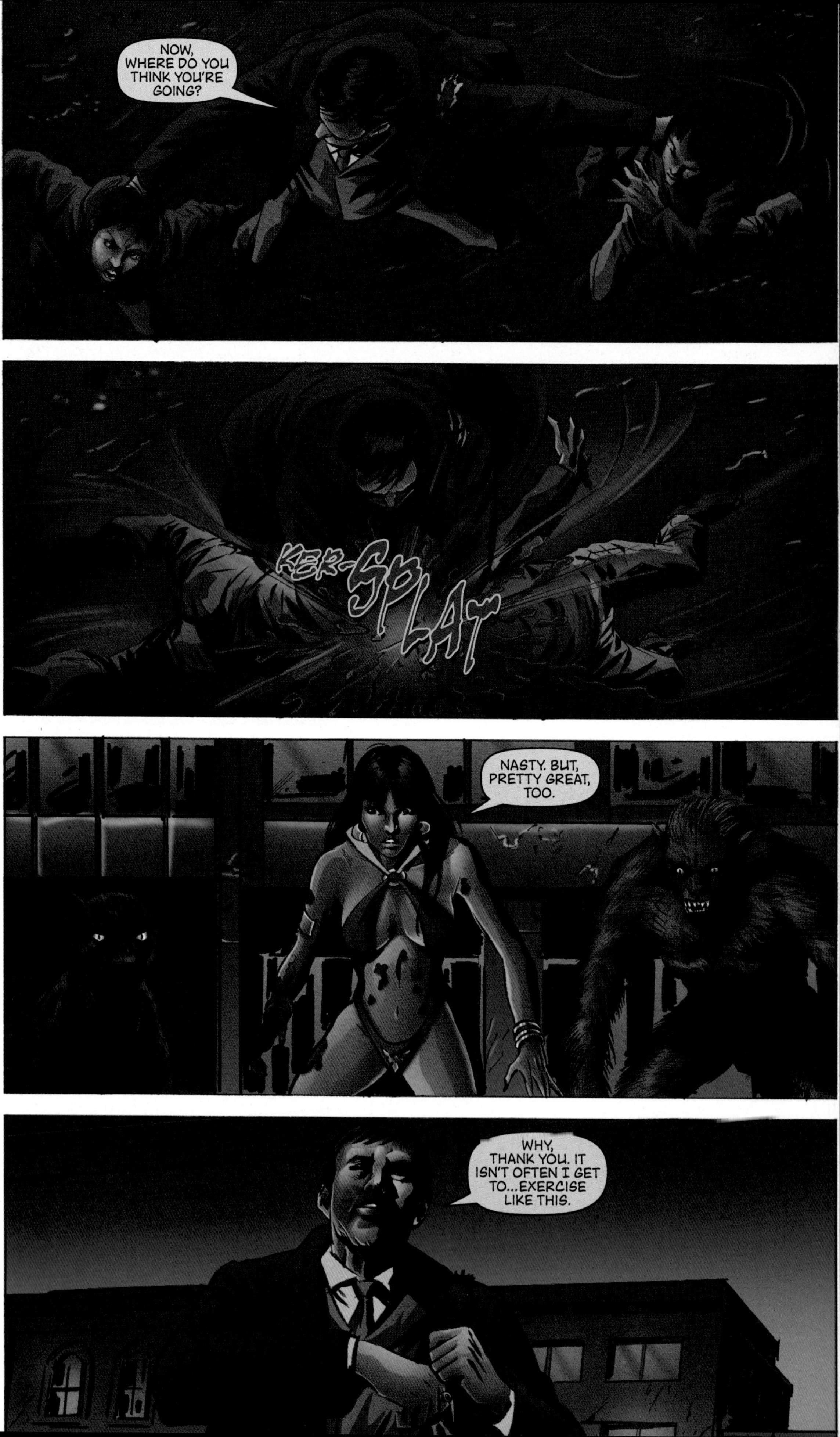
NOW, WHERE DO YOU THINK YOU'RE GOING?
KER-SPLAT
NASTY. BUT, PRETTY GREAT, TOO.
WHY, THANK YOU. IT ISN'T OFTEN I GET TO...EXERCISE LIKE THIS.

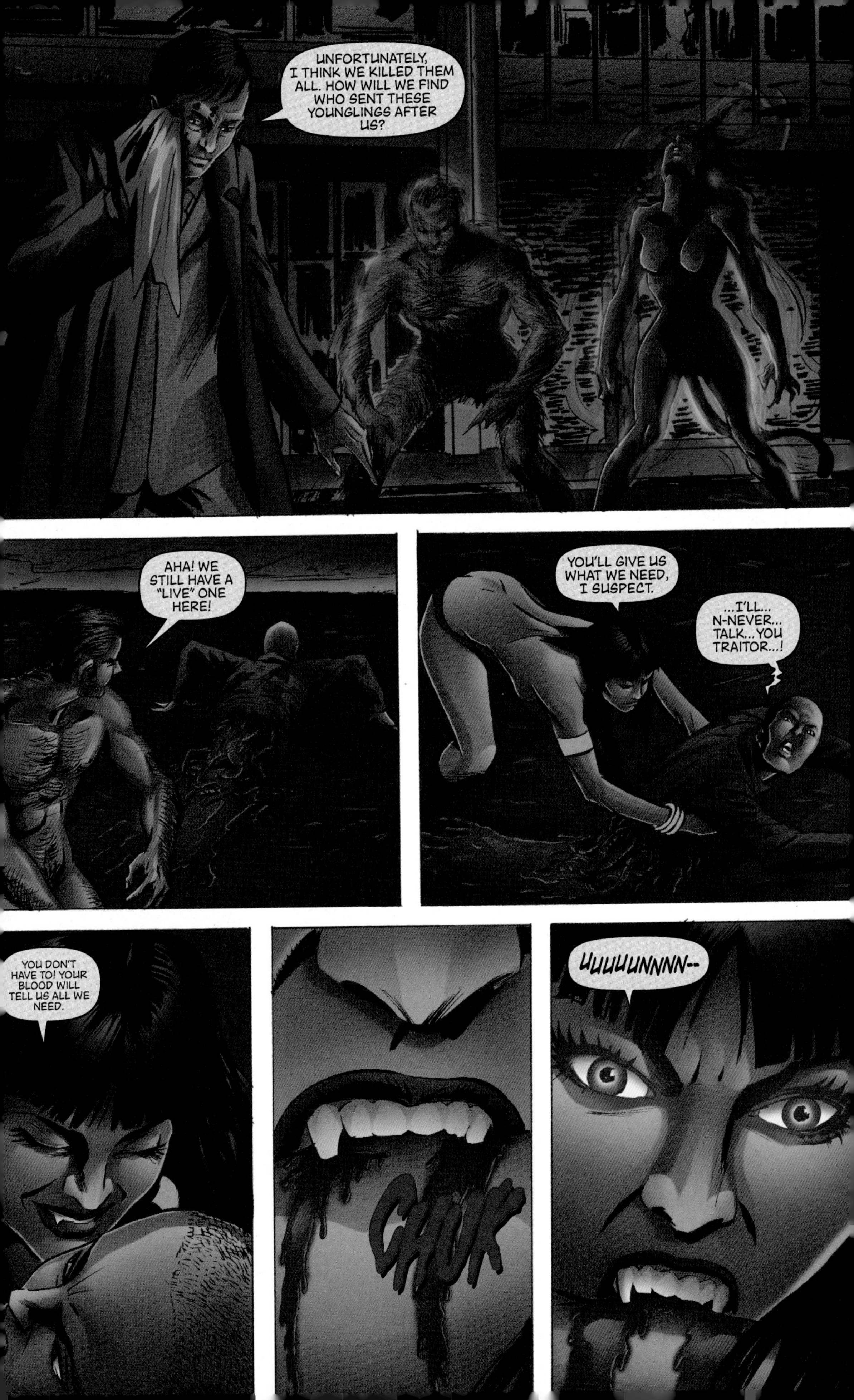
UNFORTUNATELY, I THINK WE KILLED THEM ALL. HOW WILL WE FIND WHO SENT THESE YOUNGLINGS AFTER US?
AHA! WE STILL HAVE A "LIVE" ONE HERE!
YOU'LL GIVE US WHAT WE NEED, I SUSPECT.
...I'LL... N-NEVER... TALK...YOU TRAITOR...!
YOU DON'T HAVE TO! YOUR BLOOD WILL TELL US ALL WE NEED.
CHUK
UUUUUNNNN--

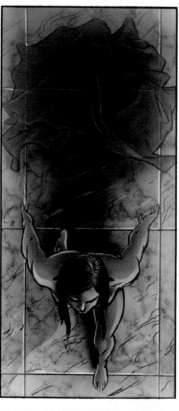

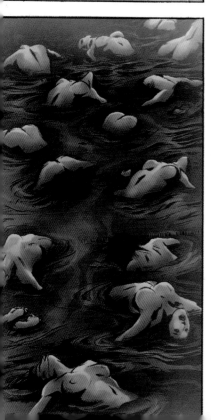

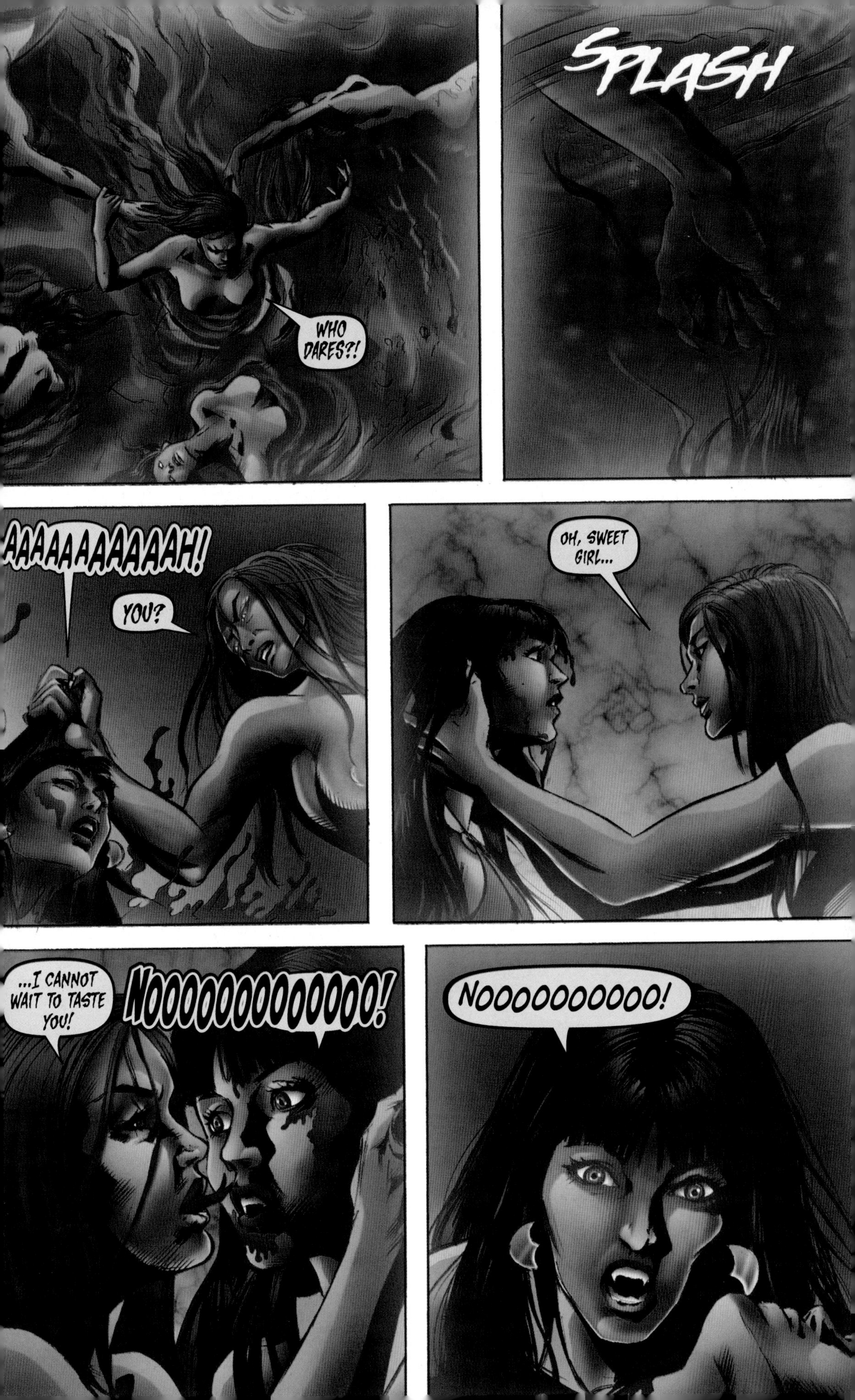
WHO DARES?!
SPLASH
AAAAAAAAAAAH!
YOU?
OH, SWEET GIRL...
...I CANNOT WAIT TO TASTE YOU!
NOOOOOOOOOOOOO!
NOOOOOOOOOO!

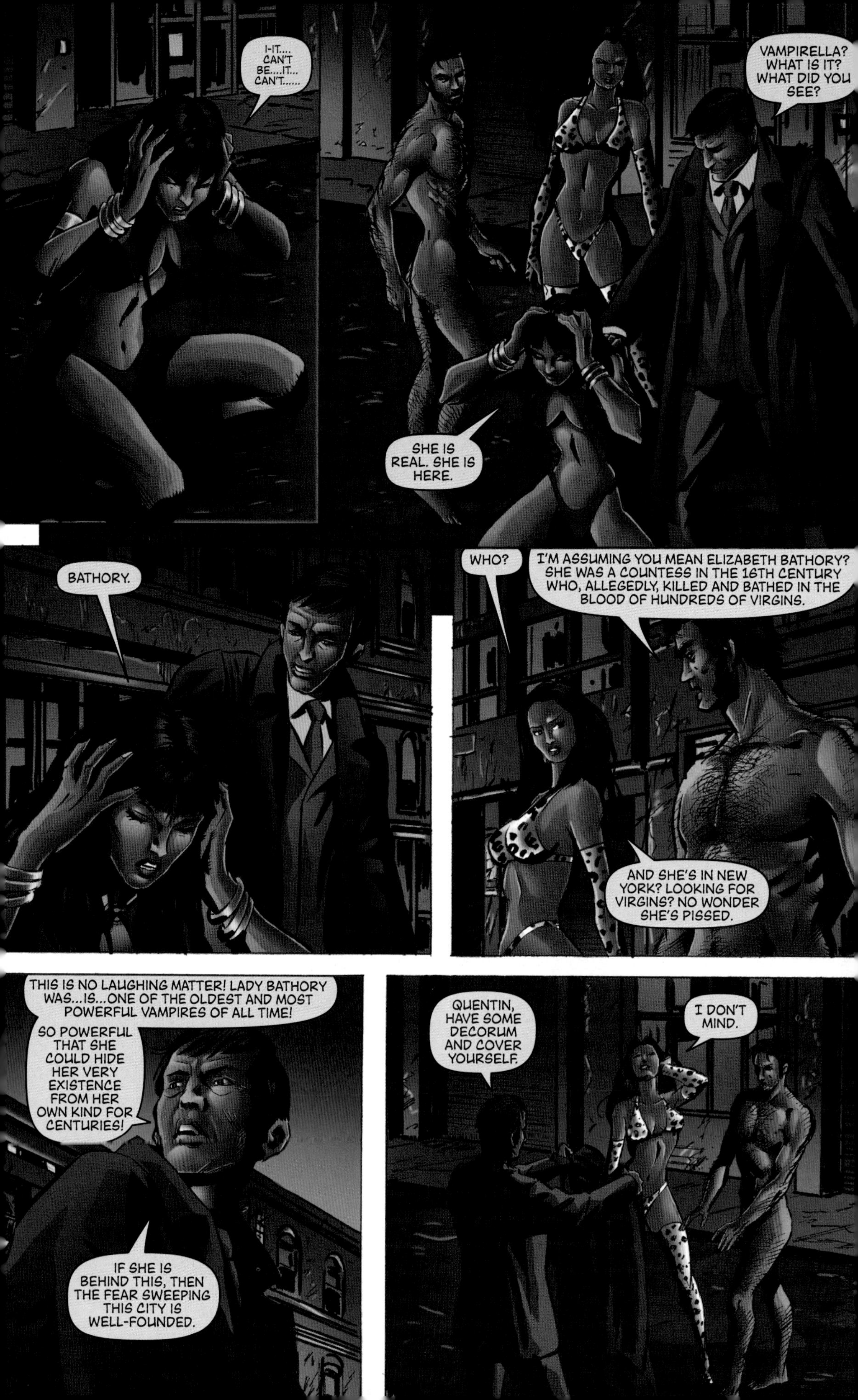
I-IT... CAN'T BE....IT... CAN'T.....
VAMPIRELLA? WHAT IS IT? WHAT DID YOU SEE?
SHE IS REAL. SHE IS HERE.
BATHORY.
WHO?
I'M ASSUMING YOU MEAN ELIZABETH BATHORY? SHE WAS A COUNTESS IN THE 16TH CENTURY WHO, ALLEGEDLY, KILLED AND BATHED IN THE BLOOD OF HUNDREDS OF VIRGINS.
AND SHE'S IN NEW YORK? LOOKING FOR VIRGINS? NO WONDER SHE'S PISSED.
THIS IS NO LAUGHING MATTER! LADY BATHORY WAS...IS...ONE OF THE OLDEST AND MOST POWERFUL VAMPIRES OF ALL TIME!
SO POWERFUL THAT SHE COULD HIDE HER VERY EXISTENCE FROM HER OWN KIND FOR CENTURIES!
IF SHE IS BEHIND THIS, THEN THE FEAR SWEEPING THIS CITY IS WELL-FOUNDED.
QUENTIN, HAVE SOME DECORUM AND COVER YOURSELF.
I DON'T MIND.

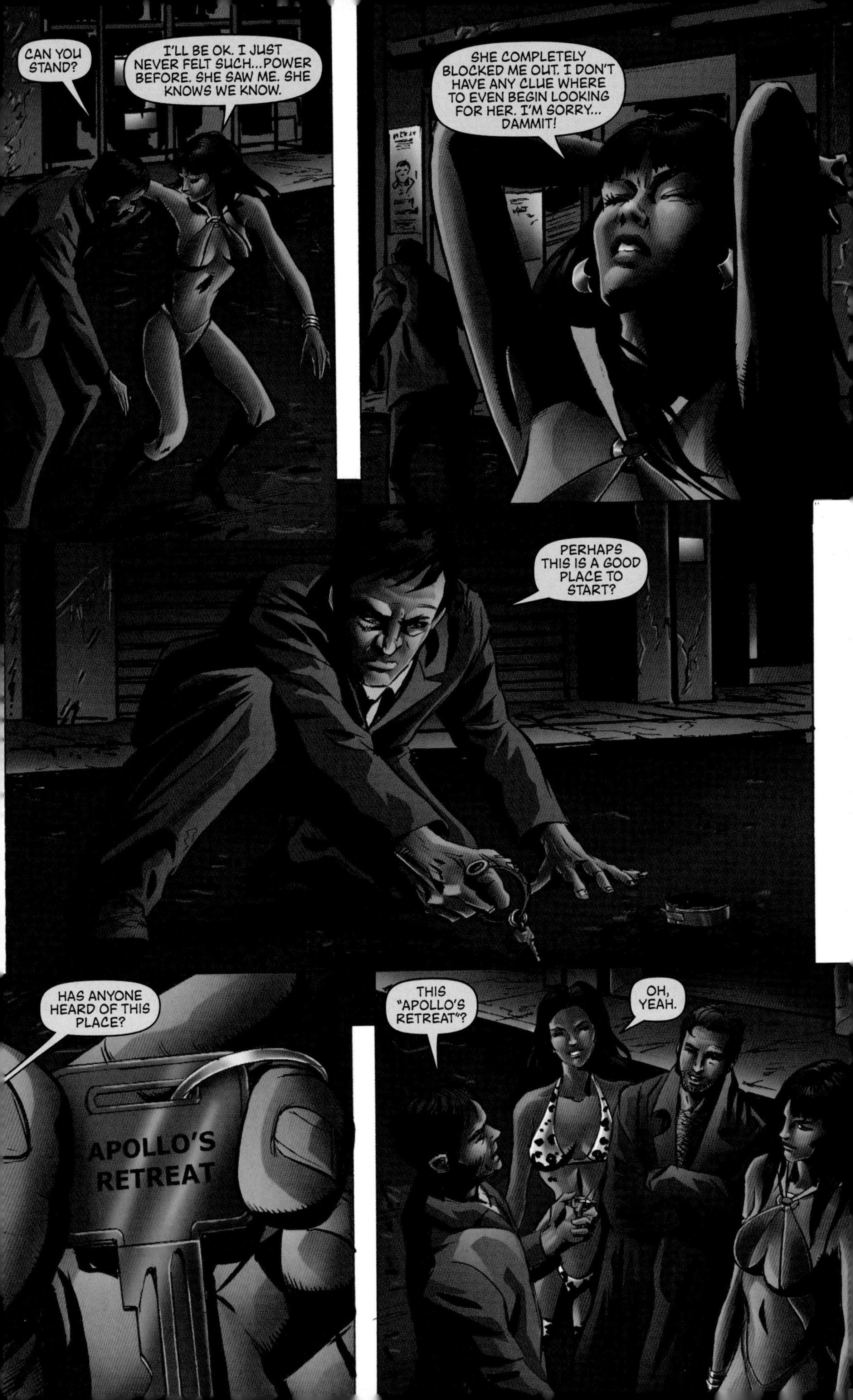
CAN YOU STAND?
I'LL BE OK. I JUST NEVER FELT SUCH...POWER BEFORE. SHE SAW ME. SHE KNOWS WE KNOW.
SHE COMPLETELY BLOCKED ME OUT. I DON'T HAVE ANY CLUE WHERE TO EVEN BEGIN LOOKING FOR HER. I'M SORRY... DAMMIT!
PERHAPS THIS IS A GOOD PLACE TO START?
HAS ANYONE HEARD OF THIS PLACE?
APOLLO'S RETREAT
THIS "APOLLO'S RETREAT"?
OH, YEAH.

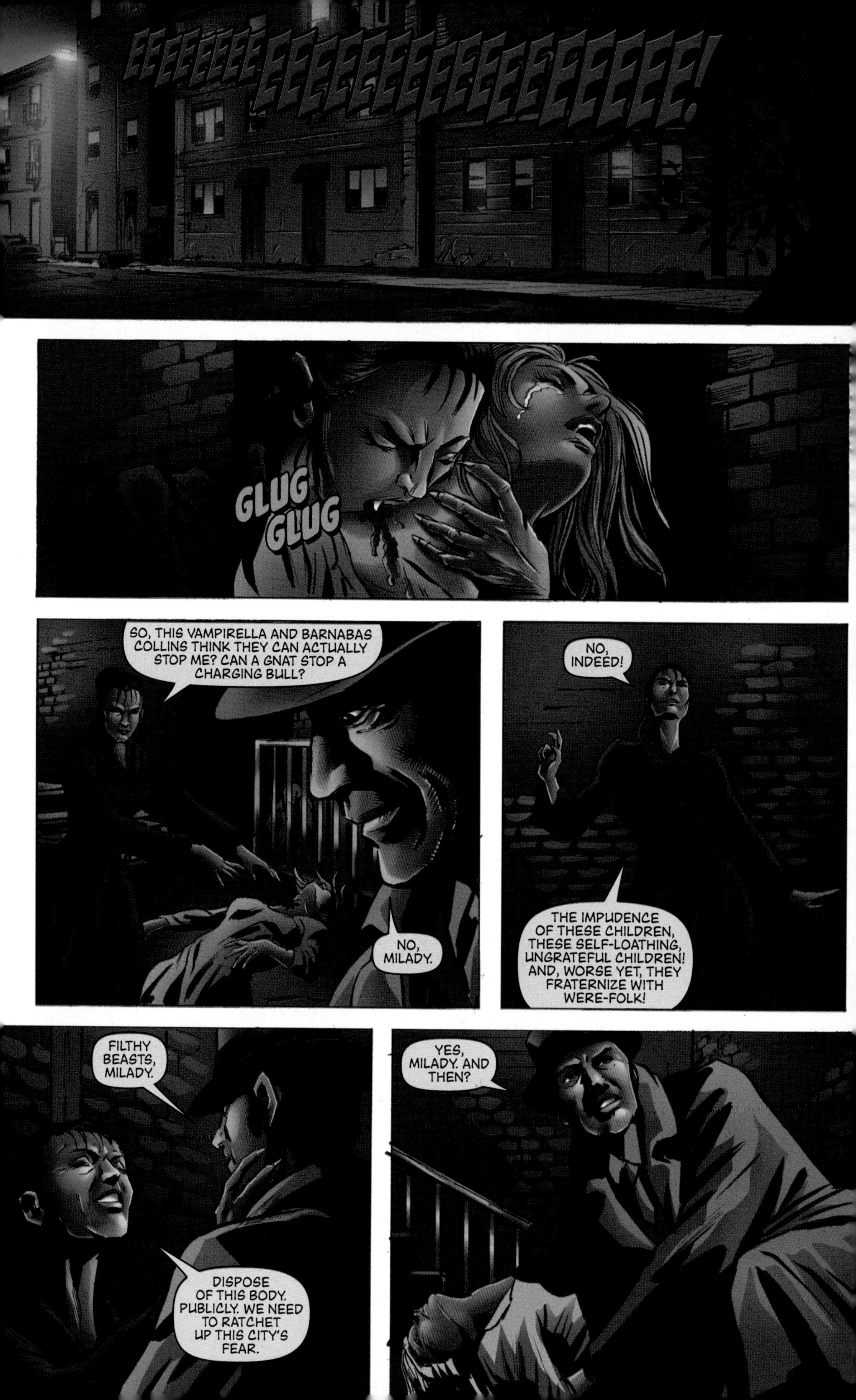
EEEEEEEEEEEEEEEEEEEEEEEEEE!
GLUG GLUG
SO, THIS VAMPIRELLA AND BARNABAS COLLINS THINK THEY CAN ACTUALLY STOP ME? CAN A GNAT STOP A CHARGING BULL?
NO, MILADY.
NO, INDEED!
THE IMPUDENCE OF THESE CHILDREN, THESE SELF-LOATHING, UNGRATEFUL CHILDREN! AND, WORSE YET, THEY FRATERNIZE WITH WERE-FOLK!
FILTHY BEASTS, MILADY.
DISPOSE OF THIS BODY. PUBLICLY. WE NEED TO RATCHET UP THIS CITY'S FEAR.
YES, MILADY. AND THEN?

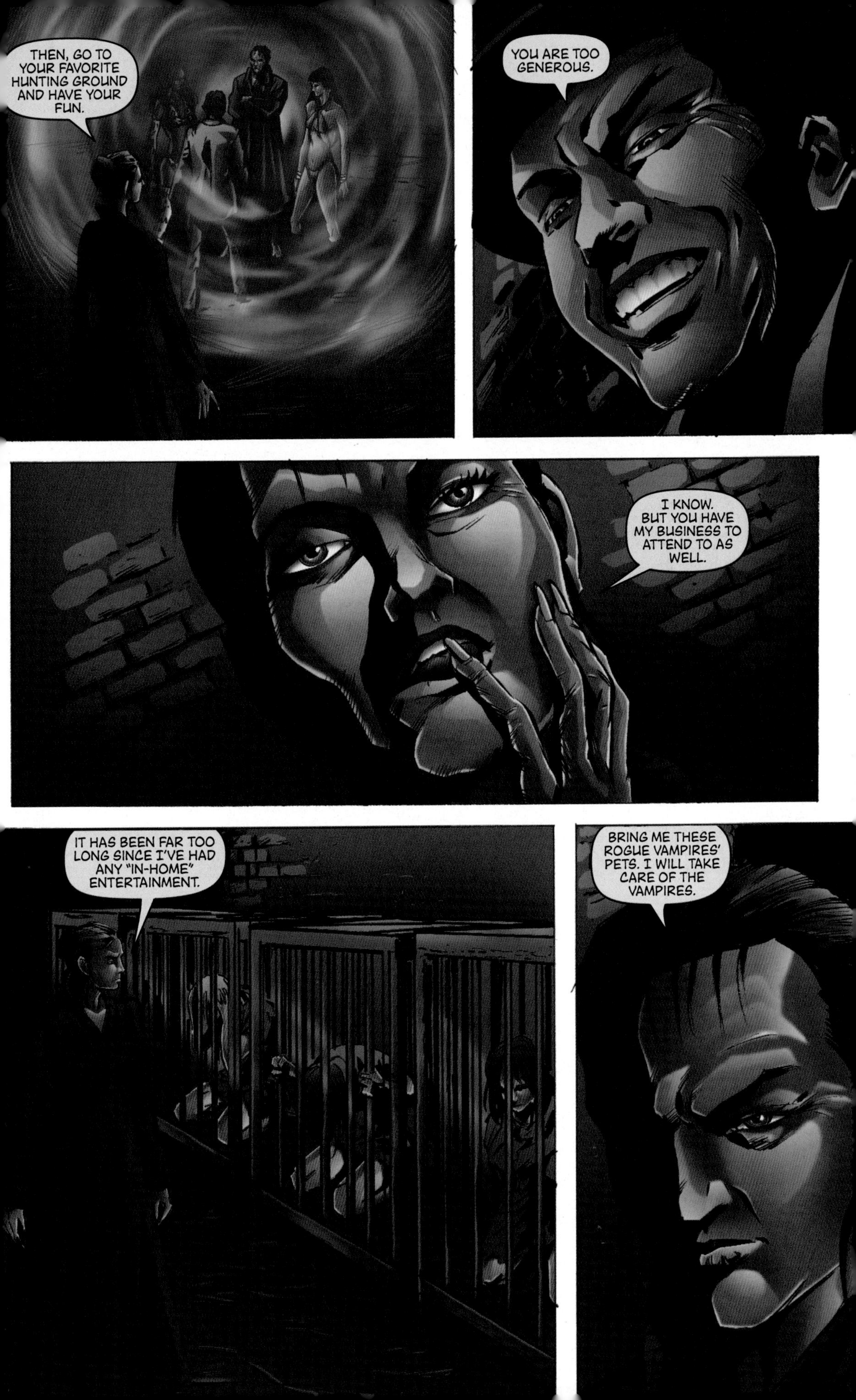
THEN, GO TO YOUR FAVORITE HUNTING GROUND AND HAVE YOUR FUN.
YOU ARE TOO GENEROUS.
I KNOW. BUT YOU HAVE MY BUSINESS TO ATTEND TO AS WELL.
IT HAS BEEN FAR TOO LONG SINCE I'VE HAD ANY "IN-HOME" ENTERTAINMENT.
BRING ME THESE ROGUE VAMPIRES' PETS. I WILL TAKE CARE OF THE VAMPIRES.

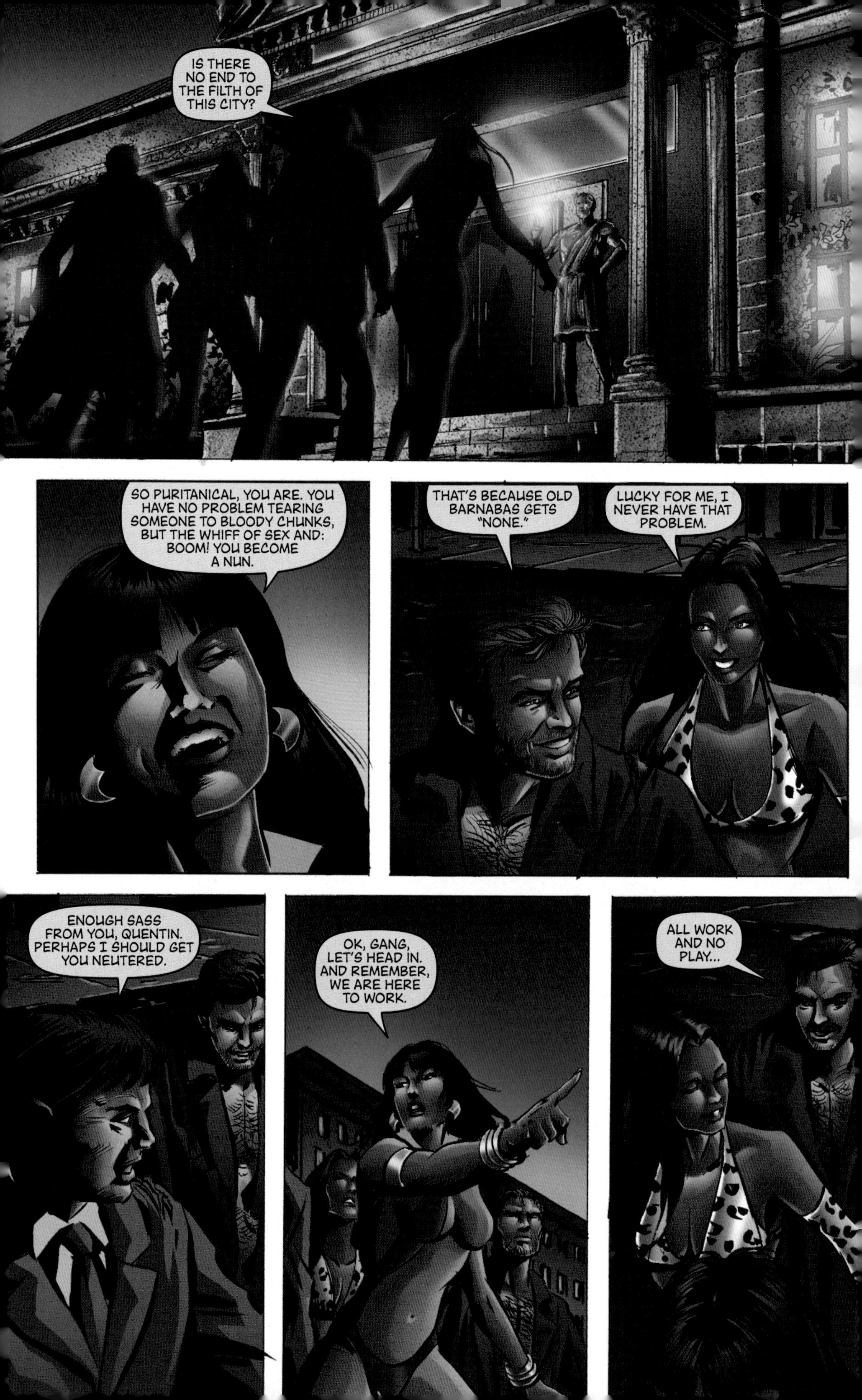
IS THERE NO END TO THE FILTH OF THIS CITY?
SO PURITANICAL, YOU ARE. YOU HAVE NO PROBLEM TEARING SOMEONE TO BLOODY CHUNKS, BUT THE WHIFF OF SEX AND: BOOM! YOU BECOME A NUN.
THAT'S BECAUSE OLD BARNABAS GETS "NONE."
LUCKY FOR ME, I NEVER HAVE THAT PROBLEM.
ENOUGH SASS FROM YOU, QUENTIN. PERHAPS I SHOULD GET YOU NEUTERED.
OK, GANG, LET'S HEAD IN. AND REMEMBER, WE ARE HERE TO WORK.
ALL WORK AND NO PLAY...

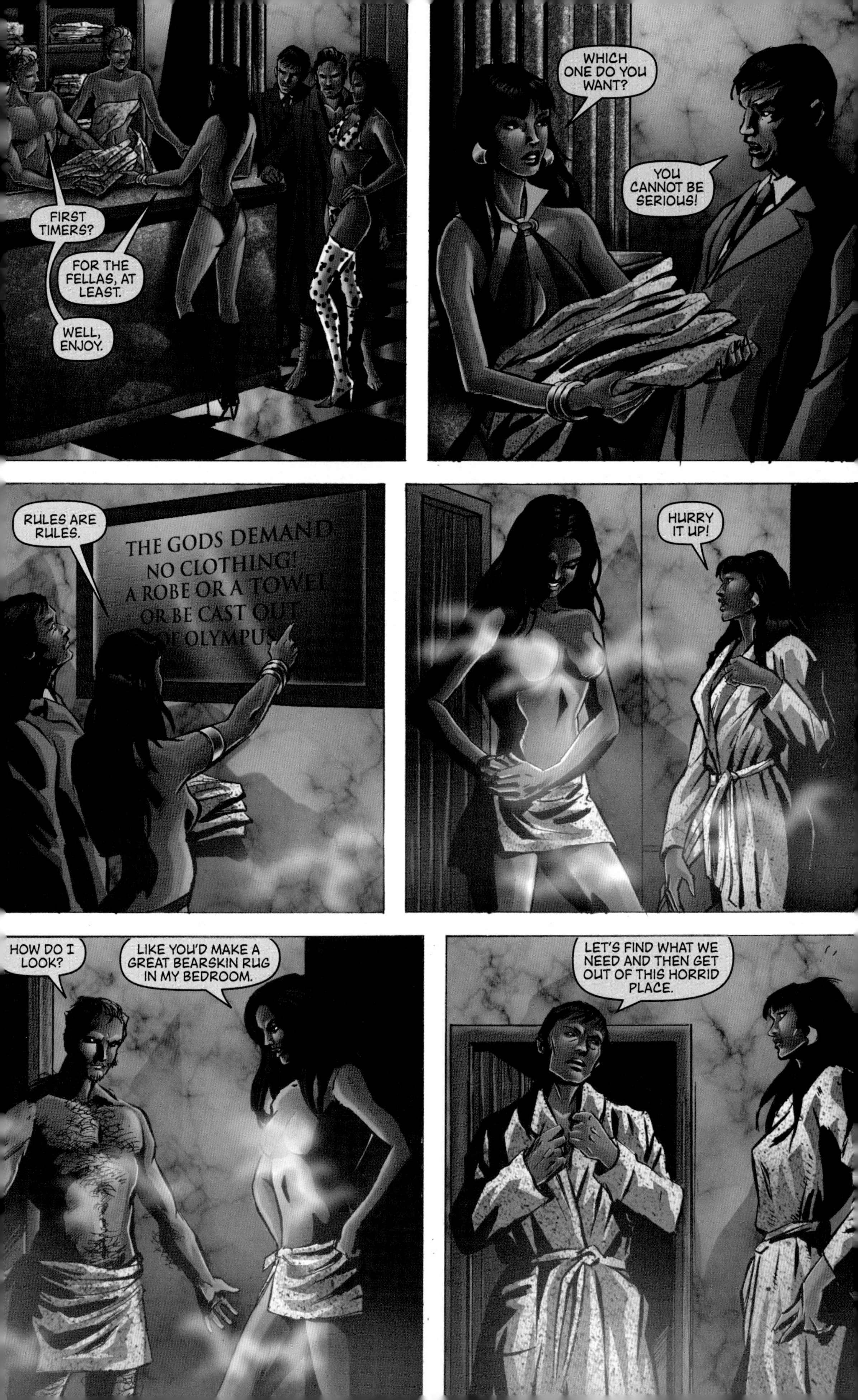
FIRST TIMERS?
FOR THE FELLAS, AT LEAST.
WELL, ENJOY.
WHICH ONE DO YOU WANT?
YOU CANNOT BE SERIOUS!
RULES ARE RULES.
THE GODS DEMAND NO CLOTHING! A ROBE OR A TOWEL OR BE CAST OUT OF OLYMPUS
HURRY IT UP!
HOW DO I LOOK?
LIKE YOU'D MAKE A GREAT BEARSKIN RUG IN MY BEDROOM.
LET'S FIND WHAT WE NEED AND THEN GET OUT OF THIS HORRID PLACE.

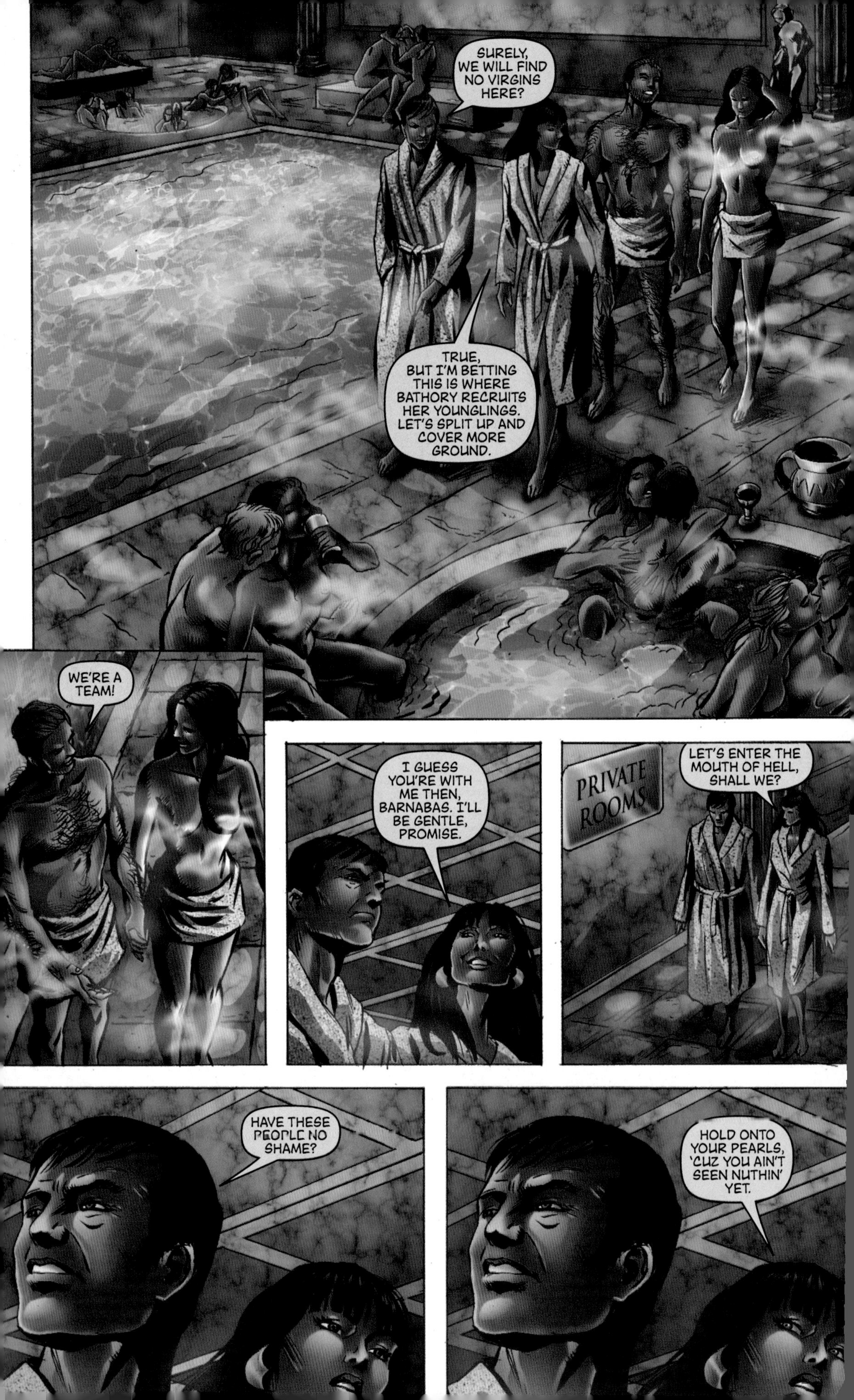
SURELY, WE WILL FIND NO VIRGINS HERE?
TRUE, BUT I'M BETTING THIS IS WHERE BATHORY RECRUITS HER YOUNGLINGS. LET'S SPLIT UP AND COVER MORE GROUND.
WE'RE A TEAM!
I GUESS YOU'RE WITH ME THEN, BARNABAS. I'LL BE GENTLE, PROMISE.
PRIVATE ROOMS
LET'S ENTER THE MOUTH OF HELL, SHALL WE?
HAVE THESE PEOPLE NO SHAME?
HOLD ONTO YOUR PEARLS, 'CUZ YOU AIN'T SEEN NUTHIN' YET.

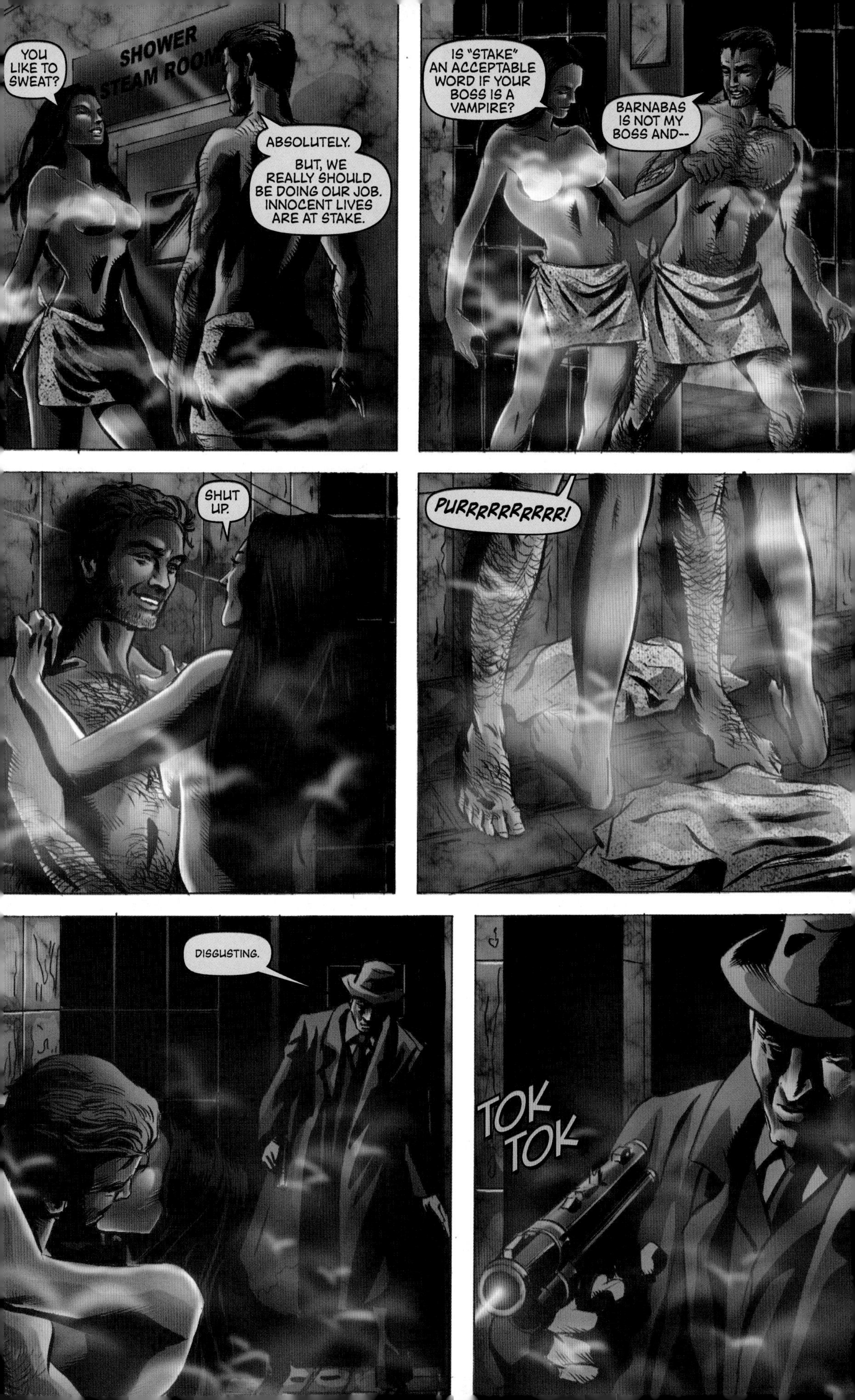
YOU LIKE TO SWEAT?
SHOWER
STEAM ROOM
ABSOLUTELY.
BUT, WE REALLY SHOULD BE DOING OUR JOB. INNOCENT LIVES ARE AT STAKE.
IS "STAKE" AN ACCEPTABLE WORD IF YOUR BOSS IS A VAMPIRE?
BARNABAS IS NOT MY BOSS AND--
SHUT UP.
PURRRRRRRRRR!
DISGUSTING.
TOK TOK

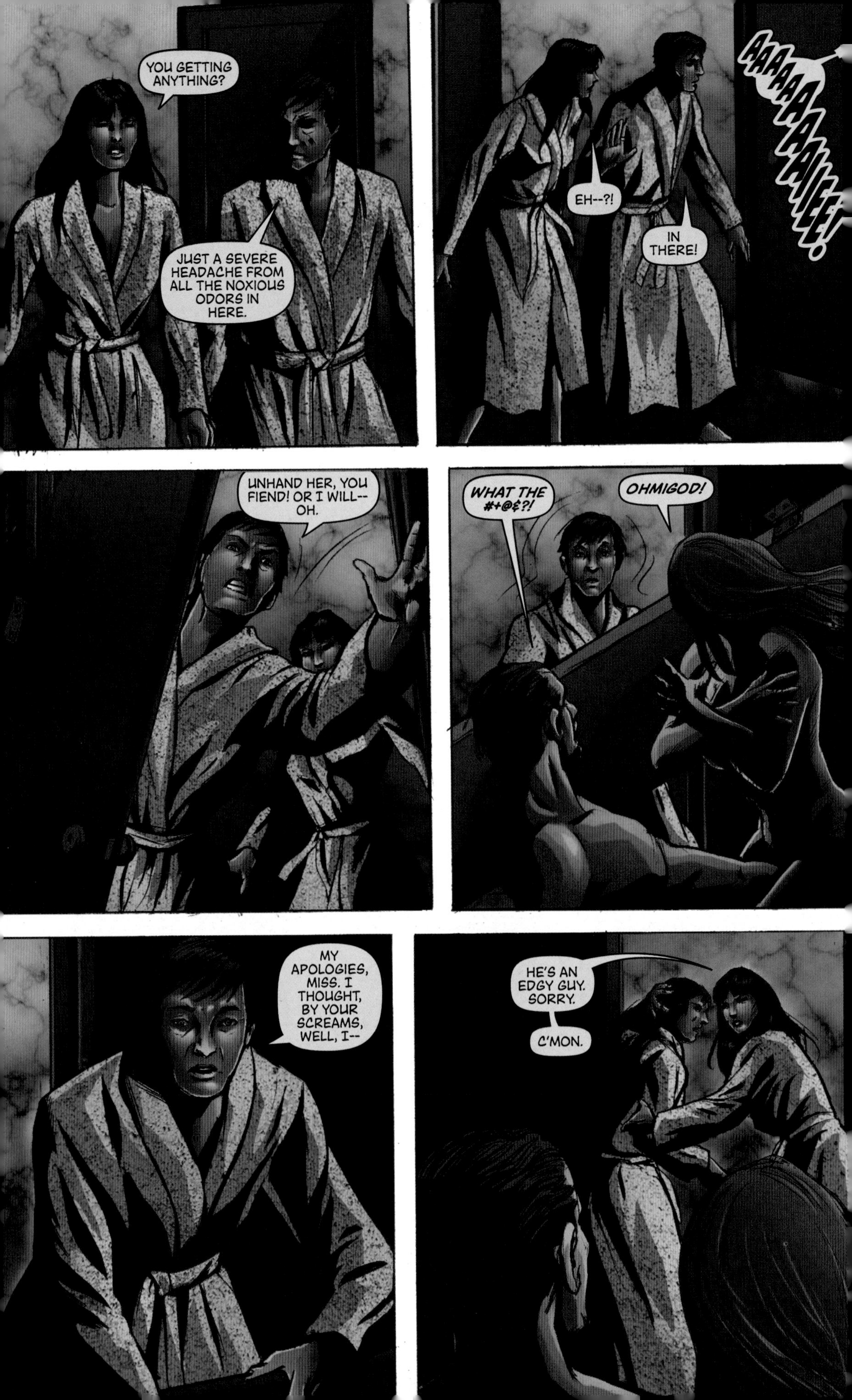
YOU GETTING ANYTHING?
JUST A SEVERE HEADACHE FROM ALL THE NOXIOUS ODORS IN HERE.
AAAAAAAIIEE!
EH--?!
IN THERE!
UNHAND HER, YOU FIEND! OR I WILL-- OH.
WHAT THE #+@$?!
OHMIGOD!
MY APOLOGIES, MISS. I THOUGHT, BY YOUR SCREAMS, WELL, I--
HE'S AN EDGY GUY. SORRY.
C'MON.

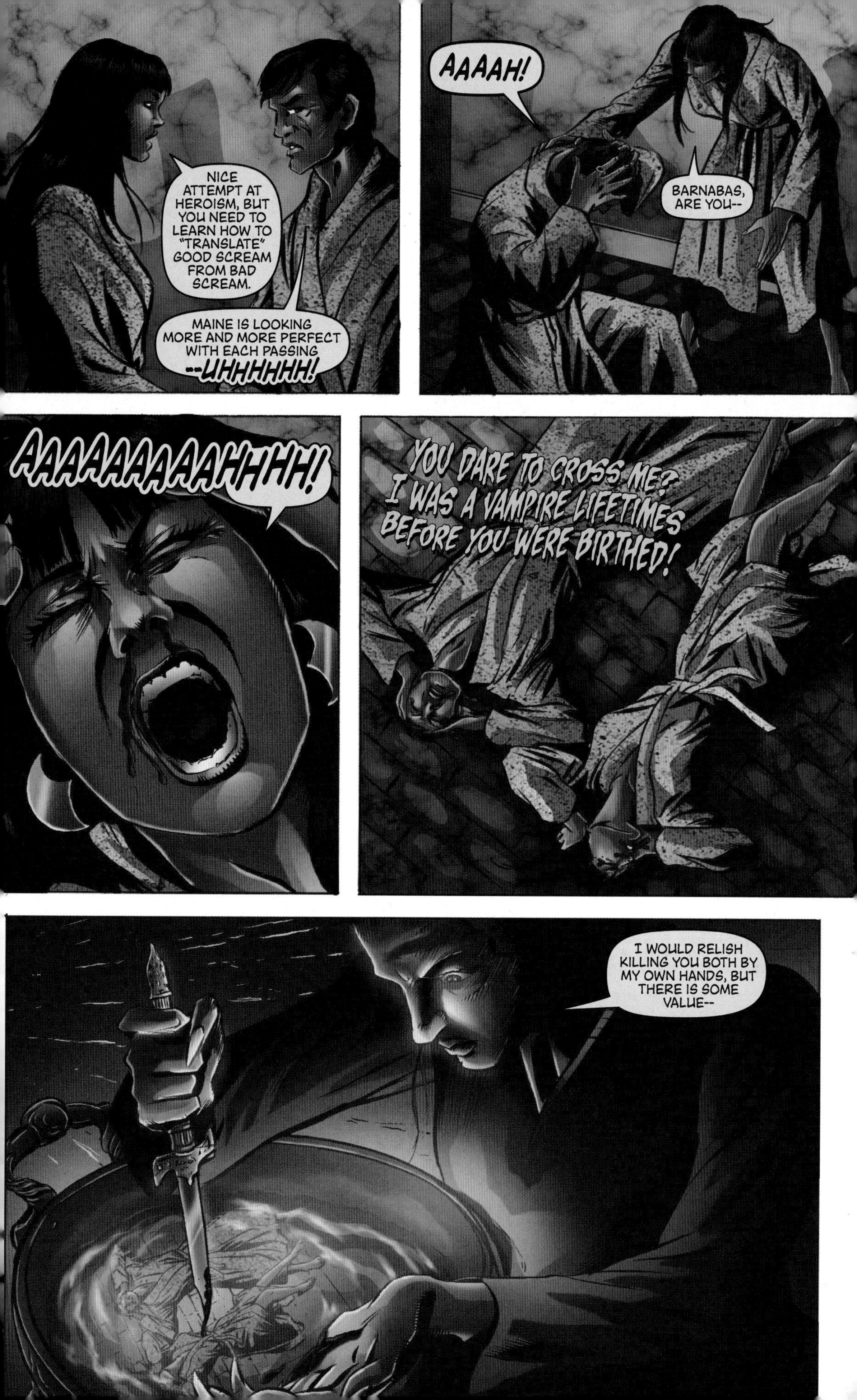
NICE ATTEMPT AT HEROISM, BUT YOU NEED TO LEARN HOW TO "TRANSLATE" GOOD SCREAM FROM BAD SCREAM.
MAINE IS LOOKING MORE AND MORE PERFECT WITH EACH PASSING --UHHHHHH!
AAAAH!
BARNABAS, ARE YOU--
AAAAAAAAAHHHH!
YOU DARE TO CROSS ME? I WAS A VAMPIRE LIFETIMES BEFORE YOU WERE BIRTHED!
I WOULD RELISH KILLING YOU BOTH BY MY OWN HANDS, BUT THERE IS SOME VALUE--

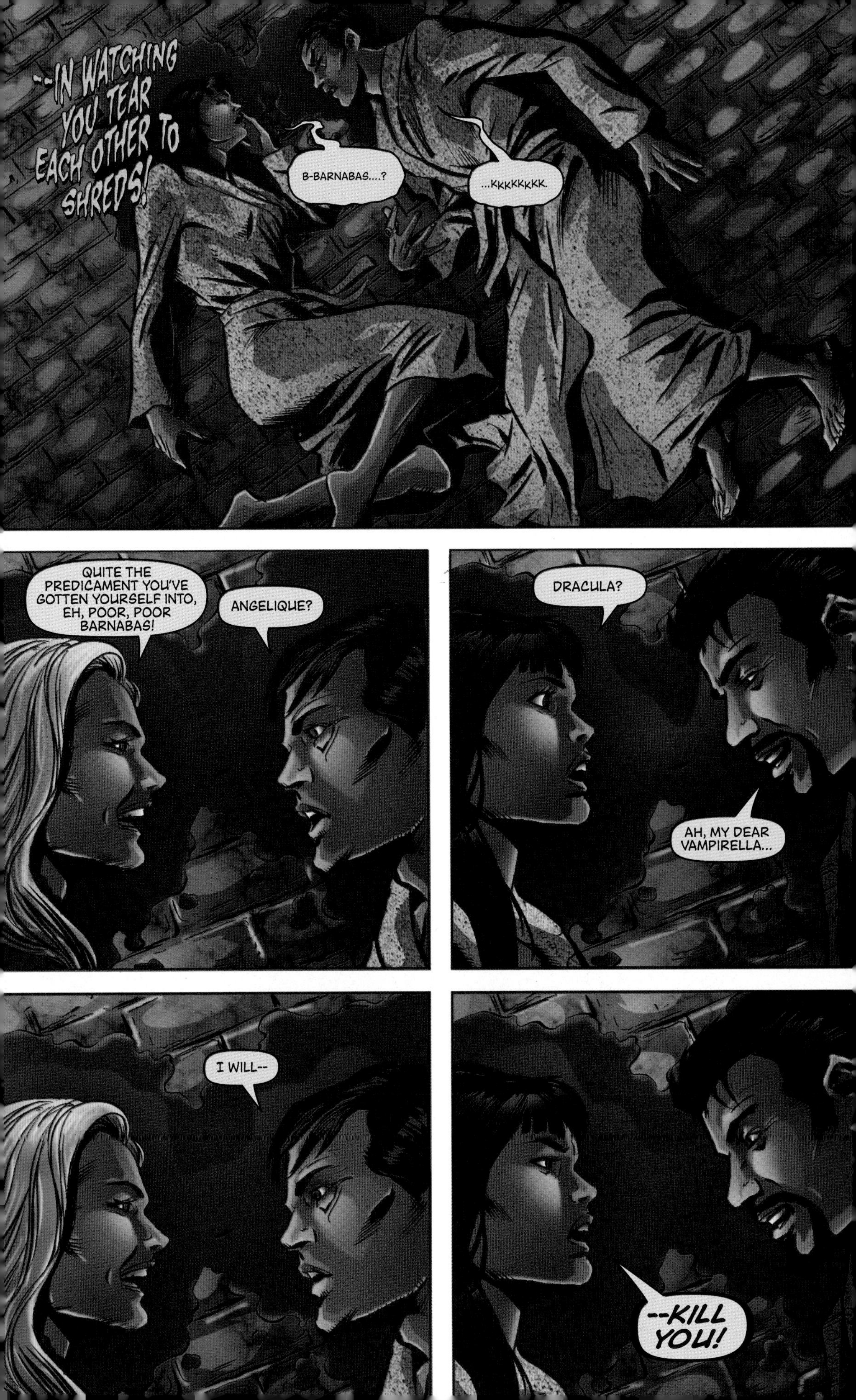
--IN WATCHING YOU TEAR EACH OTHER TO SHREDS!
B-BARNABAS....?
...KKKKKKKK.
QUITE THE PREDICAMENT YOU'VE GOTTEN YOURSELF INTO, EH, POOR, POOR BARNABAS!
ANGELIQUE?
DRACULA?
AH, MY DEAR VAMPIRELLA...
I WILL--
--KILL YOU!

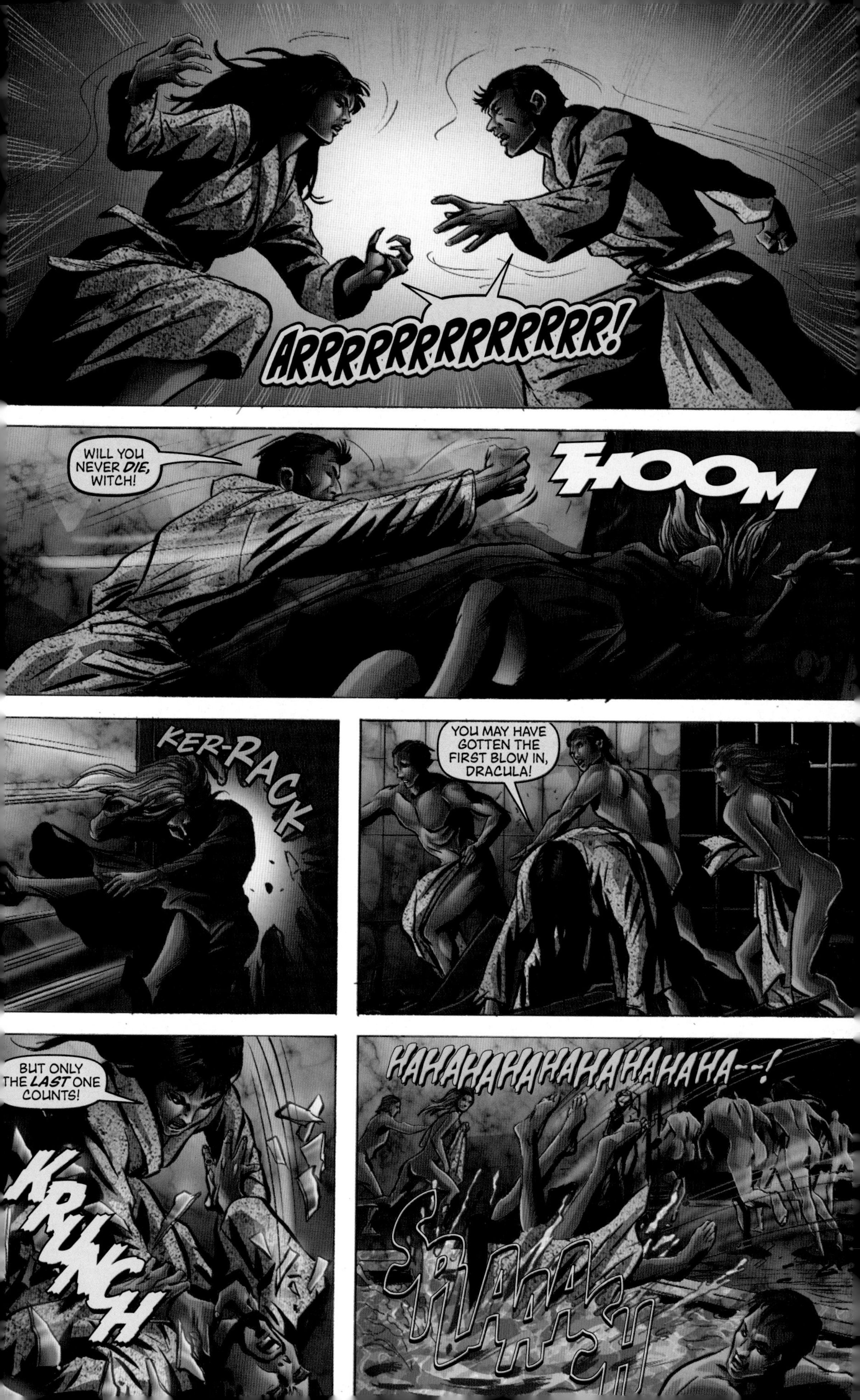
ARRRRRRRRRRRRR!
WILL YOU NEVER DIE, WITCH!
THOOM
KER-RACK
YOU MAY HAVE GOTTEN THE FIRST BLOW IN, DRACULA!
BUT ONLY THE LAST ONE COUNTS!
KRUNCH
HAHAHAHAHAHAHAHAHAHAHA--!

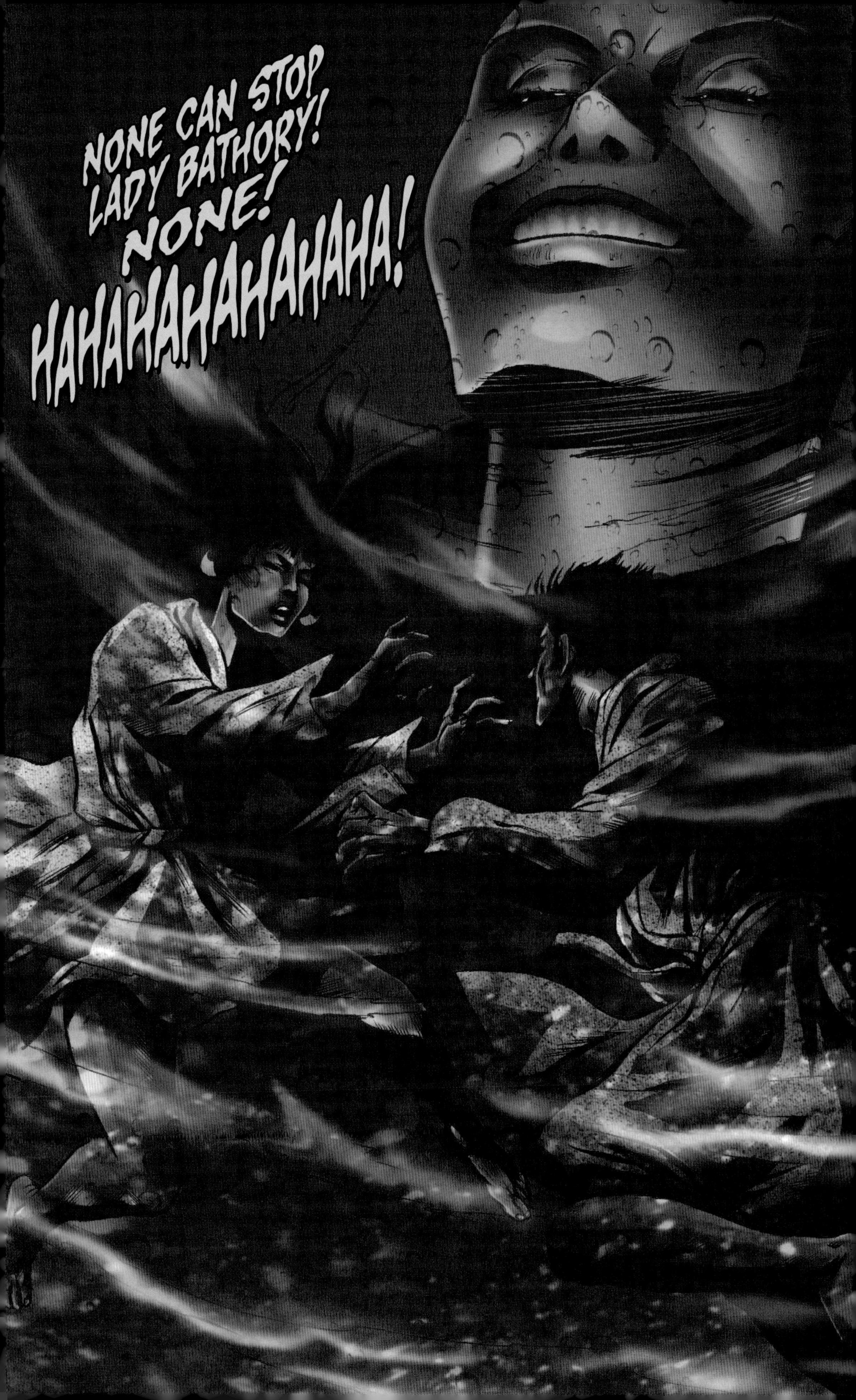
NONE CAN STOP LADY BATHORY! NONE!
HAHAHAHAHAHAHA!

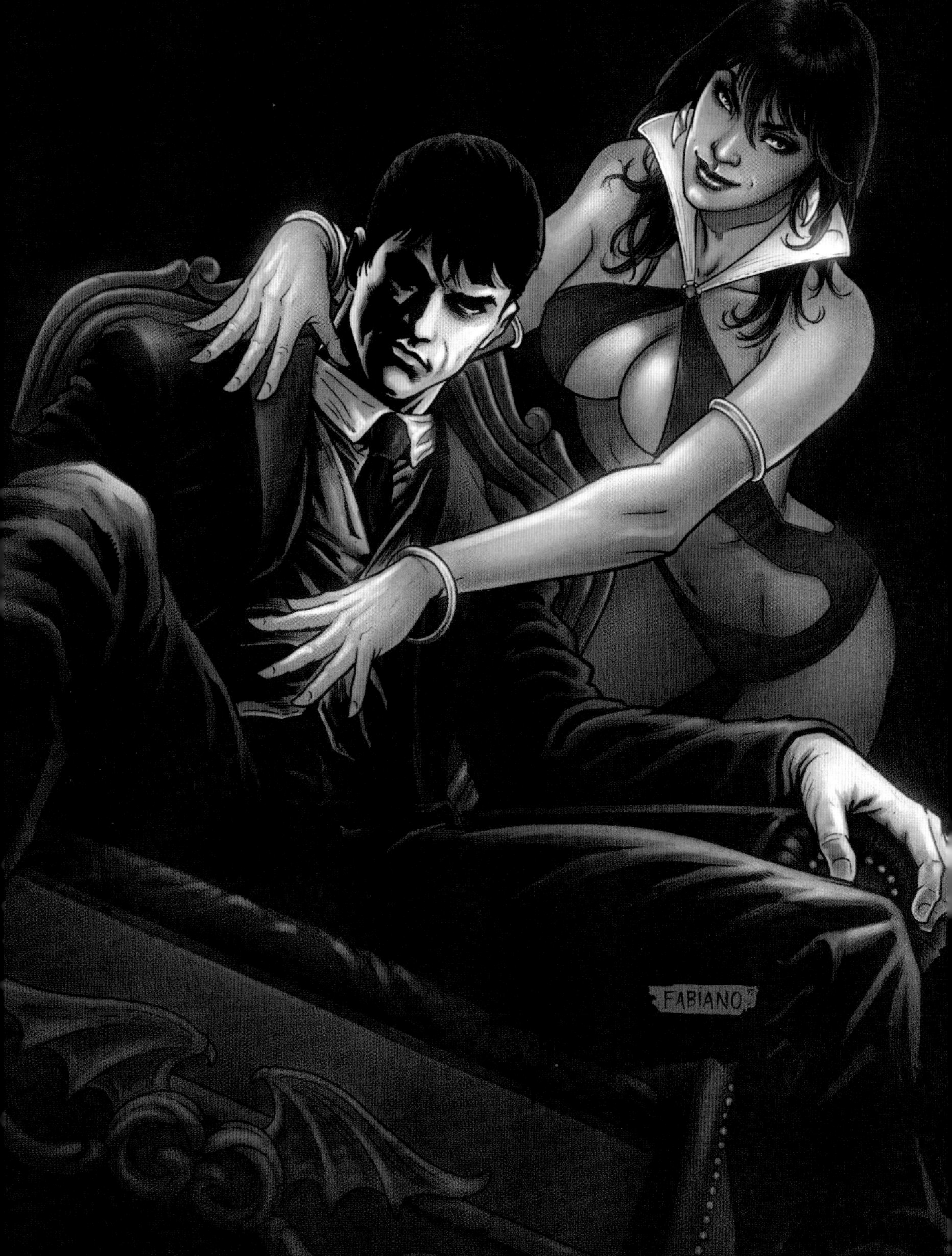
FABIANO

ISSUE #4 COVER BY FABIANO NEVES

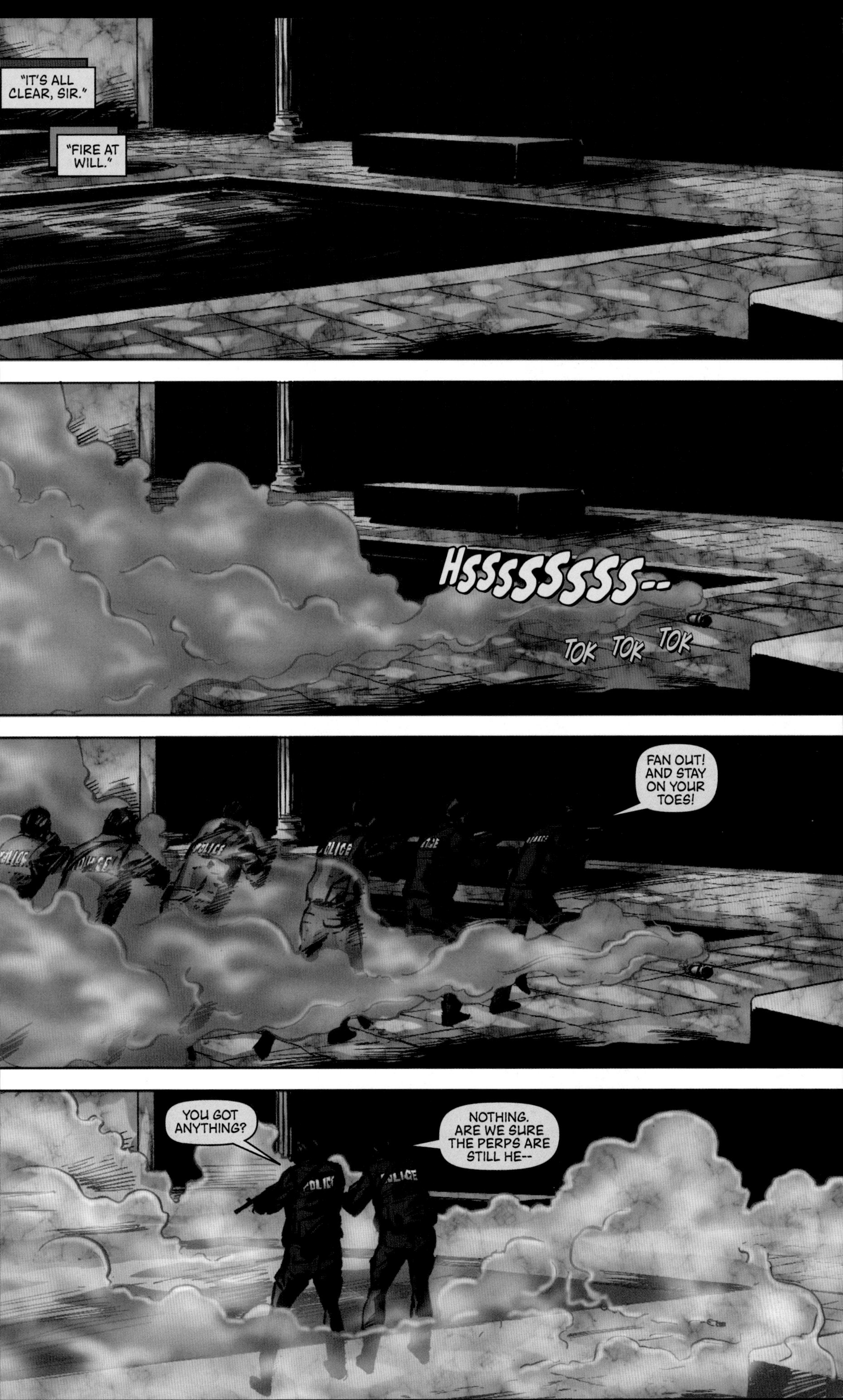
"IT'S ALL CLEAR, SIR."
"FIRE AT WILL."
HSSSSSSSS--
TOK TOK TOK
FAN OUT! AND STAY ON YOUR TOES!
YOU GOT ANYTHING?
NOTHING. ARE WE SURE THE PERPS ARE STILL HE--

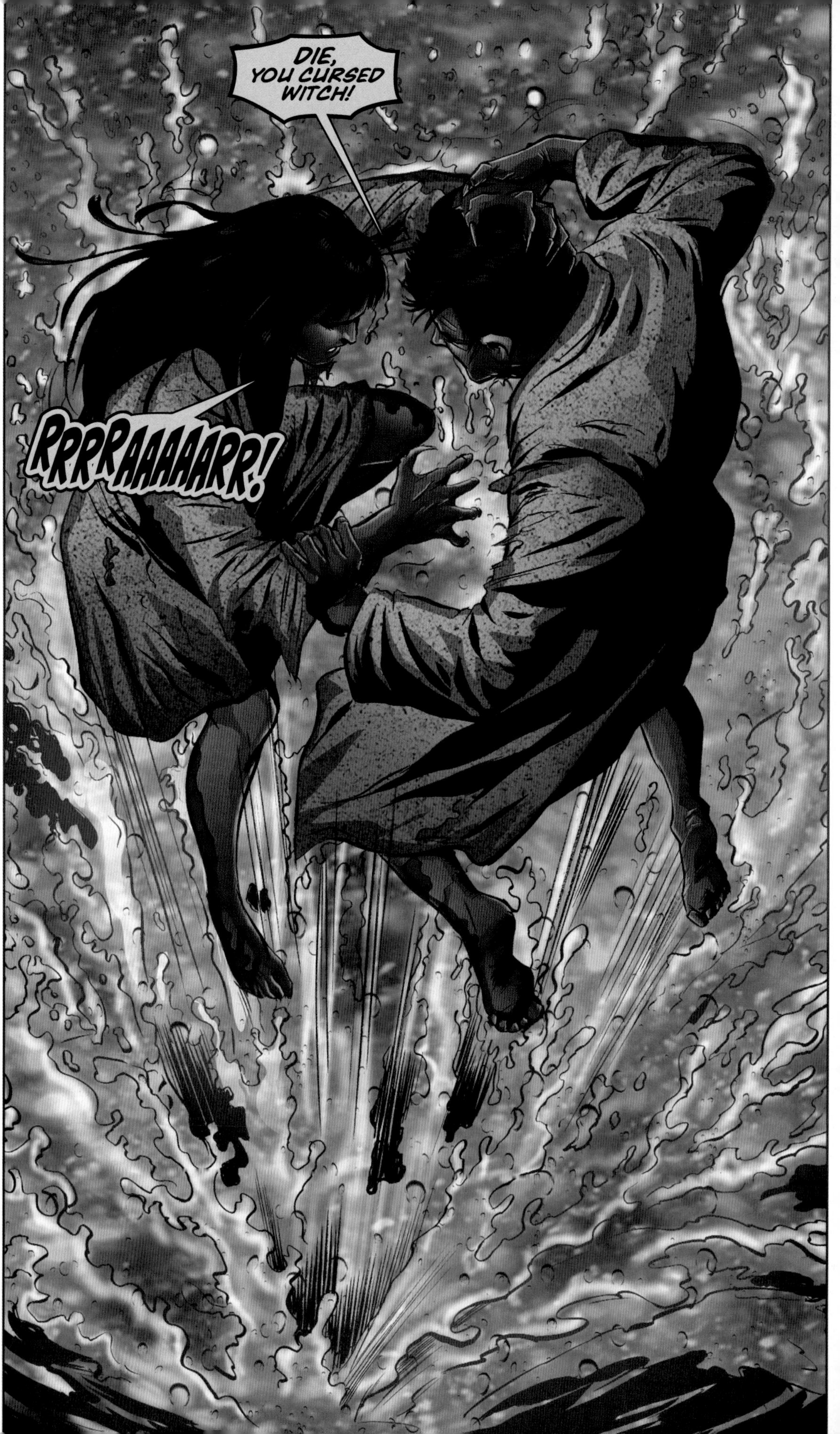
DIE, YOU CURSED WITCH!
RRRRAAAAAARR!

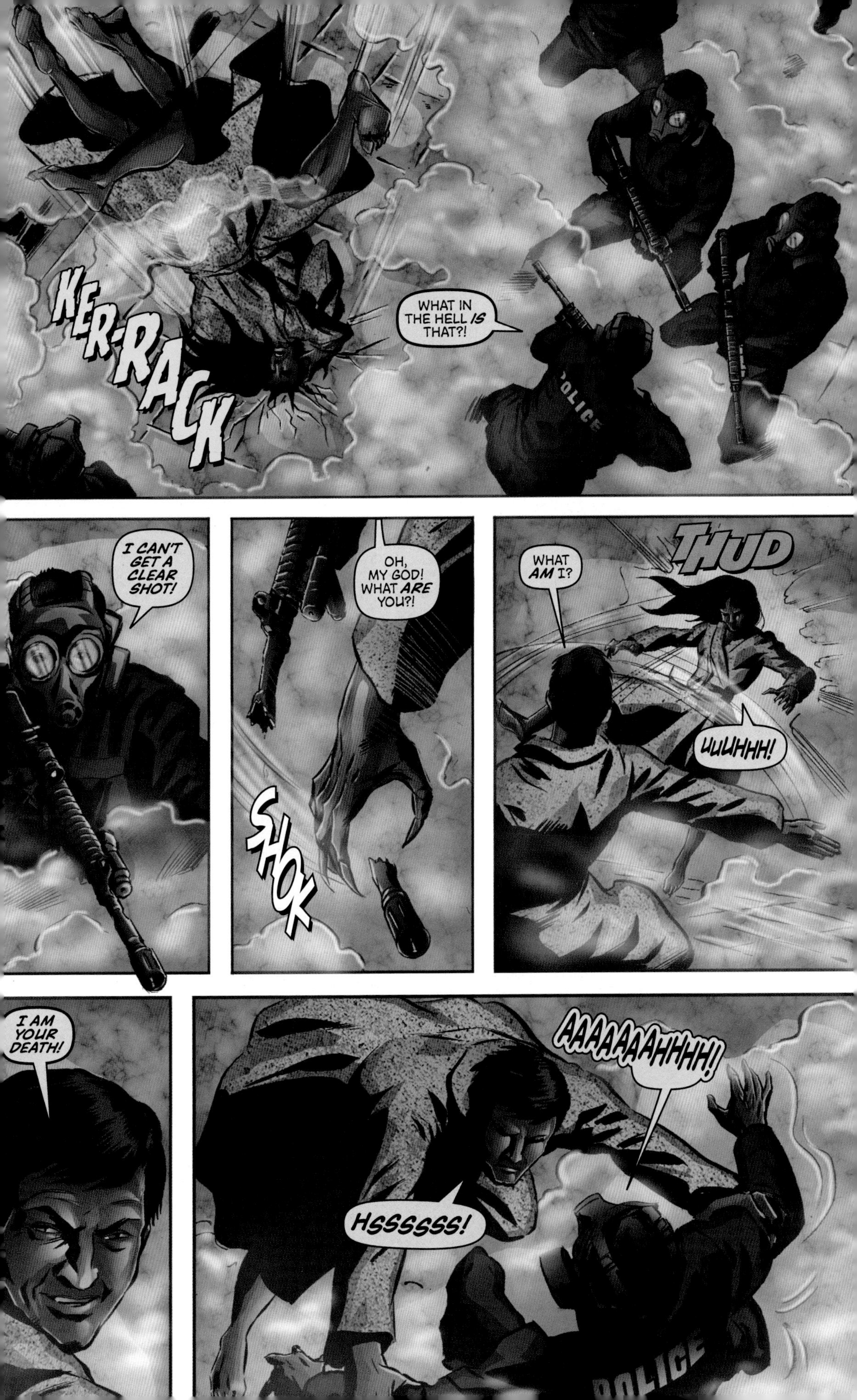
KER-RACK
WHAT IN THE HELL IS THAT?!
I CAN'T GET A CLEAR SHOT!
OH, MY GOD! WHAT ARE YOU?!
SHOK
WHAT AM I?
THUD
UUUHHH!
I AM YOUR DEATH!
AAAAAAAHHHH!
HSSSSSS!
POLICE

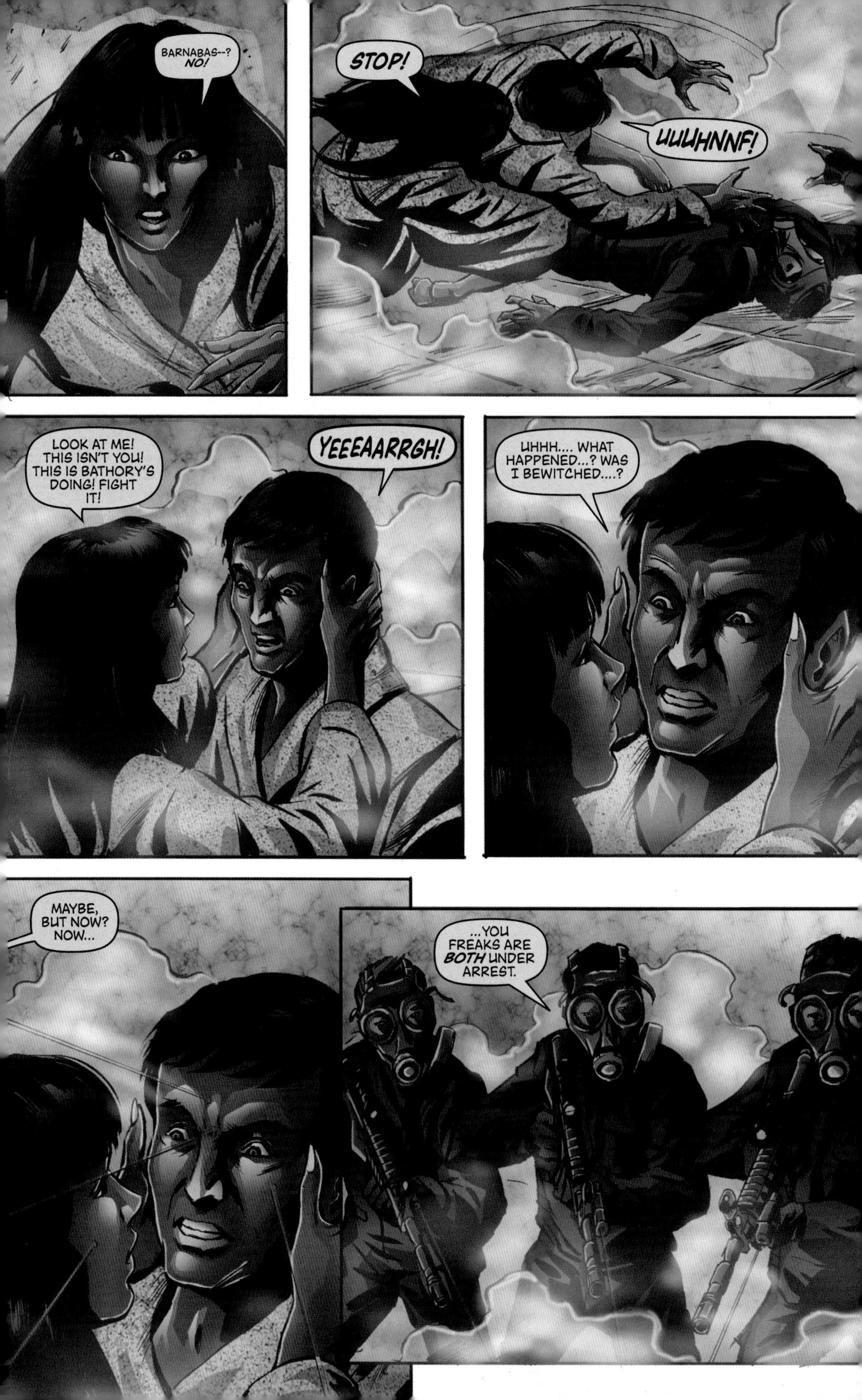
BARNABAS--? NO!
STOP!
UUUHNNF!
LOOK AT ME! THIS ISN'T YOU! THIS IS BATHORY'S DOING! FIGHT IT!
YEEEAARRGH!
UHHH.... WHAT HAPPENED...? WAS I BEWITCHED....?
MAYBE, BUT NOW? NOW...
...YOU FREAKS ARE BOTH UNDER ARREST.

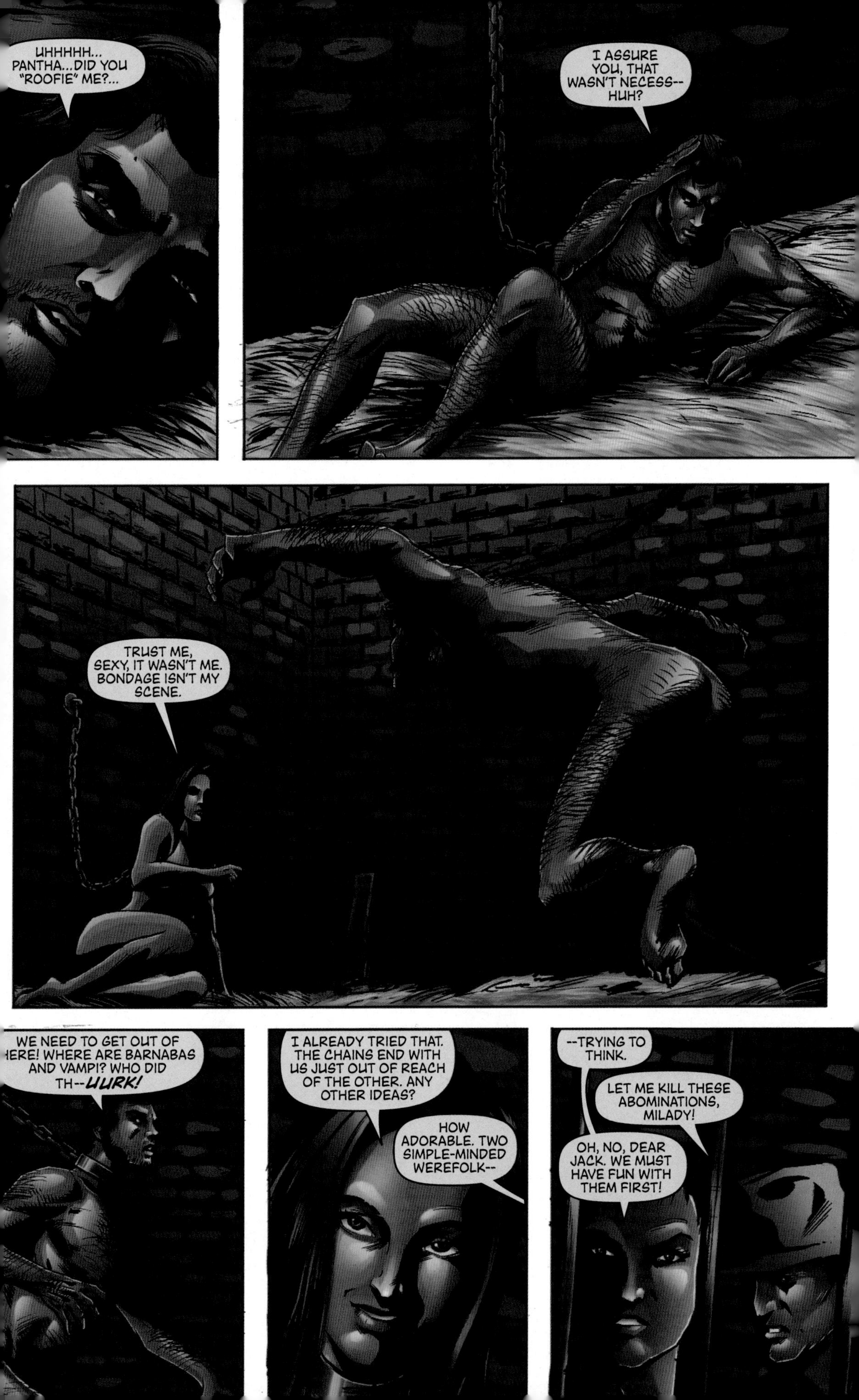
UHHHHH... PANTHA...DID YOU "ROOFIE" ME?...
I ASSURE YOU, THAT WASN'T NECESS-- HUH?
TRUST ME, SEXY, IT WASN'T ME. BONDAGE ISN'T MY SCENE.
WE NEED TO GET OUT OF HERE! WHERE ARE BARNABAS AND VAMPI? WHO DID TH--UURK!
I ALREADY TRIED THAT. THE CHAINS END WITH US JUST OUT OF REACH OF THE OTHER. ANY OTHER IDEAS?
HOW ADORABLE. TWO SIMPLE-MINDED WEREFOLK--
--TRYING TO THINK.
LET ME KILL THESE ABOMINATIONS, MILADY!
OH, NO, DEAR JACK. WE MUST HAVE FUN WITH THEM FIRST!

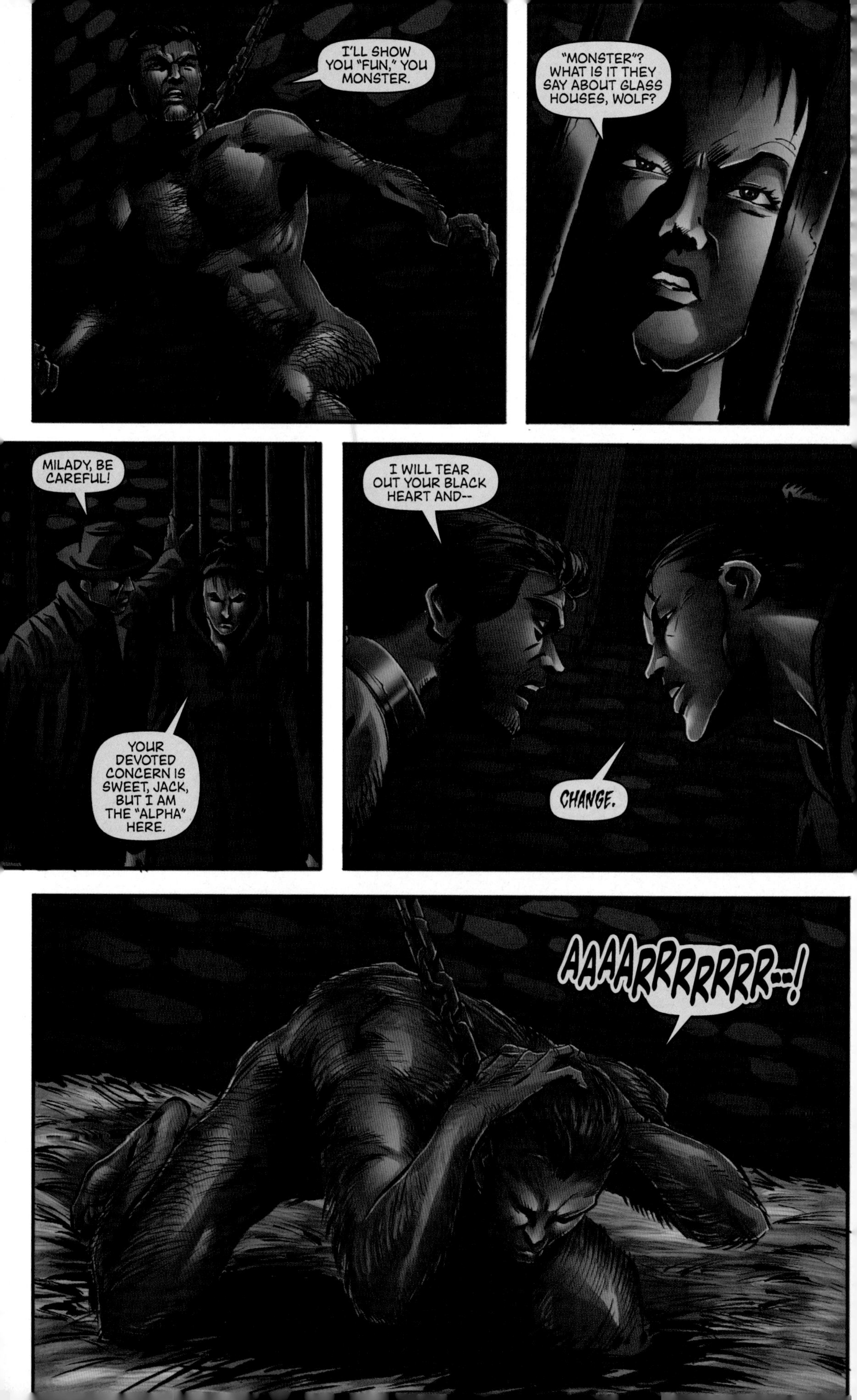
I'LL SHOW YOU "FUN," YOU MONSTER.
"MONSTER"? WHAT IS IT THEY SAY ABOUT GLASS HOUSES, WOLF?
MILADY, BE CAREFUL!
YOUR DEVOTED CONCERN IS SWEET, JACK, BUT I AM THE "ALPHA" HERE.
I WILL TEAR OUT YOUR BLACK HEART AND--
CHANGE.
AAAARRRRRRR--!

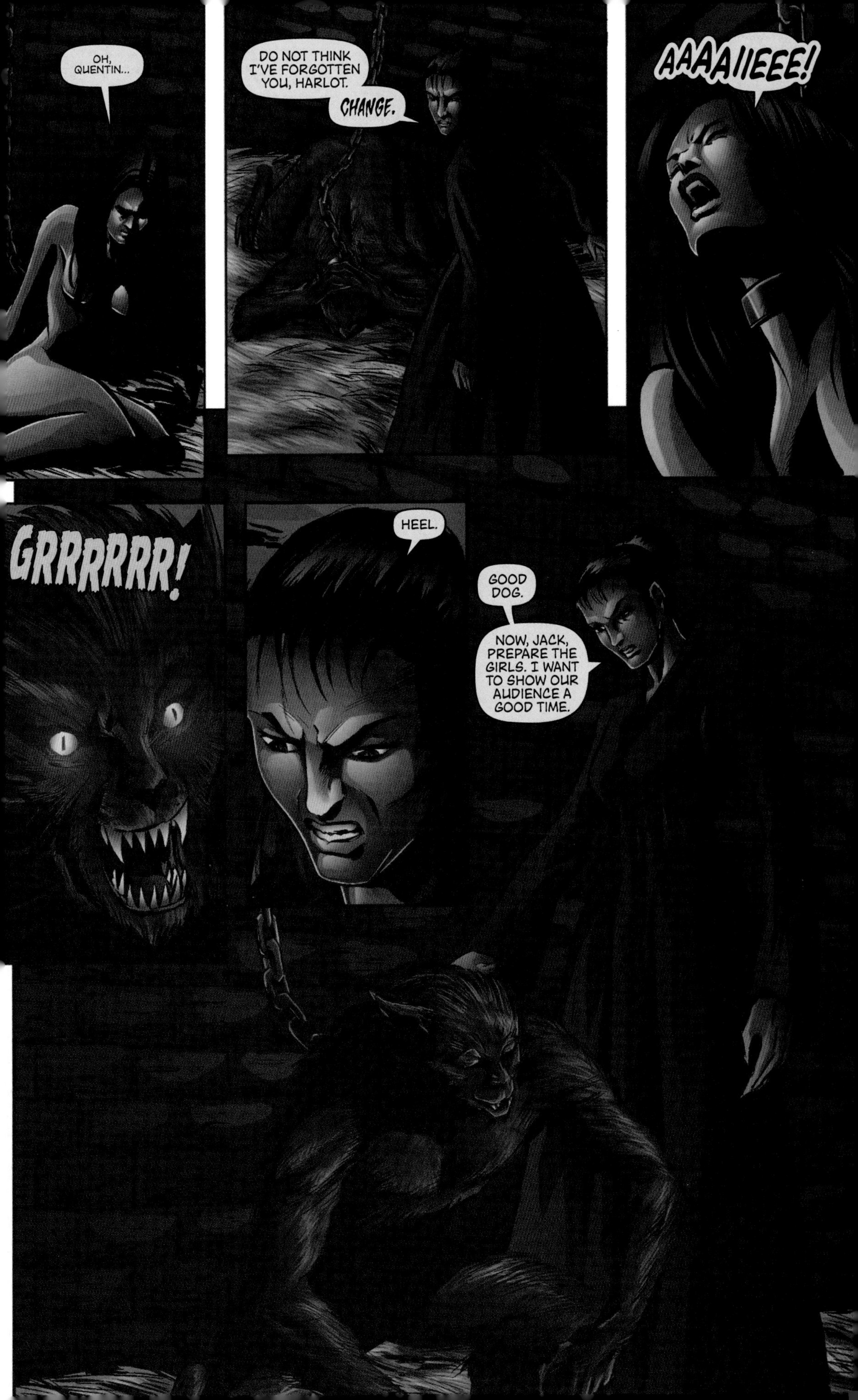
OH, QUENTIN...
DO NOT THINK I'VE FORGOTTEN YOU, HARLOT.
CHANGE.
AAAAIIEEE!
GRRRRRR!
HEEL.
GOOD DOG.
NOW, JACK, PREPARE THE GIRLS. I WANT TO SHOW OUR AUDIENCE A GOOD TIME.

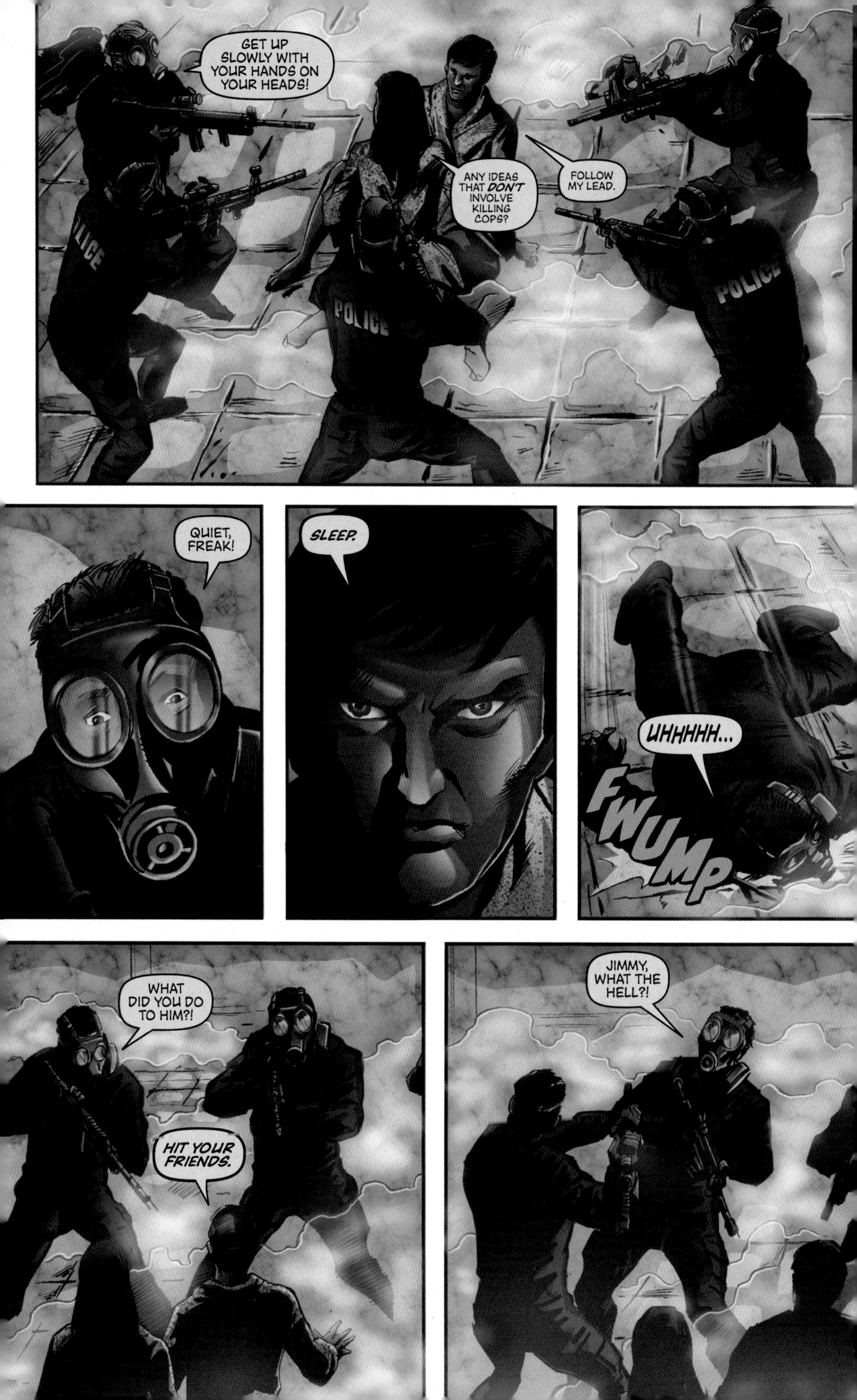
GET UP SLOWLY WITH YOUR HANDS ON YOUR HEADS!
ANY IDEAS THAT DON'T INVOLVE KILLING COPS?
FOLLOW MY LEAD.
POLICE
POLICE
POLICE
QUIET, FREAK!
SLEEP.
UHHHHH...
FWUMP
WHAT DID YOU DO TO HIM?!
HIT YOUR FRIENDS.
JIMMY, WHAT THE HELL?!

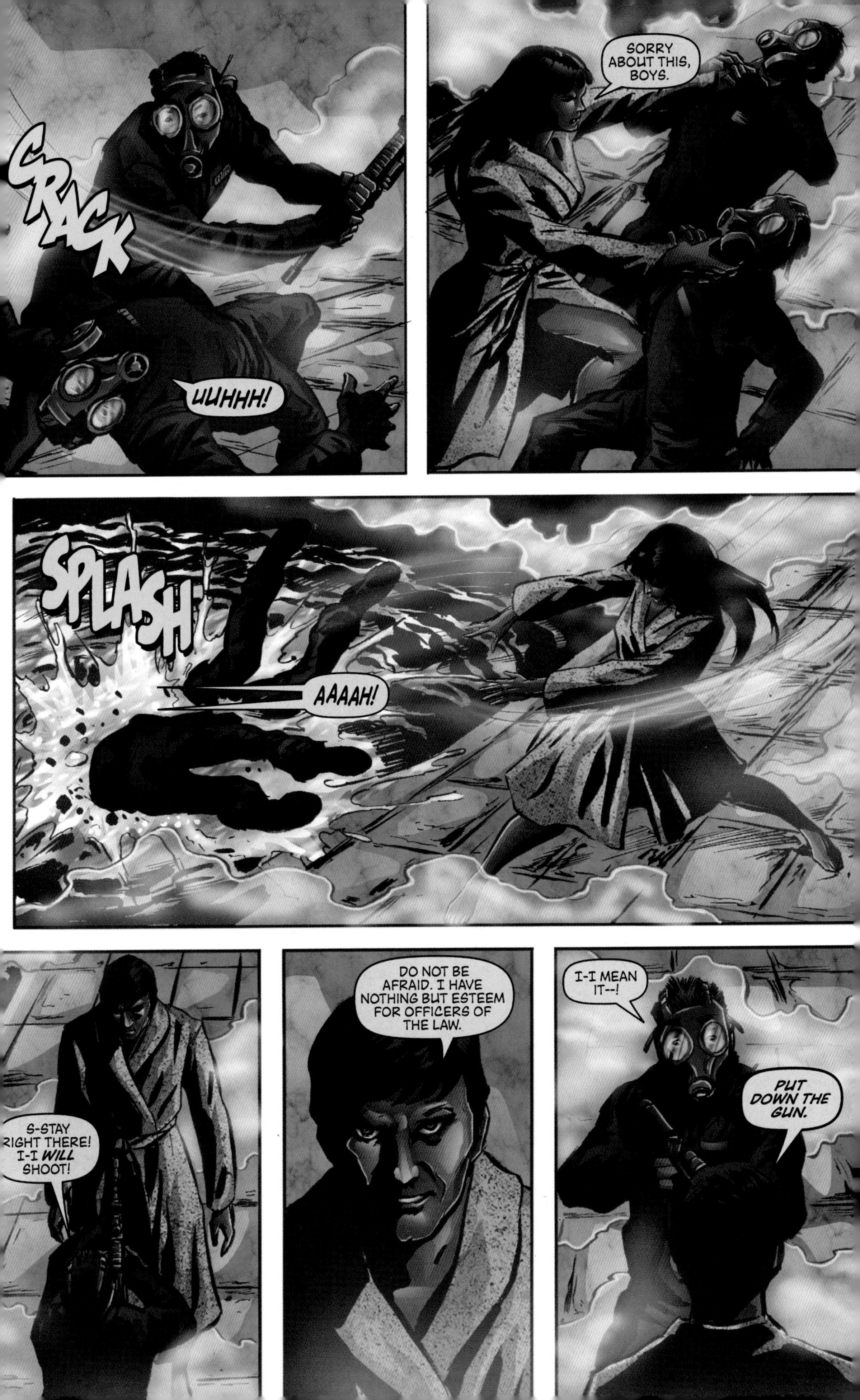
CRACK
UUHHH!
SORRY ABOUT THIS, BOYS.
SPLASH
AAAAH!
S-STAY RIGHT THERE! I-I WILL SHOOT!
DO NOT BE AFRAID. I HAVE NOTHING BUT ESTEEM FOR OFFICERS OF THE LAW.
I-I MEAN IT--!
PUT DOWN THE GUN.

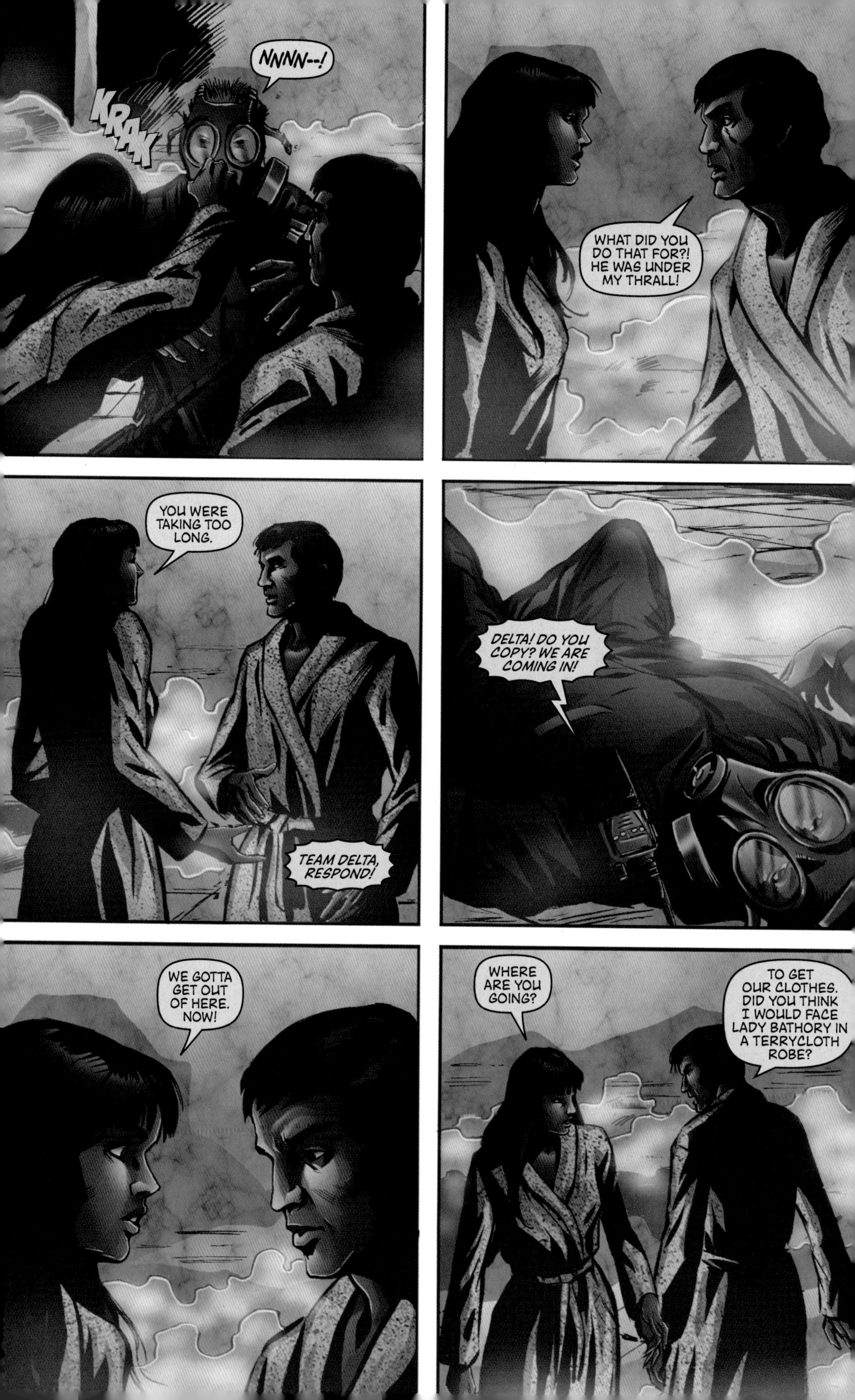
KRAK
NNNN--!
WHAT DID YOU DO THAT FOR?! HE WAS UNDER MY THRALL!
YOU WERE TAKING TOO LONG.
TEAM DELTA, RESPOND!
DELTA! DO YOU COPY? WE ARE COMING IN!
WE GOTTA GET OUT OF HERE. NOW!
WHERE ARE YOU GOING?
TO GET OUR CLOTHES. DID YOU THINK I WOULD FACE LADY BATHORY IN A TERRYCLOTH ROBE?

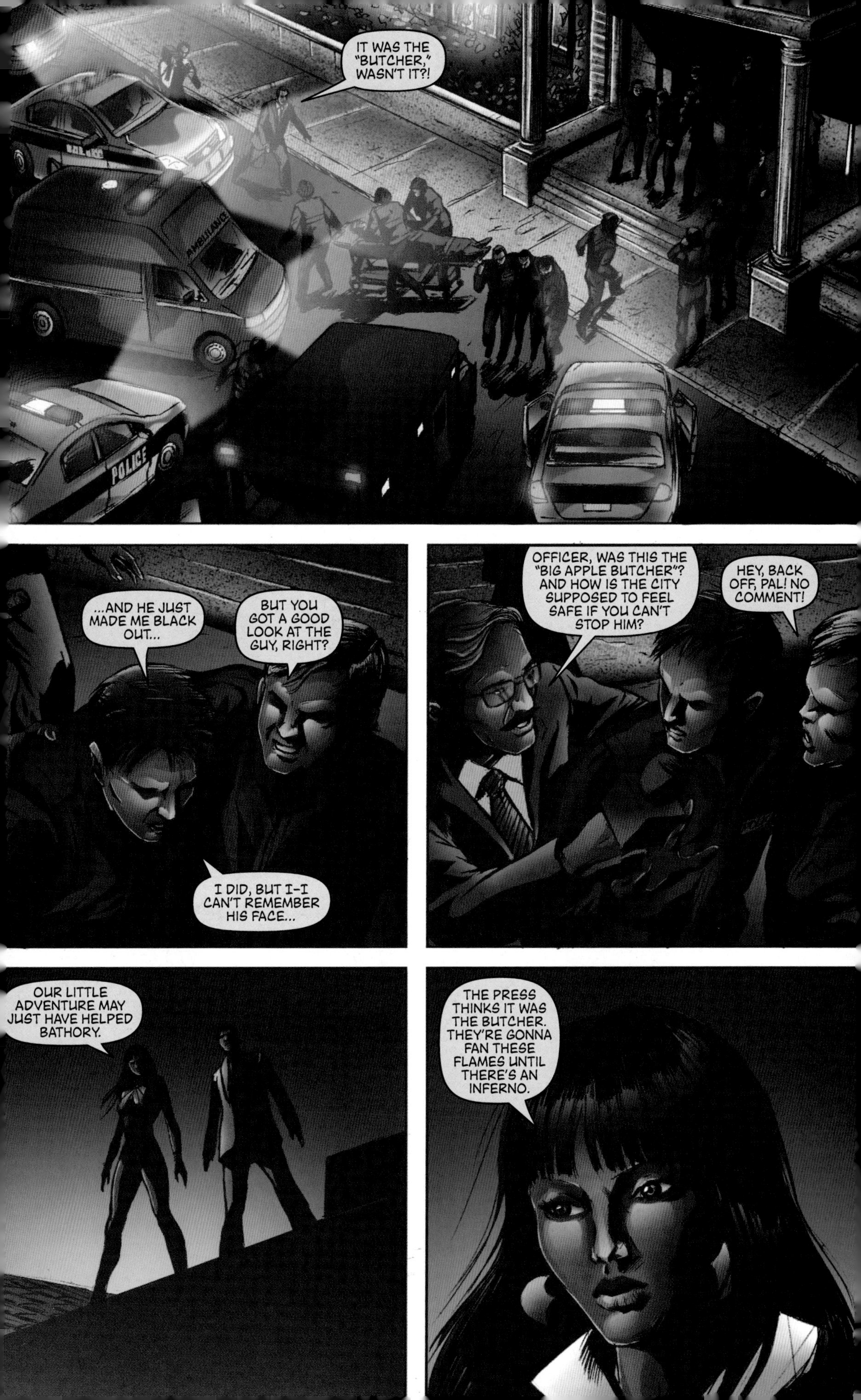
IT WAS THE "BUTCHER," WASN'T IT?!
POLICE
AMBULANCE
...AND HE JUST MADE ME BLACK OUT...
BUT YOU GOT A GOOD LOOK AT THE GUY, RIGHT?
I DID, BUT I-I CAN'T REMEMBER HIS FACE...
OFFICER, WAS THIS THE "BIG APPLE BUTCHER"? AND HOW IS THE CITY SUPPOSED TO FEEL SAFE IF YOU CAN'T STOP HIM?
HEY, BACK OFF, PAL! NO COMMENT!
OUR LITTLE ADVENTURE MAY JUST HAVE HELPED BATHORY.
THE PRESS THINKS IT WAS THE BUTCHER. THEY'RE GONNA FAN THESE FLAMES UNTIL THERE'S AN INFERNO.

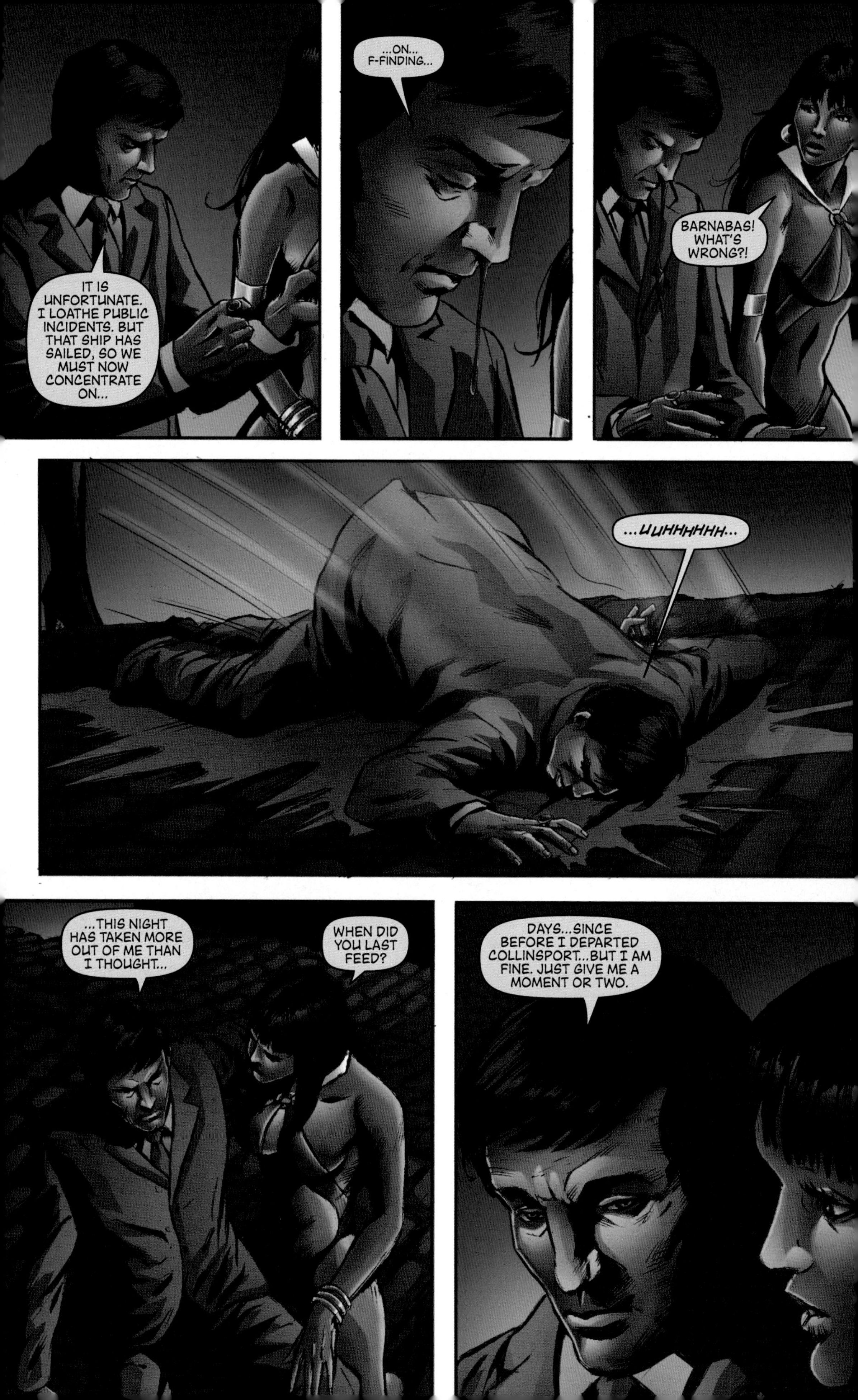
IT IS UNFORTUNATE. I LOATHE PUBLIC INCIDENTS. BUT THAT SHIP HAS SAILED, SO WE MUST NOW CONCENTRATE ON...
...ON... F-FINDING...
BARNABAS! WHAT'S WRONG?!
...UHHHHHH...
...THIS NIGHT HAS TAKEN MORE OUT OF ME THAN I THOUGHT...
WHEN DID YOU LAST FEED?
DAYS...SINCE BEFORE I DEPARTED COLLINSPORT...BUT I AM FINE. JUST GIVE ME A MOMENT OR TWO.

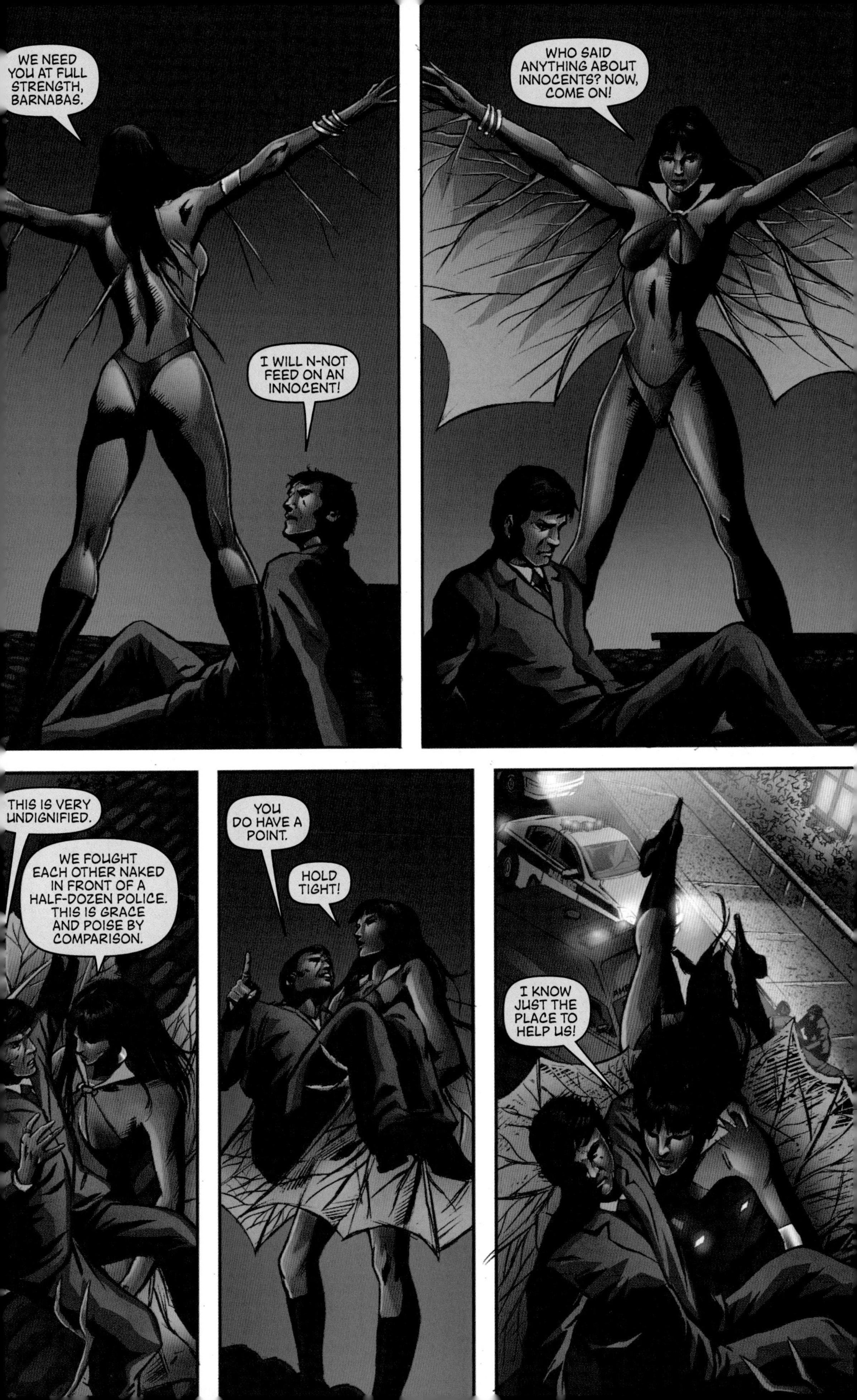
WE NEED YOU AT FULL STRENGTH, BARNABAS.
I WILL N-NOT FEED ON AN INNOCENT!
WHO SAID ANYTHING ABOUT INNOCENTS? NOW, COME ON!
THIS IS VERY UNDIGNIFIED.
WE FOUGHT EACH OTHER NAKED IN FRONT OF A HALF-DOZEN POLICE. THIS IS GRACE AND POISE BY COMPARISON.
YOU DO HAVE A POINT.
HOLD TIGHT!
I KNOW JUST THE PLACE TO HELP US!

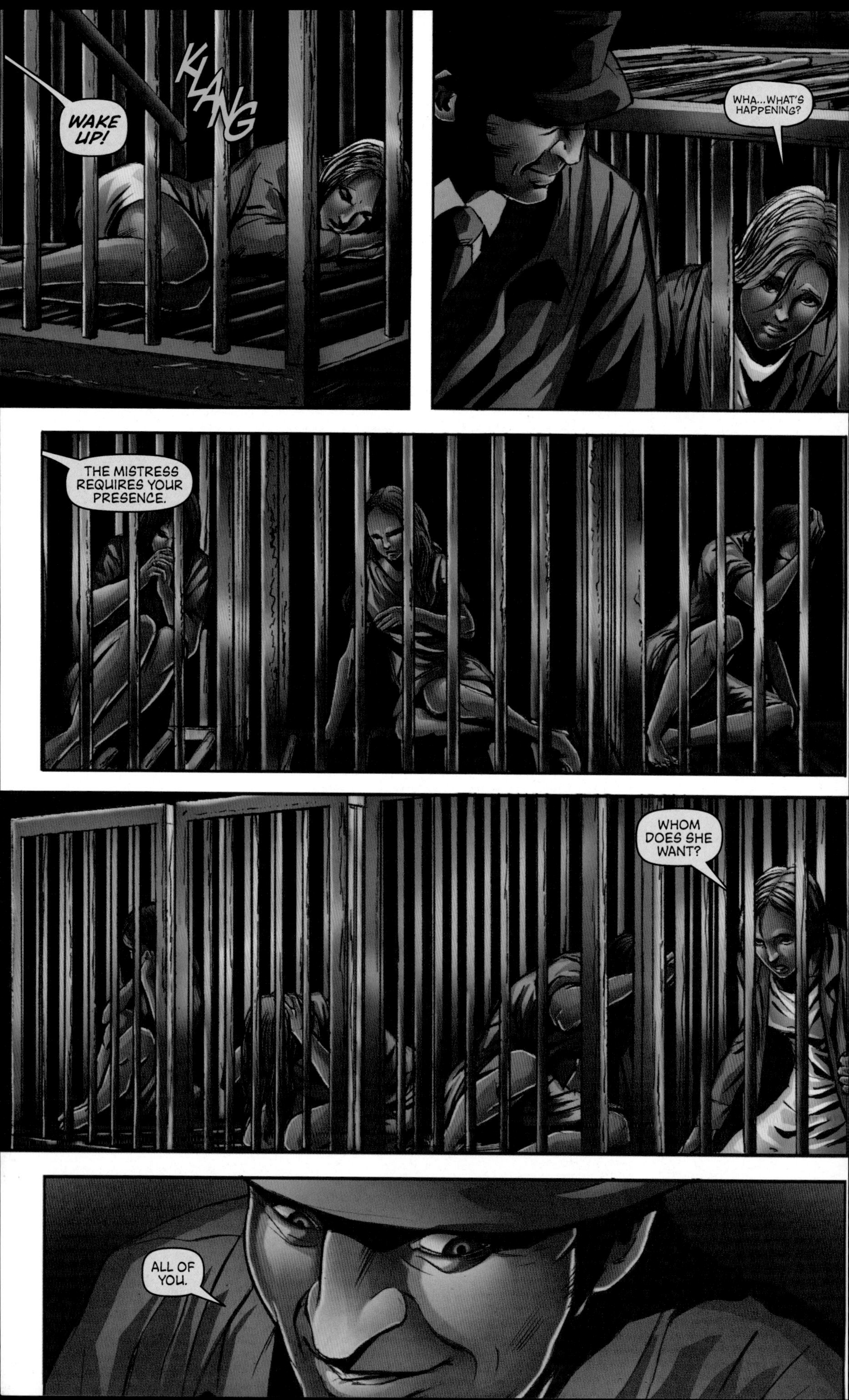
WAKE UP!
KLANG
WHA...WHAT'S HAPPENING?
THE MISTRESS REQUIRES YOUR PRESENCE.
WHOM DOES SHE WANT?
ALL OF YOU.

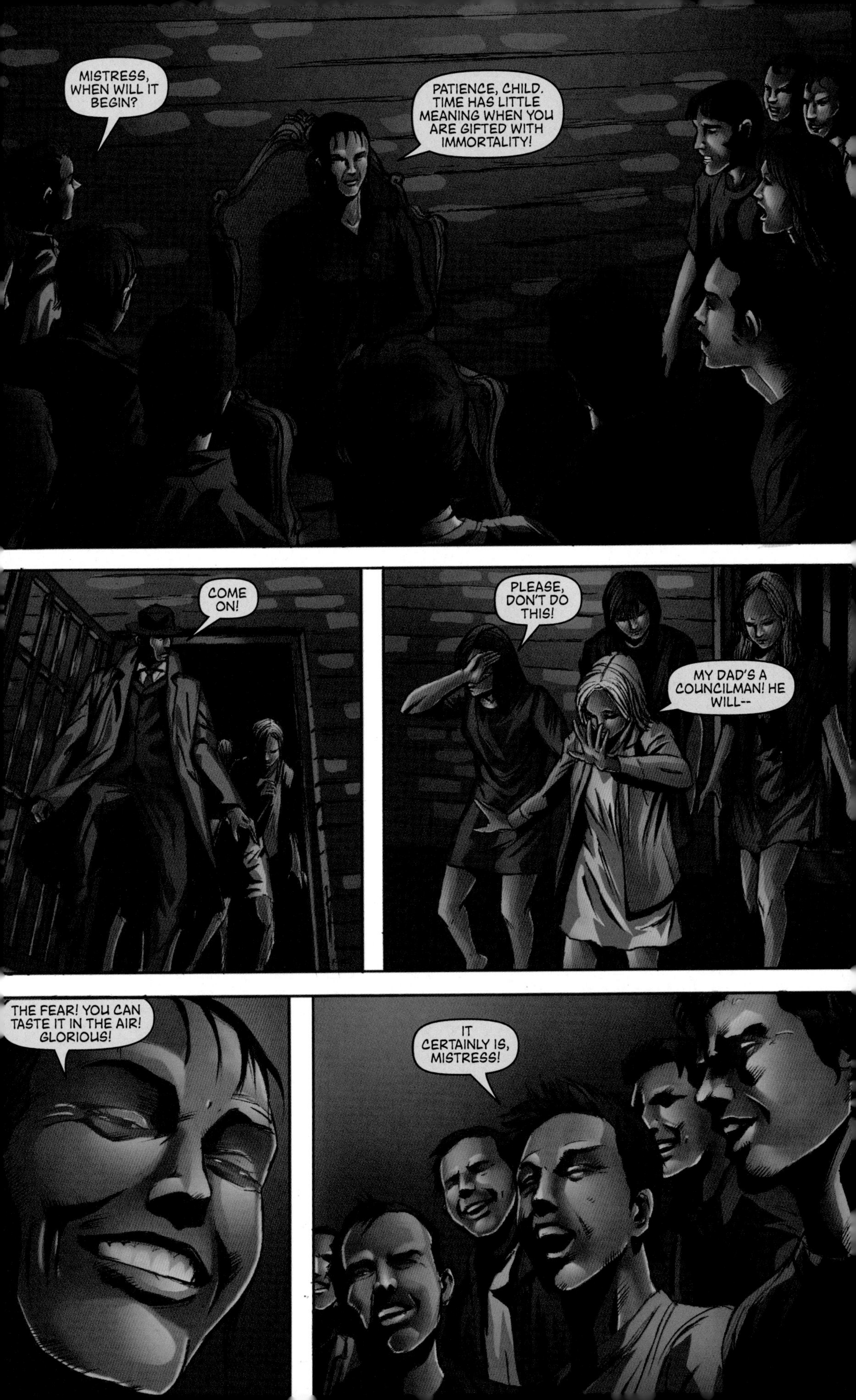
MISTRESS, WHEN WILL IT BEGIN?
PATIENCE, CHILD. TIME HAS LITTLE MEANING WHEN YOU ARE GIFTED WITH IMMORTALITY!
COME ON!
PLEASE, DON'T DO THIS!
MY DAD'S A COUNCILMAN! HE WILL--
THE FEAR! YOU CAN TASTE IT IN THE AIR! GLORIOUS!
IT CERTAINLY IS, MISTRESS!

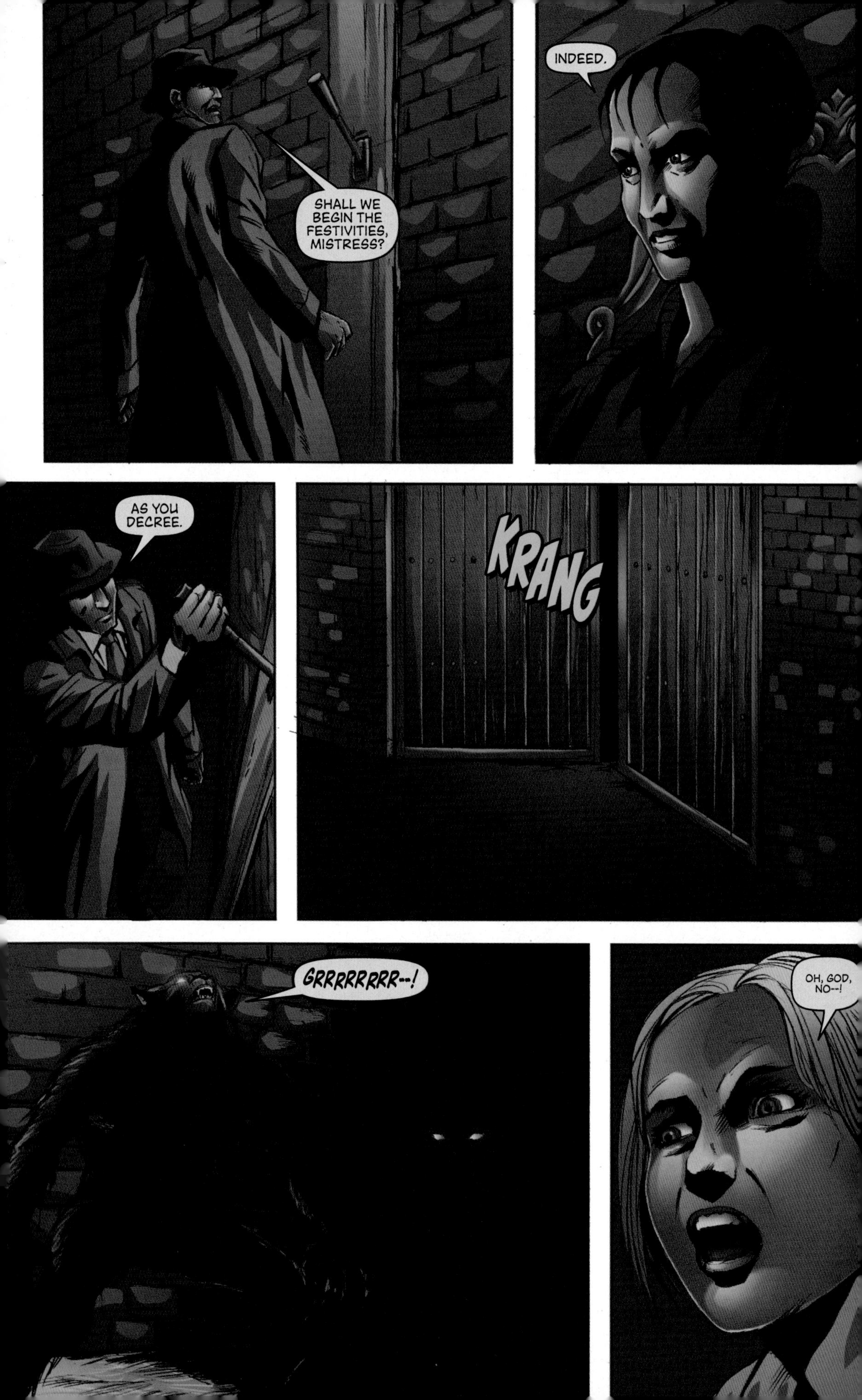
SHALL WE BEGIN THE FESTIVITIES, MISTRESS?
INDEED.
AS YOU DECREE.
KRANG
GRRRRRRRR--!
OH, GOD, NO--!

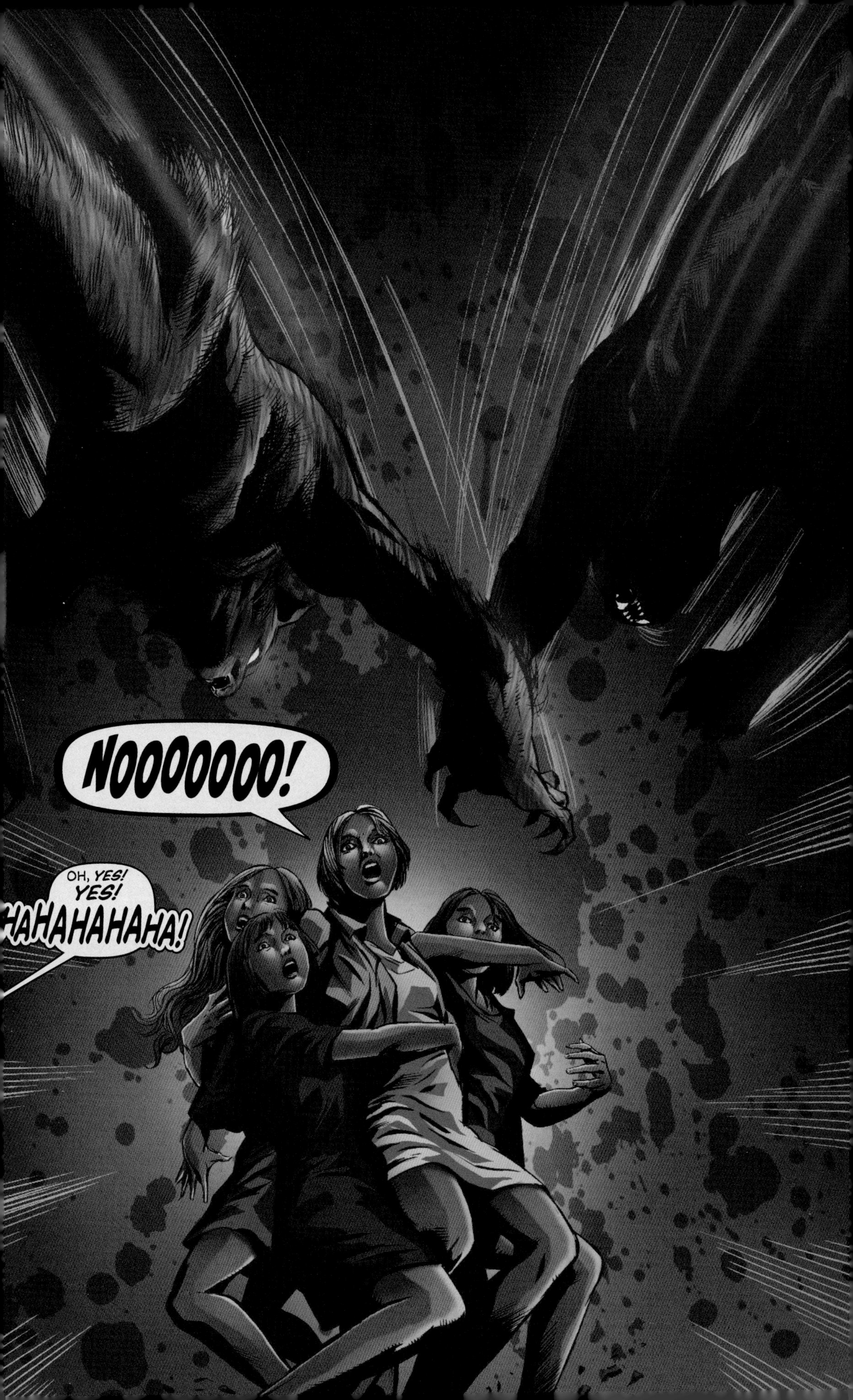
NOOOOOOO!
OH, YES! YES! HAHAHAHAHA!

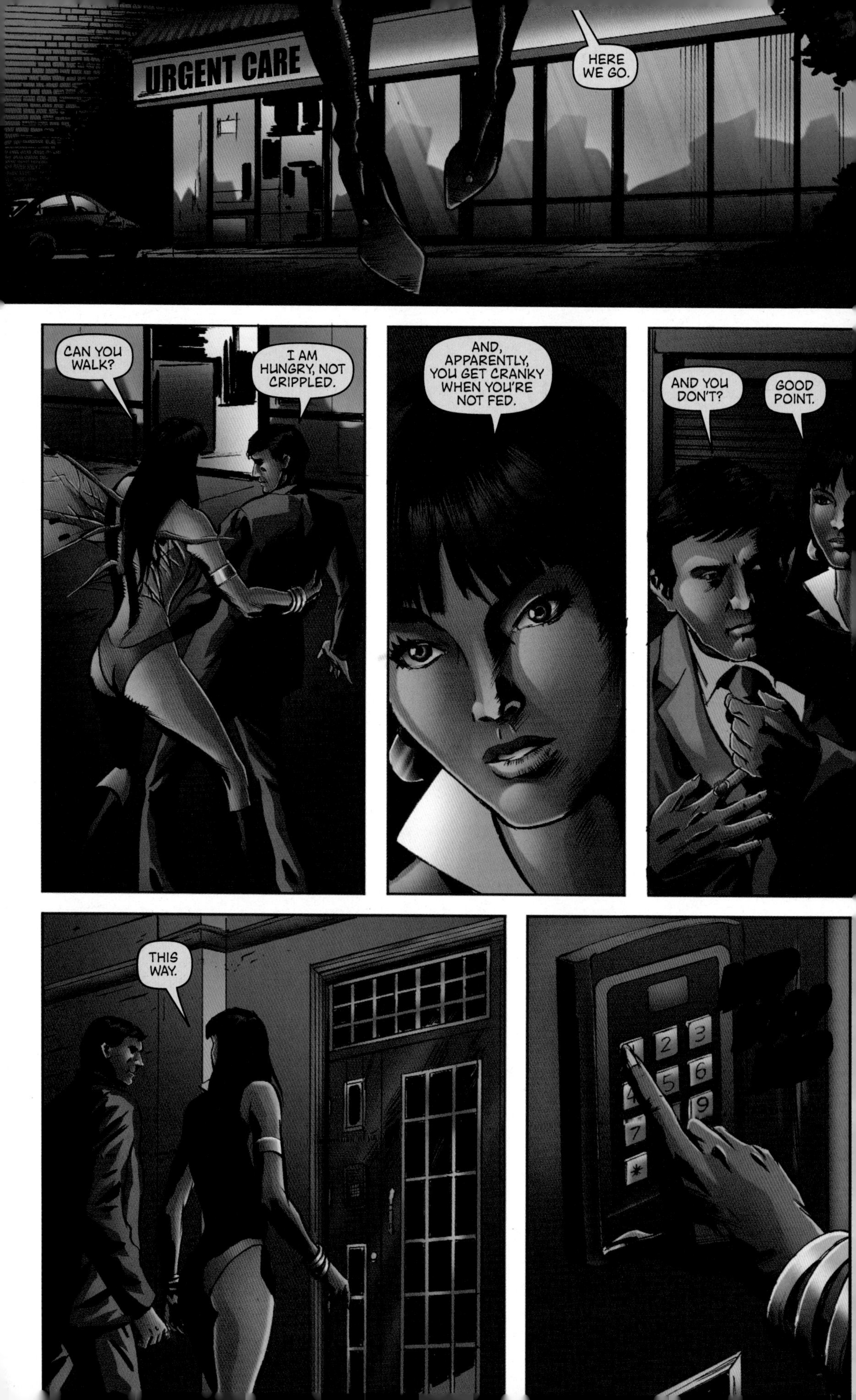
URGENT CARE
HERE WE GO.
CAN YOU WALK?
I AM HUNGRY, NOT CRIPPLED.
AND, APPARENTLY, YOU GET CRANKY WHEN YOU'RE NOT FED.
AND YOU DON'T?
GOOD POINT.
THIS WAY.
1 2 3
4 5 6
7 9
*

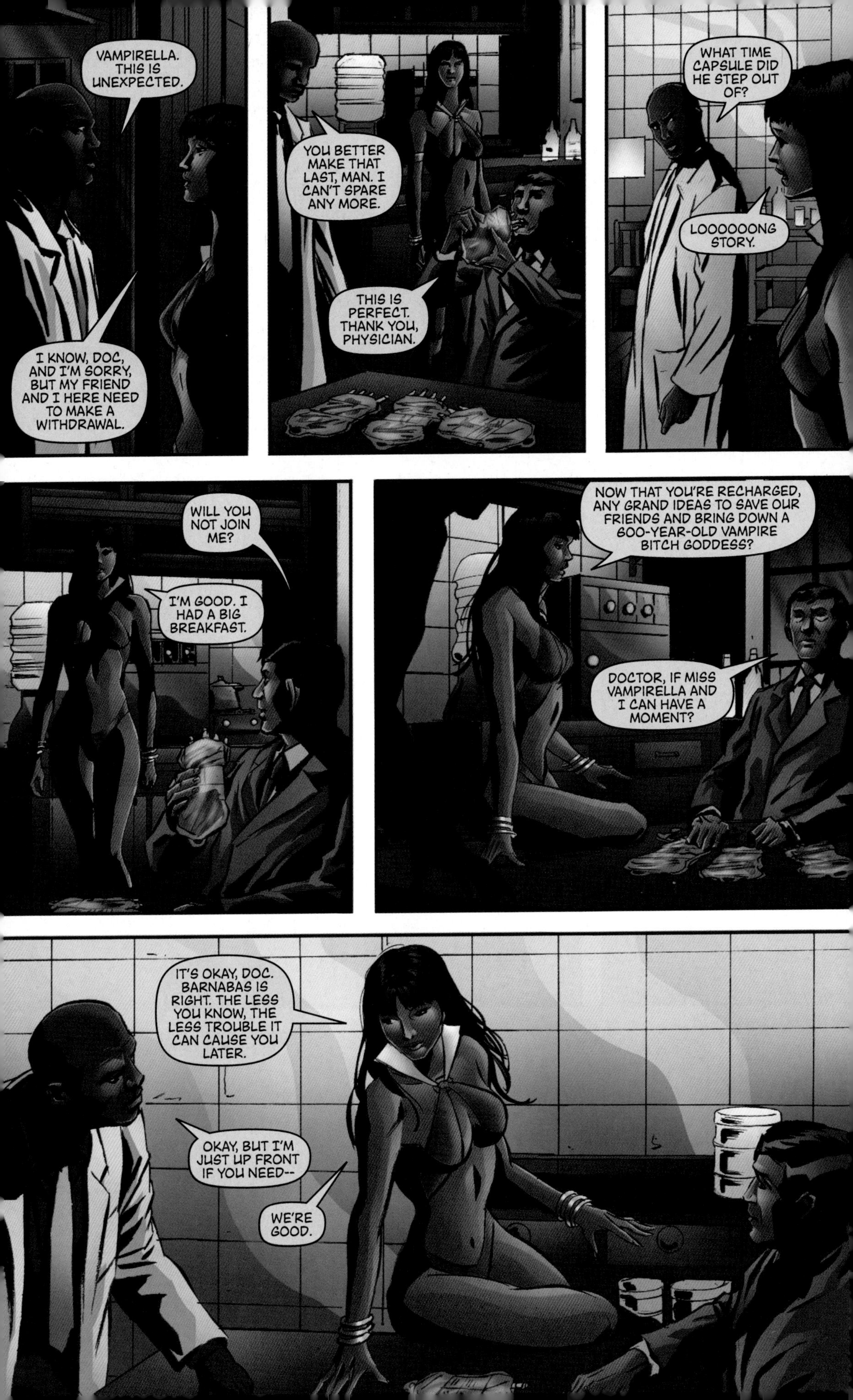
VAMPIRELLA. THIS IS UNEXPECTED.
I KNOW, DOC, AND I'M SORRY, BUT MY FRIEND AND I HERE NEED TO MAKE A WITHDRAWAL.
YOU BETTER MAKE THAT LAST, MAN. I CAN'T SPARE ANY MORE.
THIS IS PERFECT. THANK YOU, PHYSICIAN.
WHAT TIME CAPSULE DID HE STEP OUT OF?
LOOOOOONG STORY.
WILL YOU NOT JOIN ME?
I'M GOOD. I HAD A BIG BREAKFAST.
NOW THAT YOU'RE RECHARGED, ANY GRAND IDEAS TO SAVE OUR FRIENDS AND BRING DOWN A 600-YEAR-OLD VAMPIRE BITCH GODDESS?
DOCTOR, IF MISS VAMPIRELLA AND I CAN HAVE A MOMENT?
IT'S OKAY, DOC. BARNABAS IS RIGHT. THE LESS YOU KNOW, THE LESS TROUBLE IT CAN CAUSE YOU LATER.
OKAY, BUT I'M JUST UP FRONT IF YOU NEED--
WE'RE GOOD.

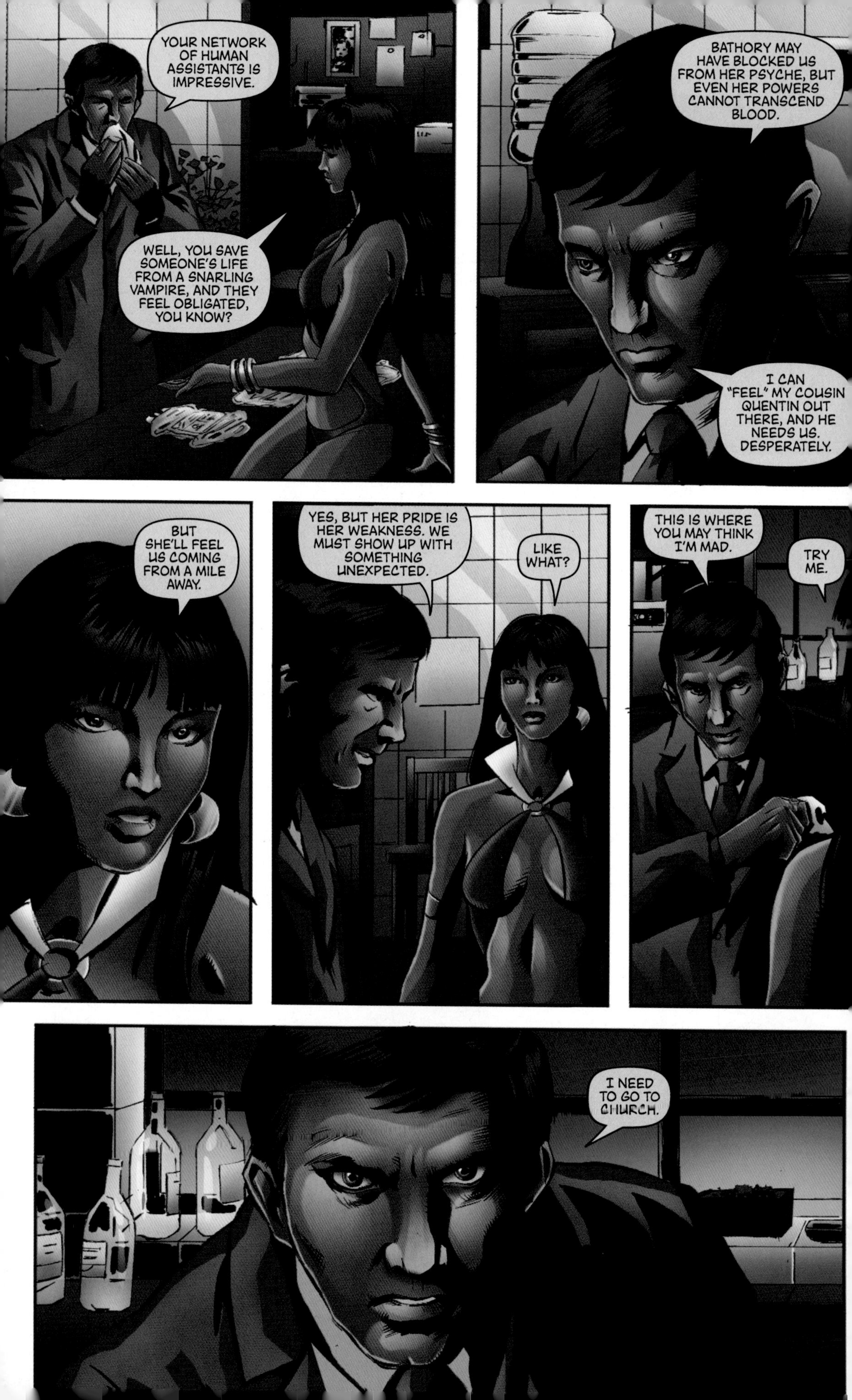
YOUR NETWORK OF HUMAN ASSISTANTS IS IMPRESSIVE.
WELL, YOU SAVE SOMEONE'S LIFE FROM A SNARLING VAMPIRE, AND THEY FEEL OBLIGATED, YOU KNOW?
BATHORY MAY HAVE BLOCKED US FROM HER PSYCHE, BUT EVEN HER POWERS CANNOT TRANSCEND BLOOD.
I CAN "FEEL" MY COUSIN QUENTIN OUT THERE, AND HE NEEDS US. DESPERATELY.
BUT SHE'LL FEEL US COMING FROM A MILE AWAY.
YES, BUT HER PRIDE IS HER WEAKNESS. WE MUST SHOW UP WITH SOMETHING UNEXPECTED.
LIKE WHAT?
THIS IS WHERE YOU MAY THINK I'M MAD.
TRY ME.
I NEED TO GO TO CHURCH.

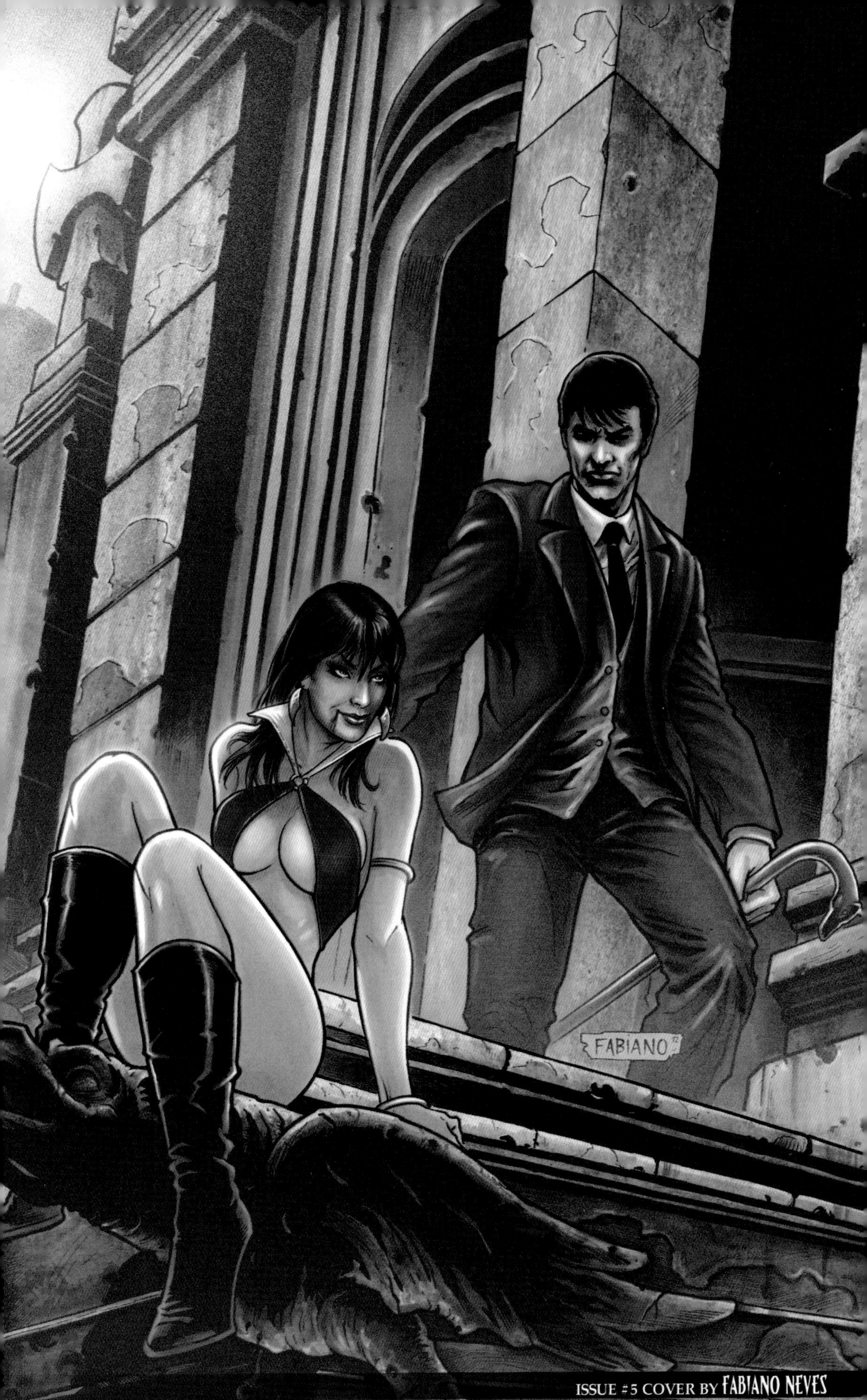
FABIANO

ISSUE #5 COVER BY FABIANO NEVES

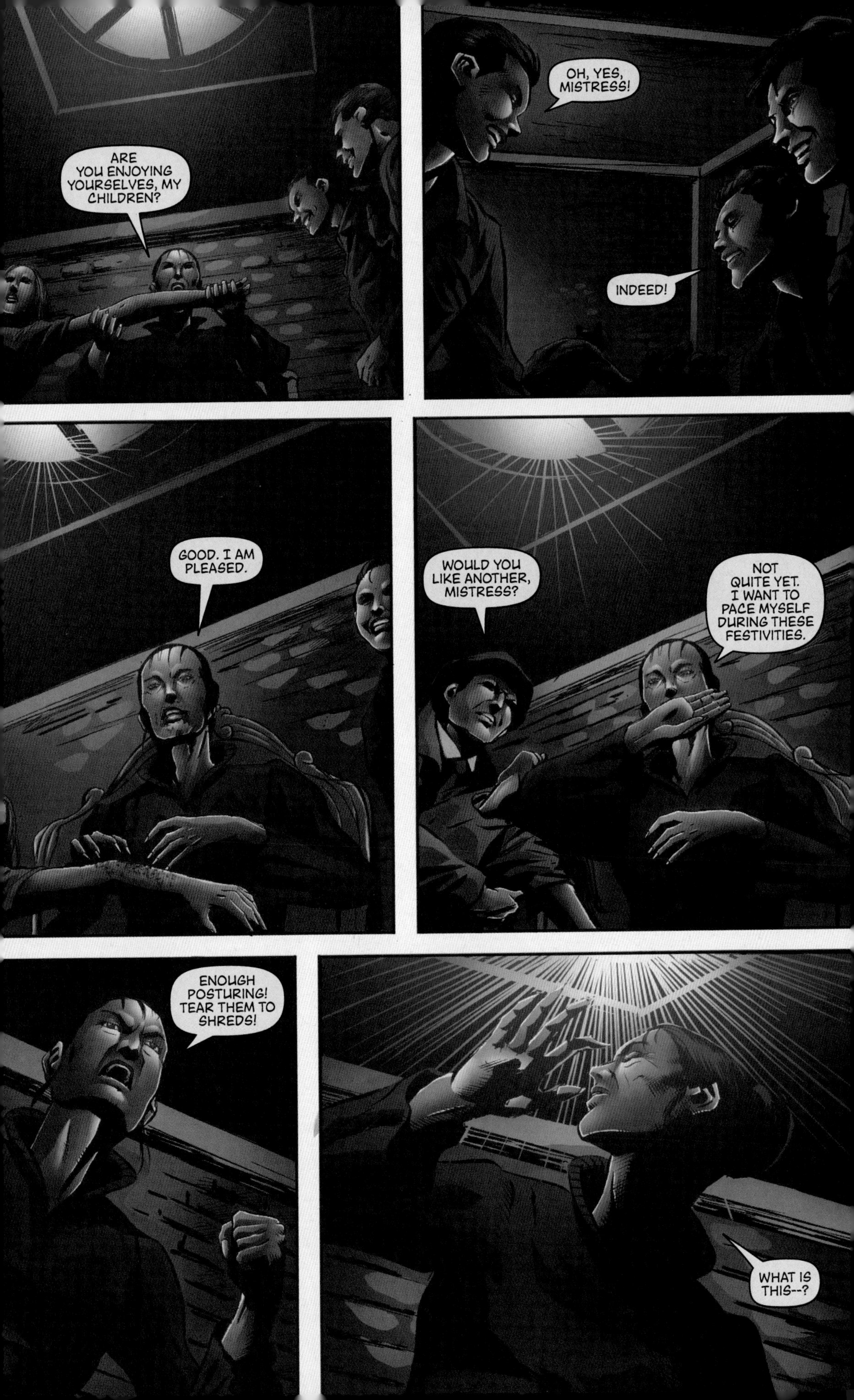
ARE YOU ENJOYING YOURSELVES, MY CHILDREN?
OH, YES, MISTRESS!
INDEED!
GOOD. I AM PLEASED.
WOULD YOU LIKE ANOTHER, MISTRESS?
NOT QUITE YET. I WANT TO PACE MYSELF DURING THESE FESTIVITIES.
ENOUGH POSTURING! TEAR THEM TO SHREDS!
WHAT IS THIS--?

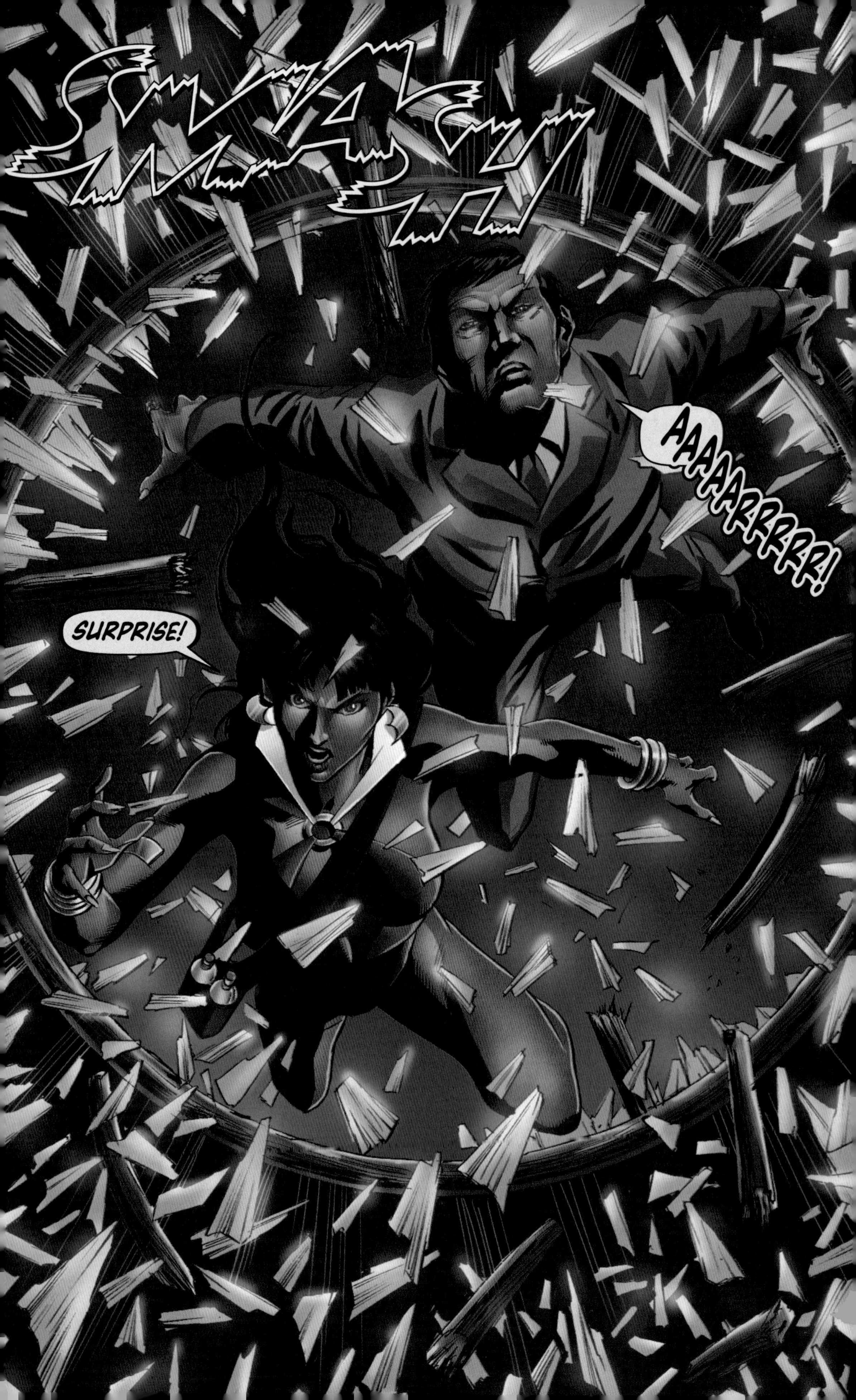
SMASH
AAAAARRRRR!
SURPRISE!

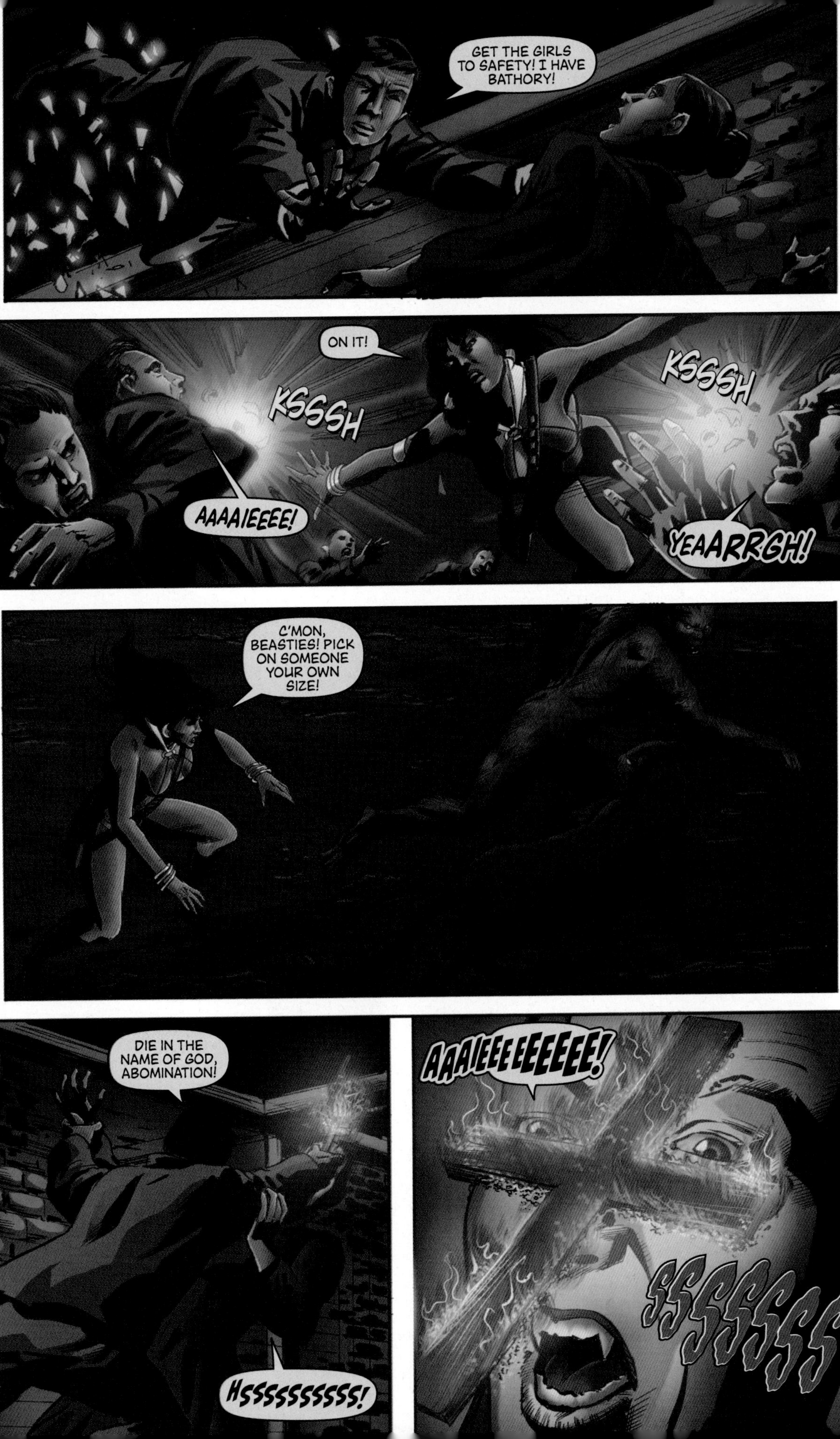
GET THE GIRLS TO SAFETY! I HAVE BATHORY!
ON IT!
KSSSH
KSSSH
AAAAIEEEE!
YEAARRGH!
C'MON, BEASTIES! PICK ON SOMEONE YOUR OWN SIZE!
DIE IN THE NAME OF GOD, ABOMINATION!
HSSSSSSSSS!
AAAIEEE EEEEEE!
SSSSSSS

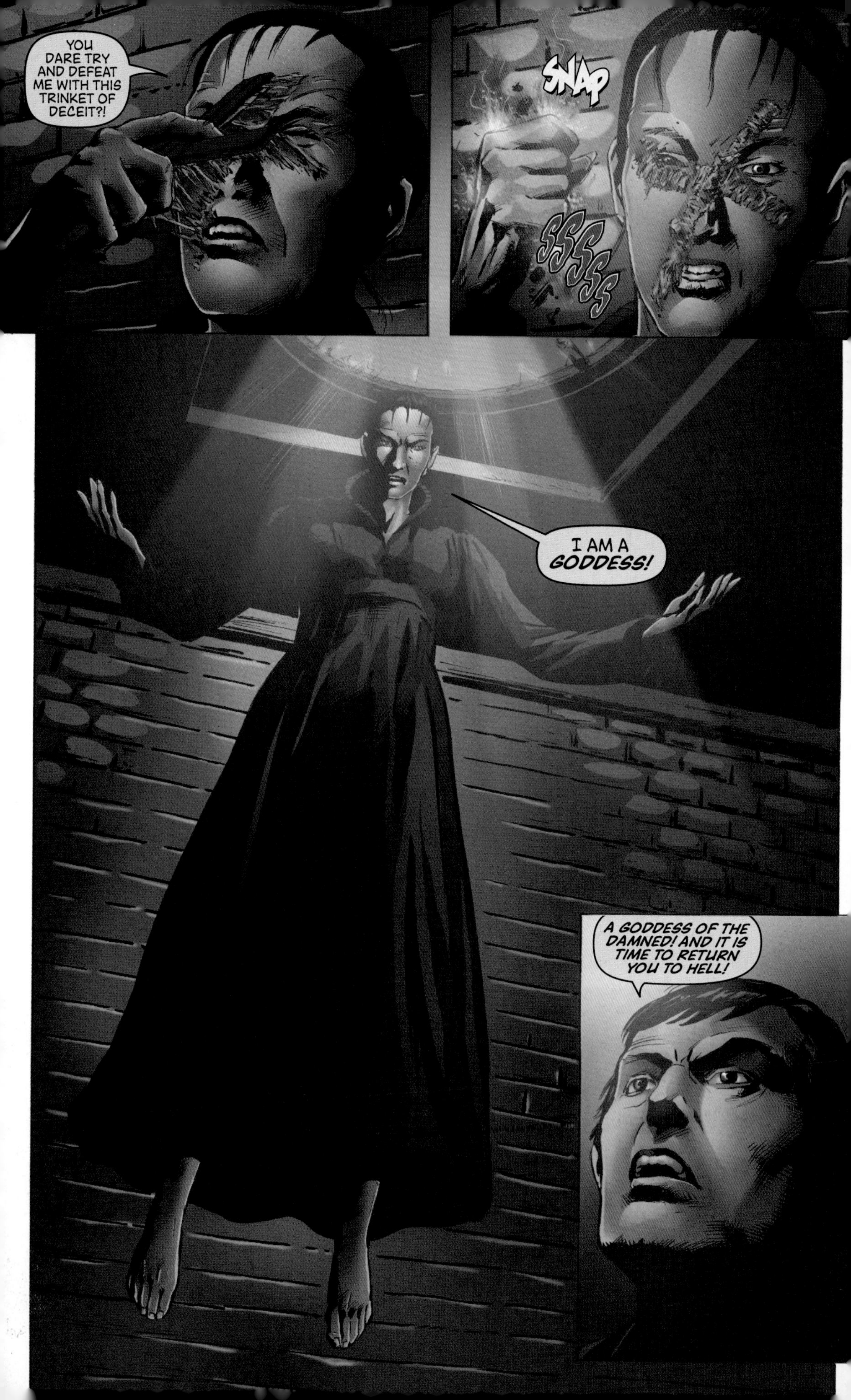
YOU DARE TRY AND DEFEAT ME WITH THIS TRINKET OF DECEIT?!
SNAP
SSSSSS
I AM A GODDESS!
A GODDESS OF THE DAMNED! AND IT IS TIME TO RETURN YOU TO HELL!

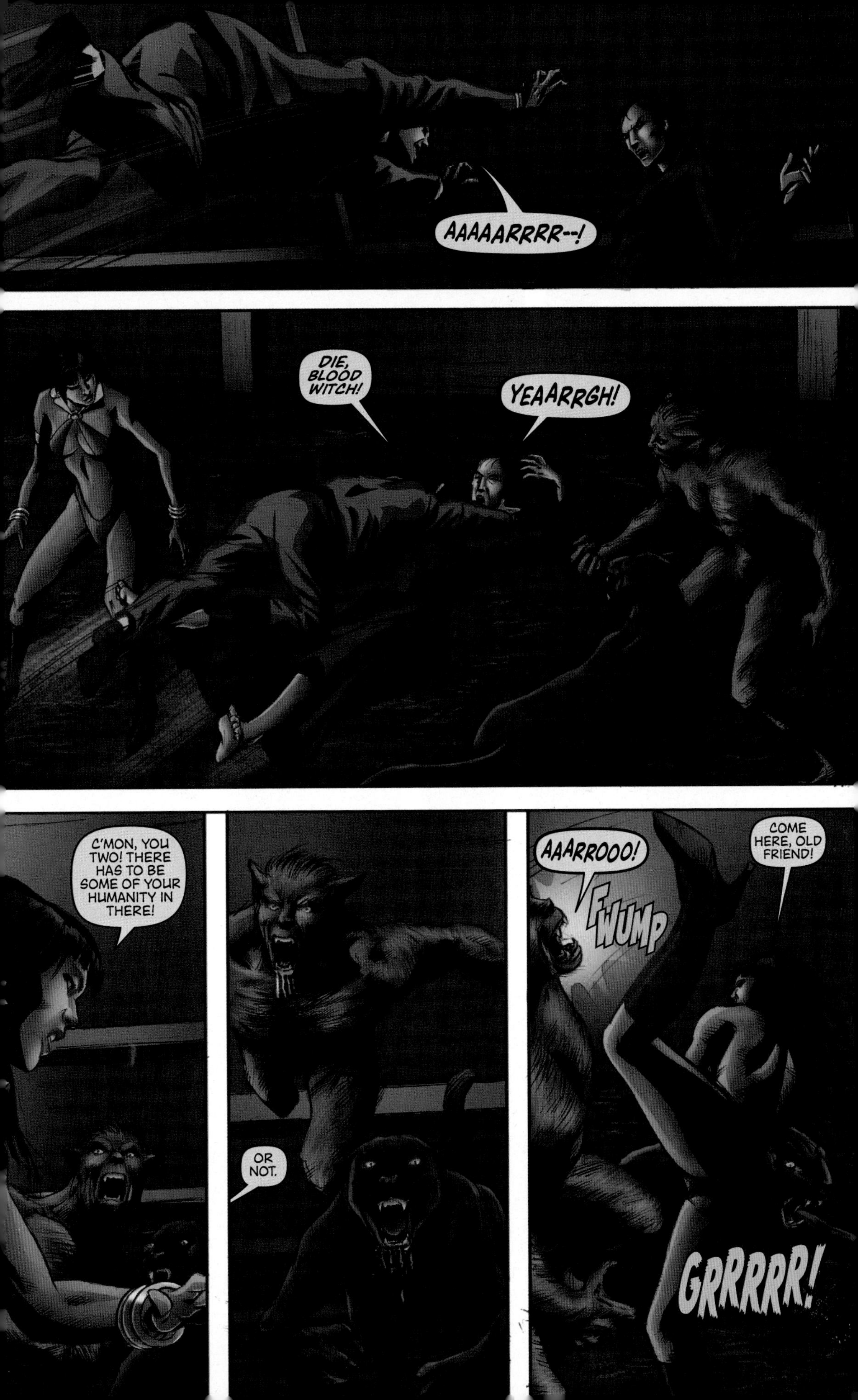
AAAAARRRR--!
DIE, BLOOD WITCH!
YEAARRGH!
C'MON, YOU TWO! THERE HAS TO BE SOME OF YOUR HUMANITY IN THERE!
OR NOT.
AAARROOO!
FWUMP
COME HERE, OLD FRIEND!
GRRRRR!

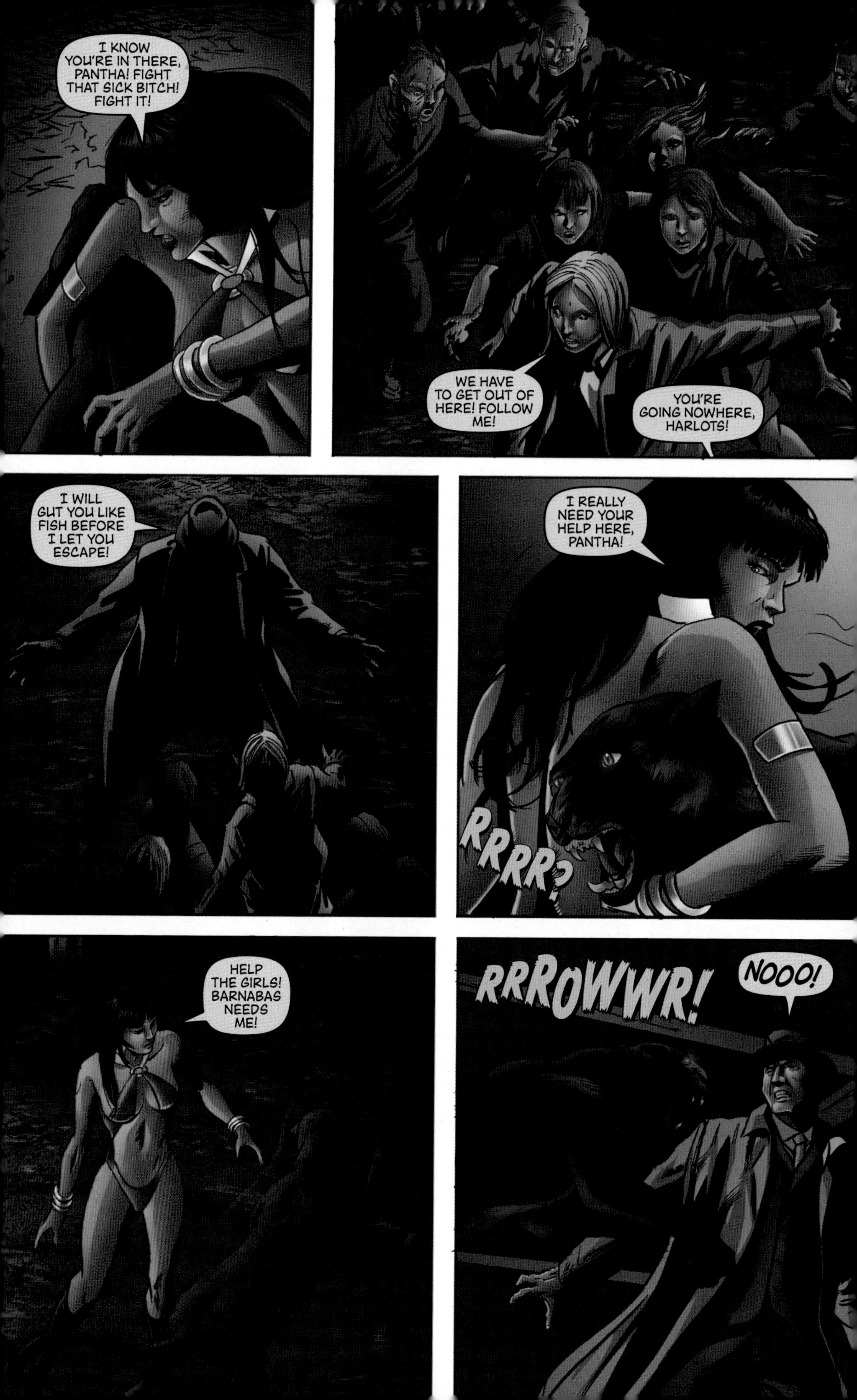
I KNOW YOU'RE IN THERE, PANTHA! FIGHT THAT SICK BITCH! FIGHT IT!
WE HAVE TO GET OUT OF HERE! FOLLOW ME!
YOU'RE GOING NOWHERE, HARLOTS!
I WILL GUT YOU LIKE FISH BEFORE I LET YOU ESCAPE!
I REALLY NEED YOUR HELP HERE, PANTHA!
RRRR?
HELP THE GIRLS! BARNABAS NEEDS ME!
RRROWWR!
NOOO!

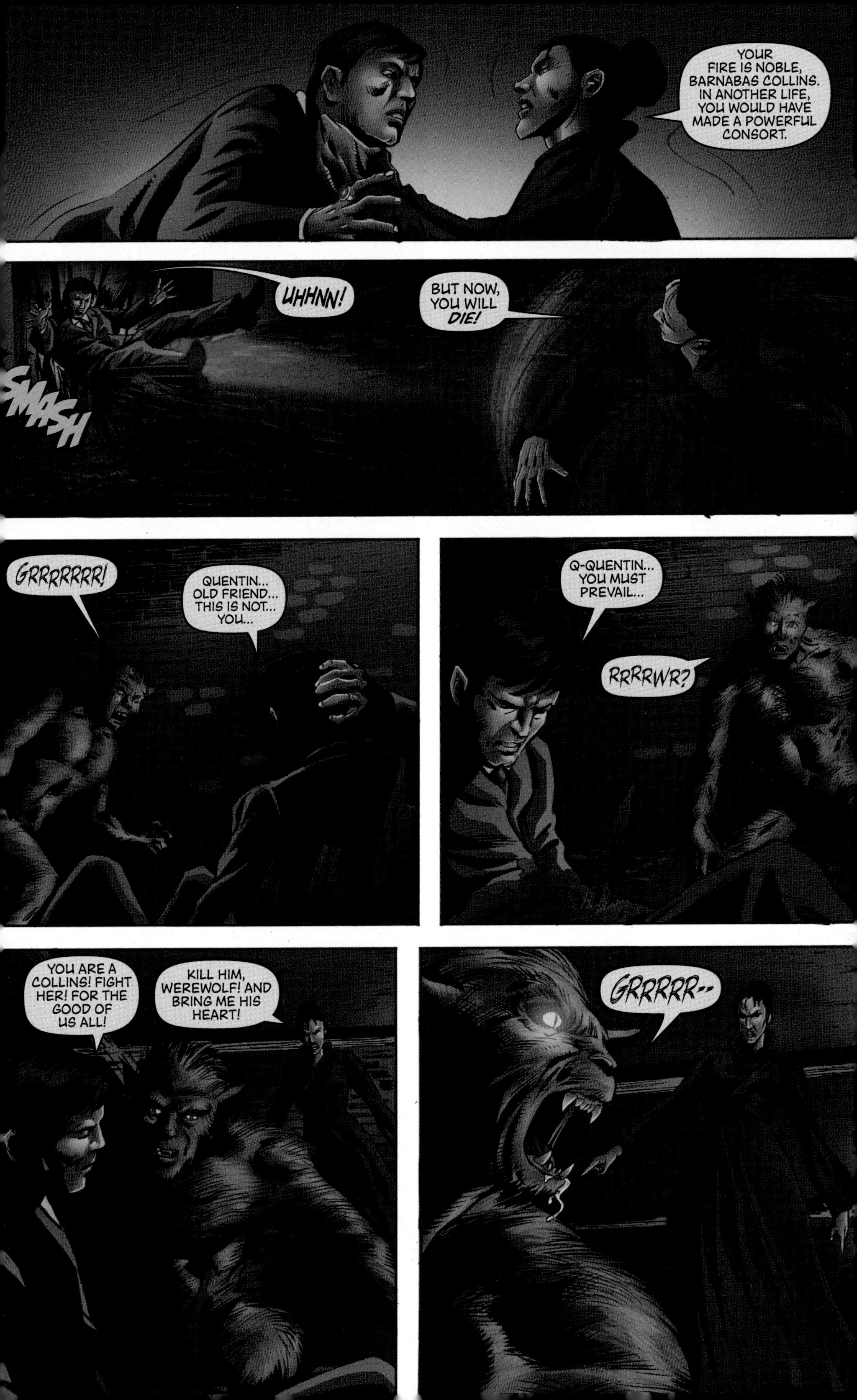
YOUR FIRE IS NOBLE, BARNABAS COLLINS. IN ANOTHER LIFE, YOU WOULD HAVE MADE A POWERFUL CONSORT.
SMASH
UHHNN!
BUT NOW, YOU WILL DIE!
GRRRRRRR!
QUENTIN... OLD FRIEND... THIS IS NOT... YOU...
Q-QUENTIN... YOU MUST PREVAIL...
RRRRWR?
YOU ARE A COLLINS! FIGHT HER! FOR THE GOOD OF US ALL!
KILL HIM, WEREWOLF! AND BRING ME HIS HEART!
GRRRRR--

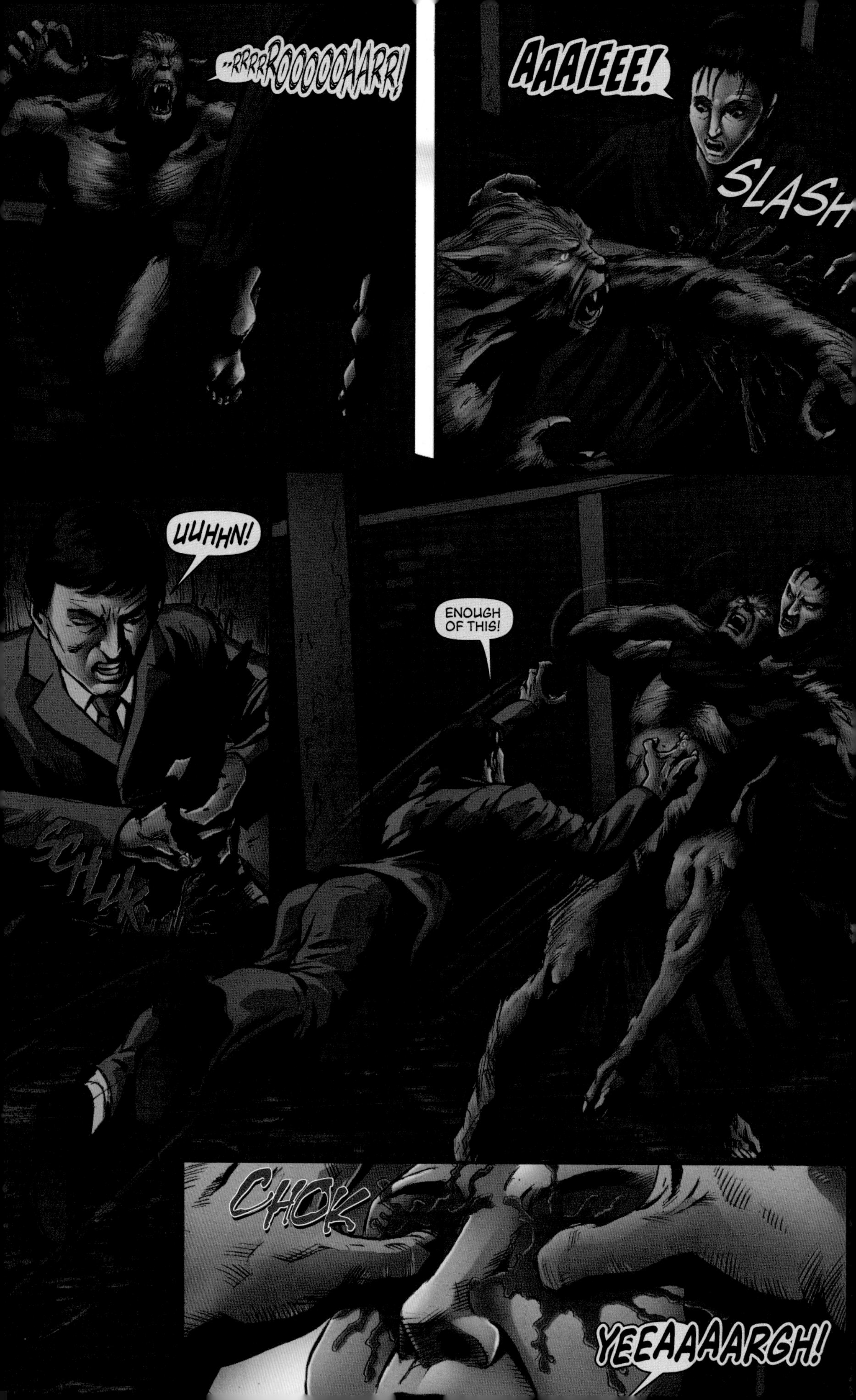
--RRRRROOOOOOAARR!
AAAIEEE!
SLASH
UUHHN!
SCHLUK
ENOUGH OF THIS!
CHOK
YEEAAAARGH!

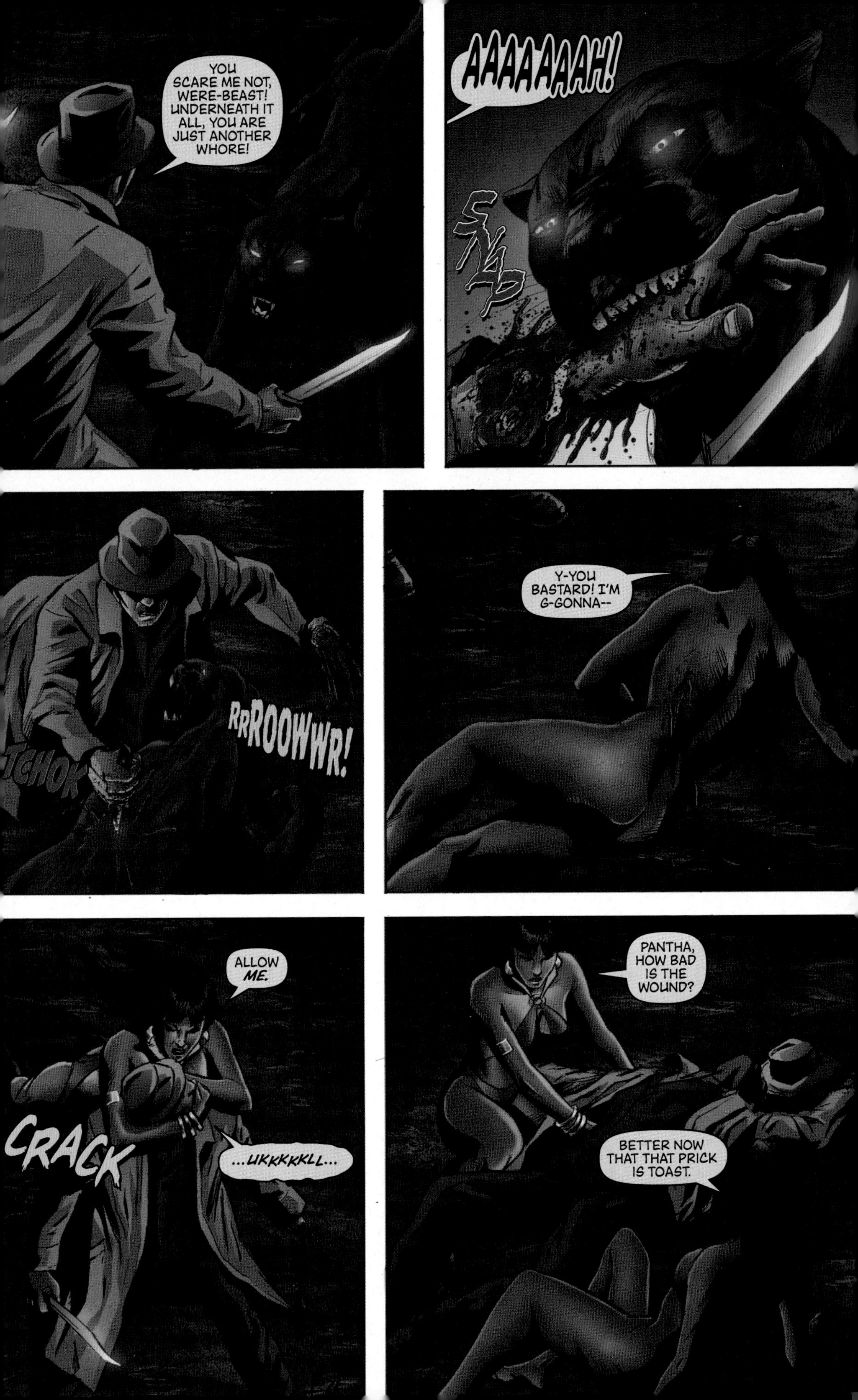
YOU SCARE ME NOT, WERE-BEAST! UNDERNEATH IT ALL, YOU ARE JUST ANOTHER WHORE!
AAAAAAAH!
SNAP
TCHOK
RRROOWWR!
Y-YOU BASTARD! I'M G-GONNA--
ALLOW ME.
CRACK
...UKKKKKLL...
PANTHA, HOW BAD IS THE WOUND?
BETTER NOW THAT THAT PRICK IS TOAST.

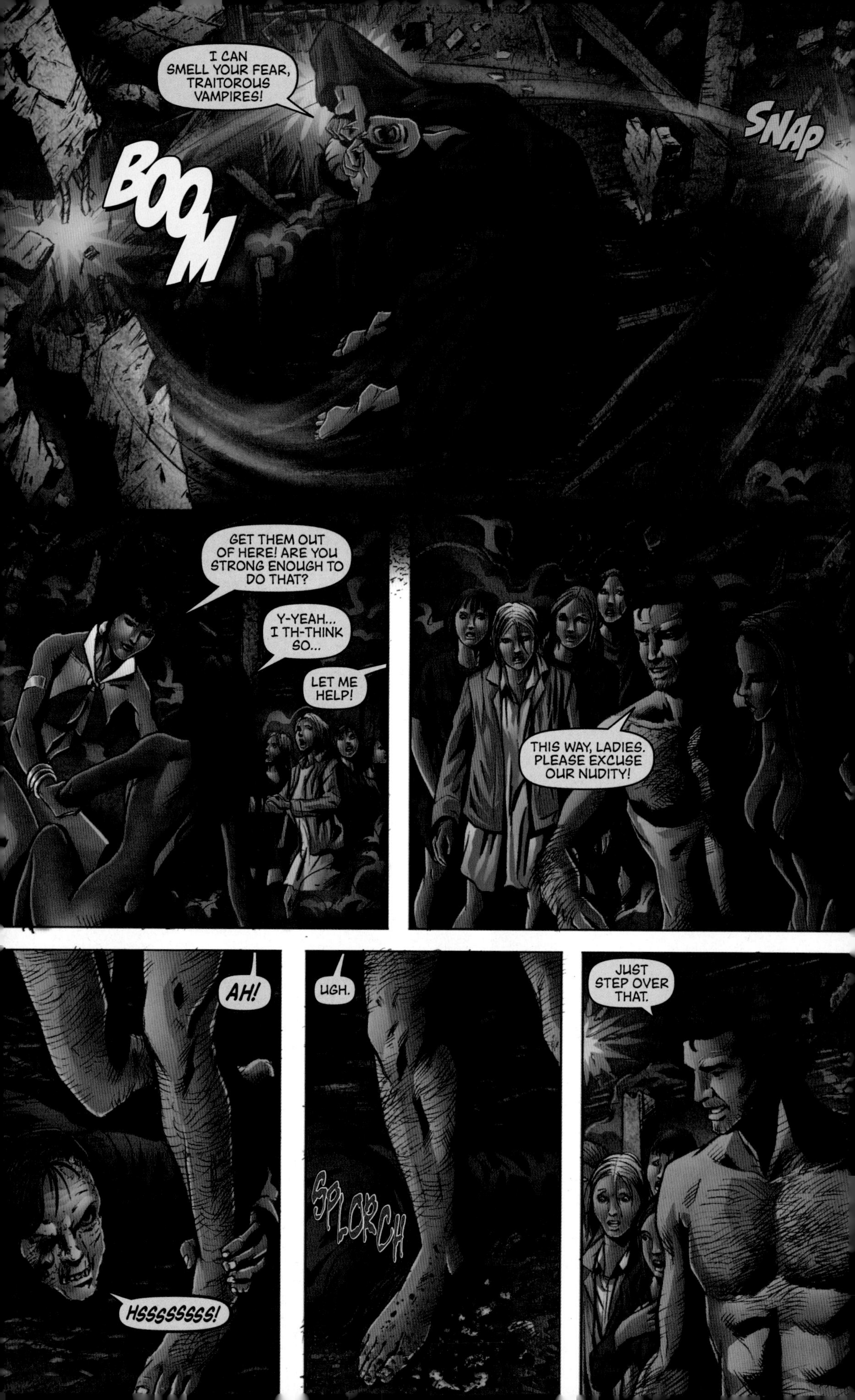
I CAN SMELL YOUR FEAR, TRAITOROUS VAMPIRES!
SNAP
BOOM
GET THEM OUT OF HERE! ARE YOU STRONG ENOUGH TO DO THAT?
Y-YEAH... I TH-THINK SO...
LET ME HELP!
THIS WAY, LADIES. PLEASE EXCUSE OUR NUDITY!
AH!
HSSSSSSSS!
UGH.
SPLORCH
JUST STEP OVER THAT.

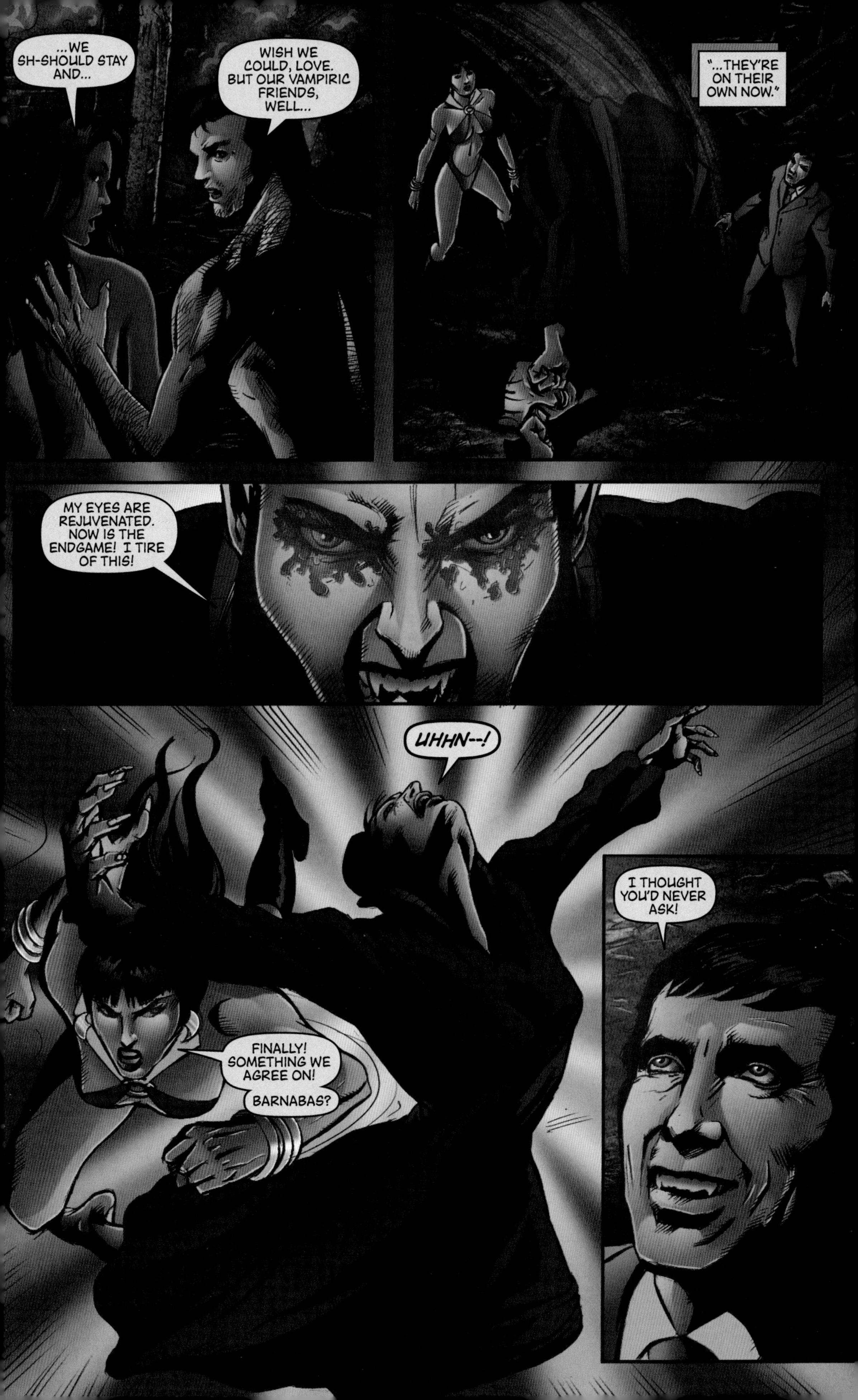
...WE SH-SHOULD STAY AND...
WISH WE COULD, LOVE. BUT OUR VAMPIRIC FRIENDS, WELL...
"...THEY'RE ON THEIR OWN NOW."
MY EYES ARE REJUVENATED. NOW IS THE ENDGAME! I TIRE OF THIS!
UHHN--!
FINALLY! SOMETHING WE AGREE ON!
BARNABAS?
I THOUGHT YOU'D NEVER ASK!

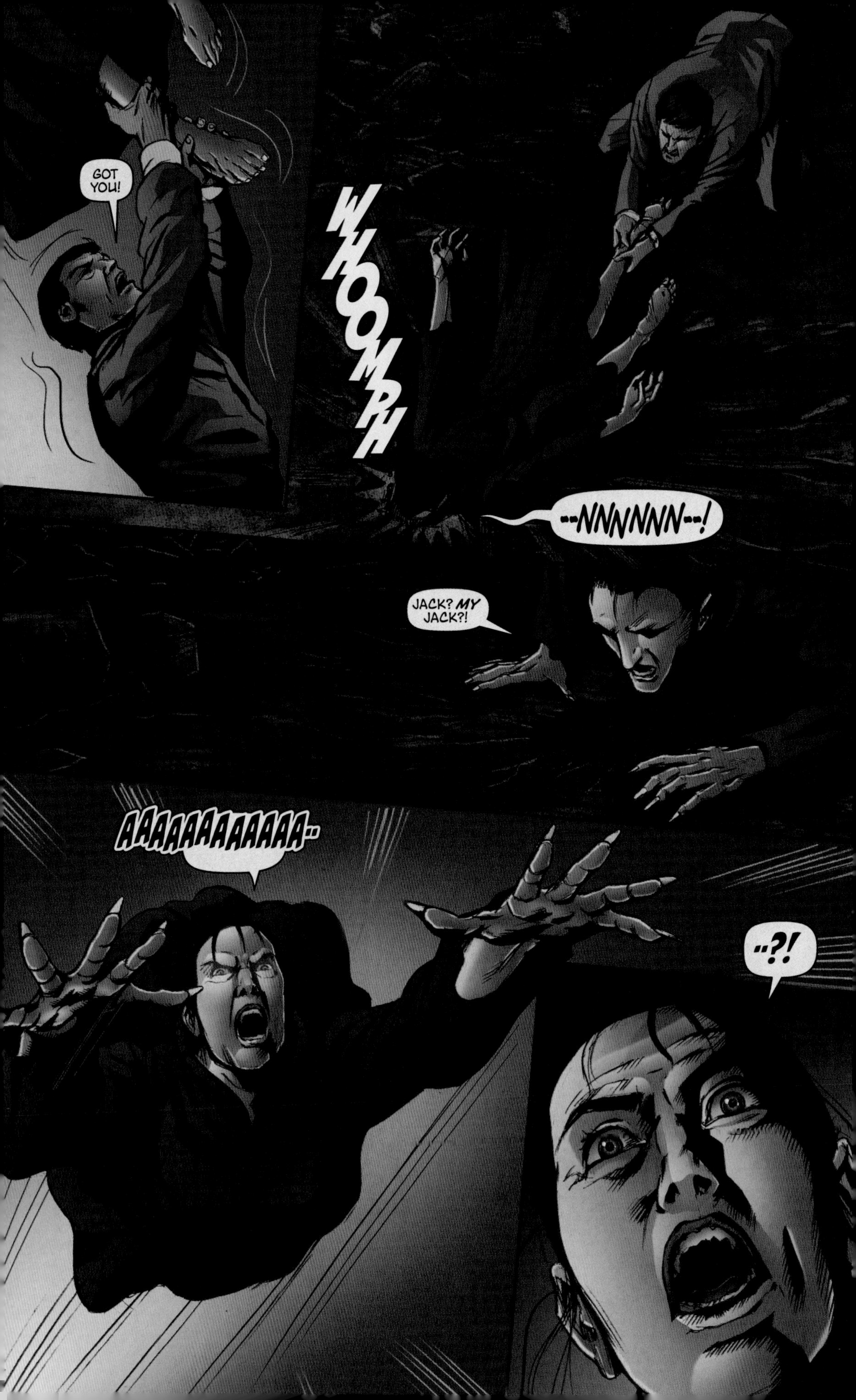
GOT YOU!
WHOOMPH
--NNNNNN--!
JACK? MY JACK?!
AAAAAAAAAAAA--
--?!

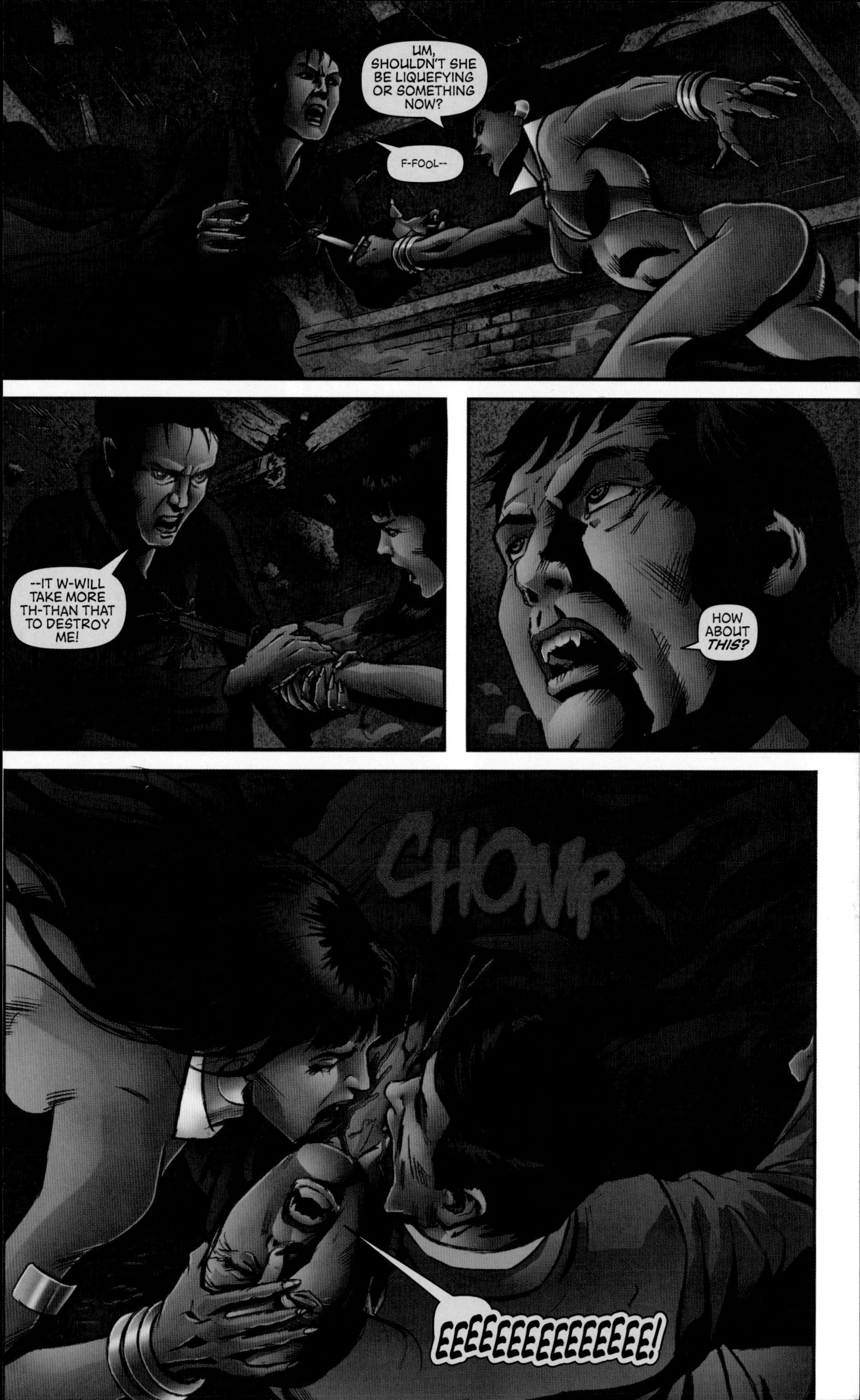
UM, SHOULDN'T SHE BE LIQUEFYING OR SOMETHING NOW?
F-FOOL--
--IT W-WILL TAKE MORE TH-THAN THAT TO DESTROY ME!
HOW ABOUT *THIS?*
CHOMP
EEEEEEEEEEEEEEEE!

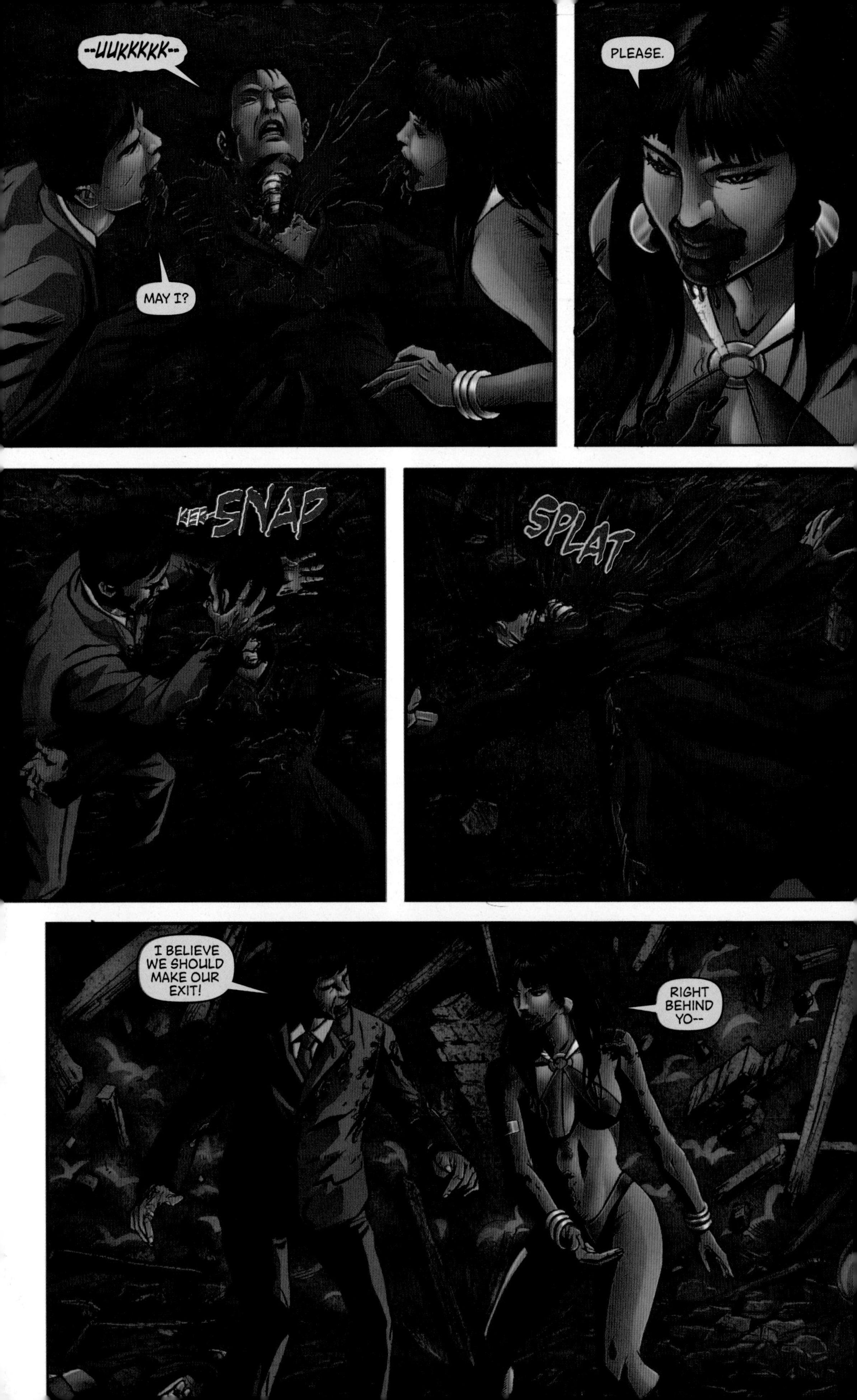
--UUKKKKK--
MAY I?
PLEASE.
KEE-SNAP
SPLAT
I BELIEVE WE SHOULD MAKE OUR EXIT!
RIGHT BEHIND YO--

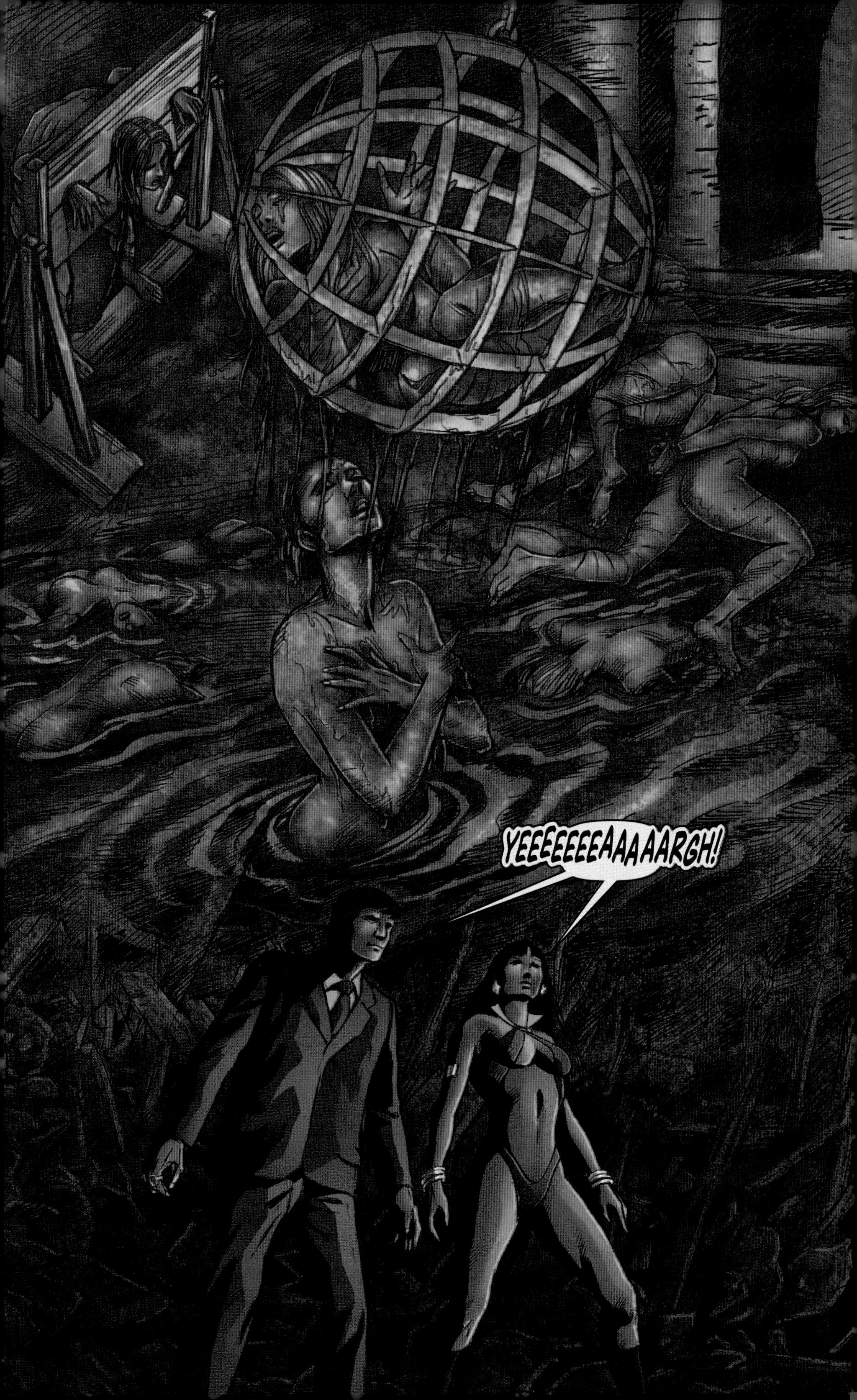
YEEEEEEEAAAAARGH!

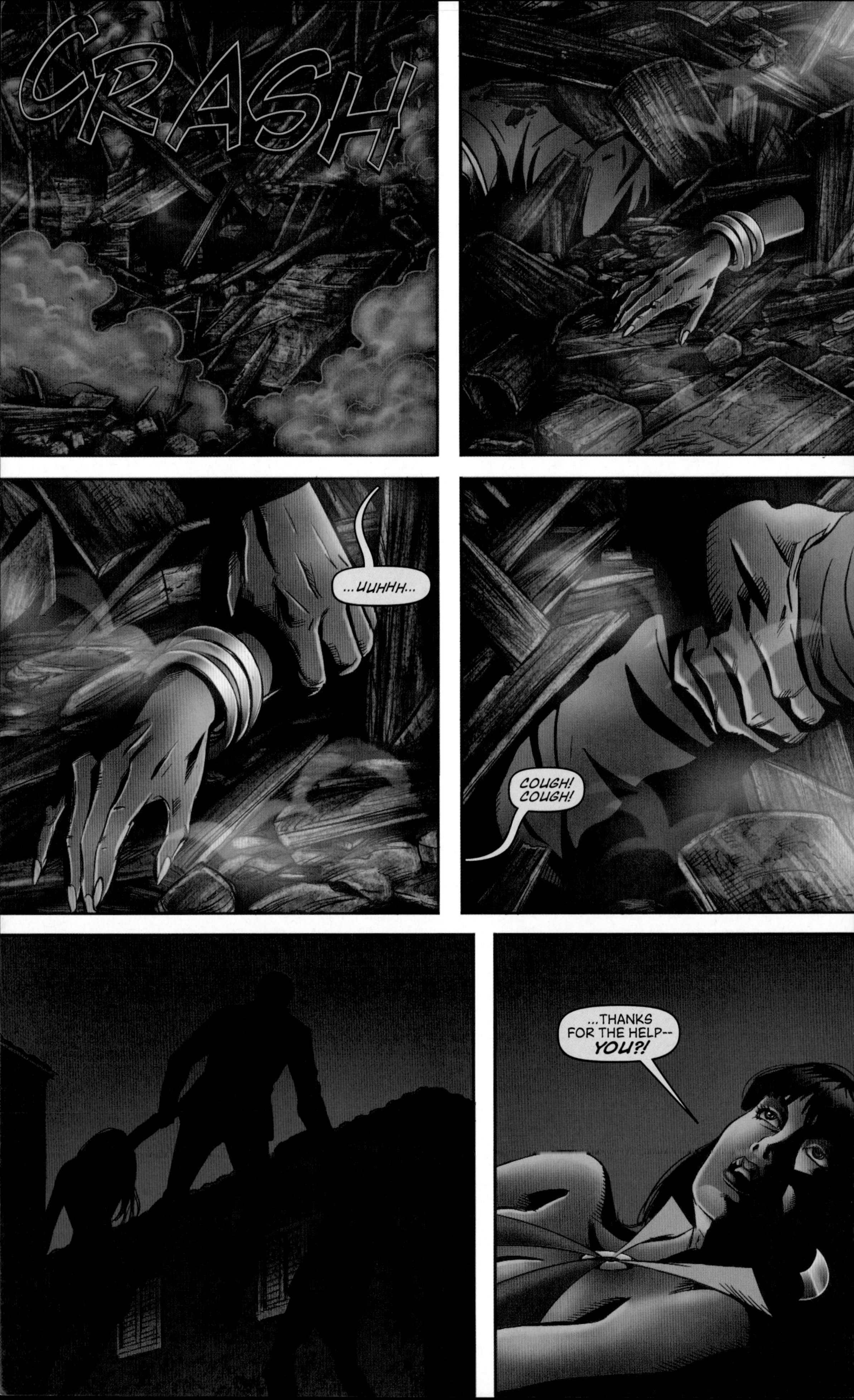
CRASH
...UUHHH...
COUGH! COUGH!
...THANKS FOR THE HELP-- YOU?!

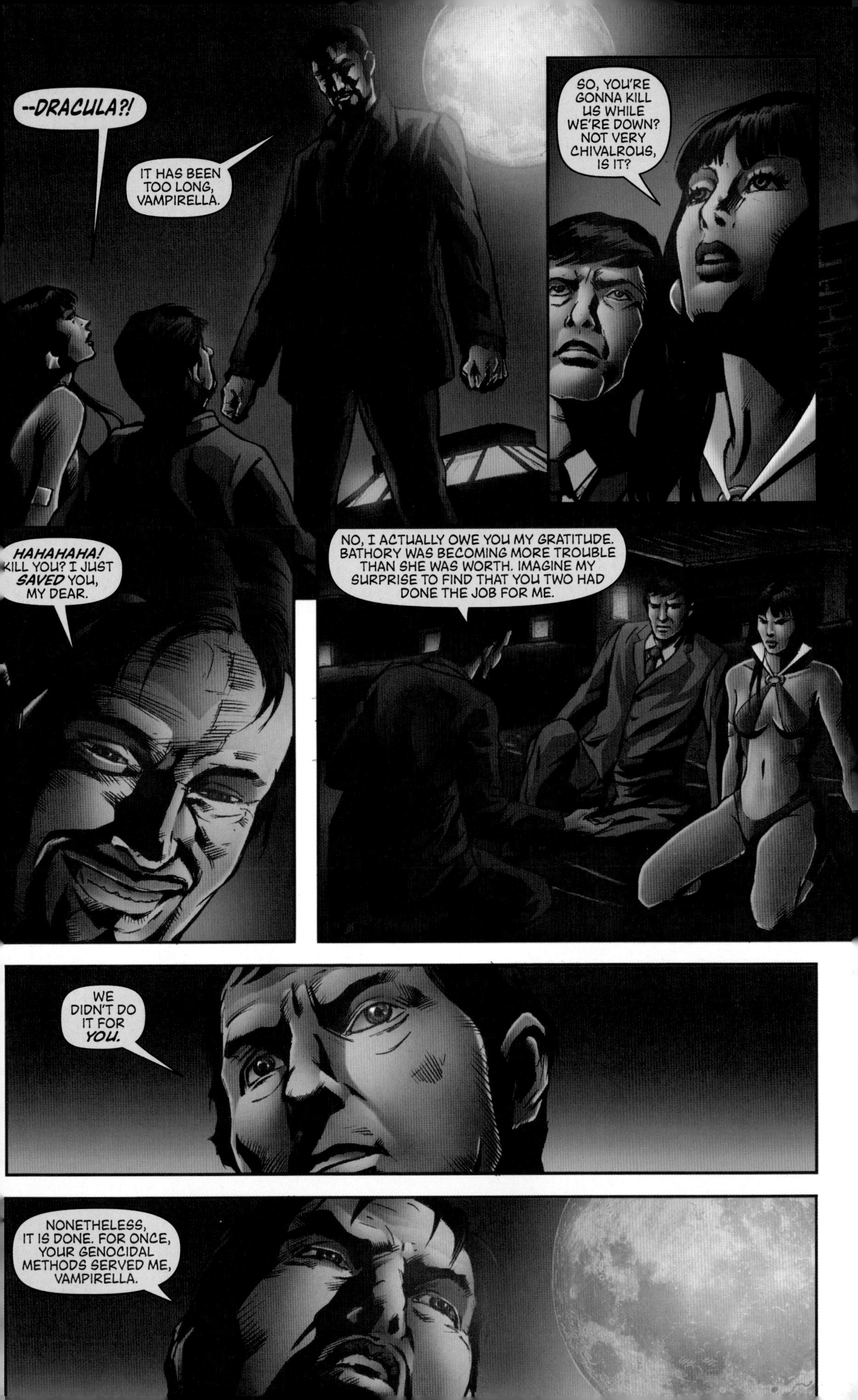
--DRACULA?!
IT HAS BEEN TOO LONG, VAMPIRELLA.
SO, YOU'RE GONNA KILL US WHILE WE'RE DOWN? NOT VERY CHIVALROUS, IS IT?
HAHAHAHA! KILL YOU? I JUST SAVED YOU, MY DEAR.
NO, I ACTUALLY OWE YOU MY GRATITUDE. BATHORY WAS BECOMING MORE TROUBLE THAN SHE WAS WORTH. IMAGINE MY SURPRISE TO FIND THAT YOU TWO HAD DONE THE JOB FOR ME.
WE DIDN'T DO IT FOR YOU.
NONETHELESS, IT IS DONE. FOR ONCE, YOUR GENOCIDAL METHODS SERVED ME, VAMPIRELLA.

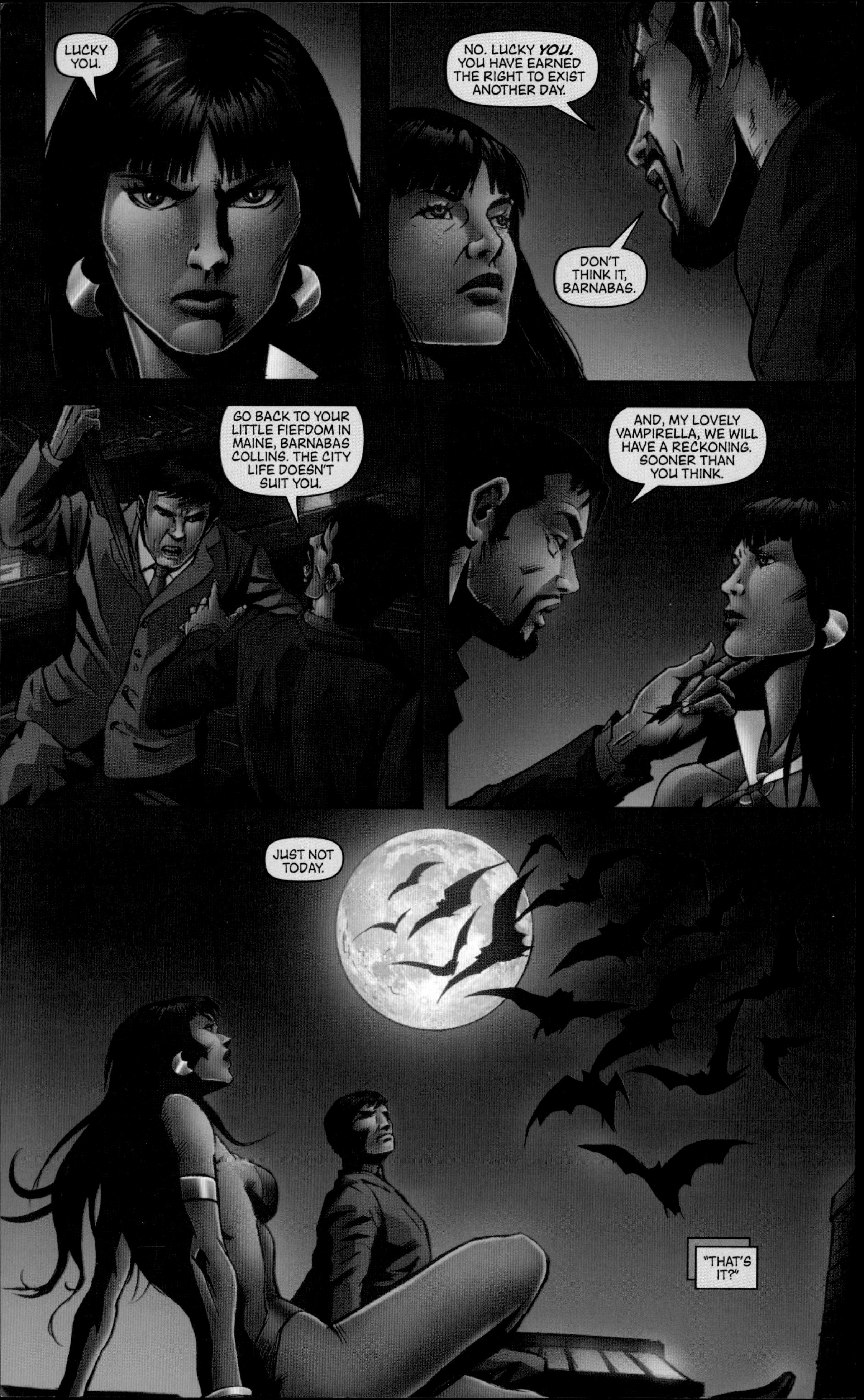
LUCKY YOU.
NO. LUCKY *YOU.* YOU HAVE EARNED THE RIGHT TO EXIST ANOTHER DAY.
DON'T THINK IT, BARNABAS.
GO BACK TO YOUR LITTLE FIEFDOM IN MAINE, BARNABAS COLLINS. THE CITY LIFE DOESN'T SUIT YOU.
AND, MY LOVELY VAMPIRELLA, WE WILL HAVE A RECKONING. SOONER THAN YOU THINK.
JUST NOT TODAY.
"THAT'S IT?"

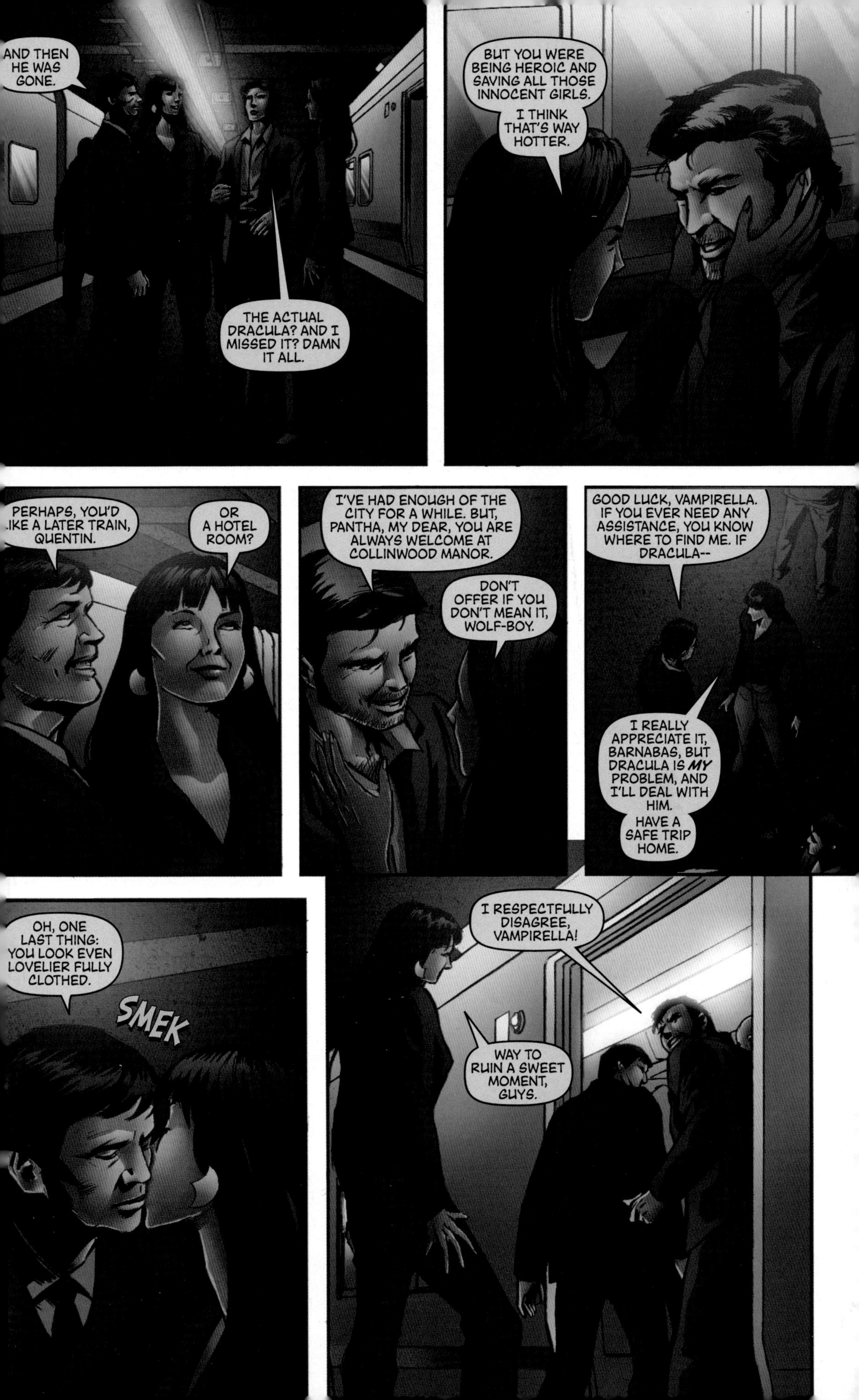
AND THEN HE WAS GONE.
THE ACTUAL DRACULA? AND I MISSED IT? DAMN IT ALL.
BUT YOU WERE BEING HEROIC AND SAVING ALL THOSE INNOCENT GIRLS.
I THINK THAT'S WAY HOTTER.
PERHAPS, YOU'D LIKE A LATER TRAIN, QUENTIN.
OR A HOTEL ROOM?
I'VE HAD ENOUGH OF THE CITY FOR A WHILE. BUT, PANTHA, MY DEAR, YOU ARE ALWAYS WELCOME AT COLLINWOOD MANOR.
DON'T OFFER IF YOU DON'T MEAN IT, WOLF-BOY.
GOOD LUCK, VAMPIRELLA. IF YOU EVER NEED ANY ASSISTANCE, YOU KNOW WHERE TO FIND ME. IF DRACULA--
I REALLY APPRECIATE IT, BARNABAS, BUT DRACULA IS *MY* PROBLEM, AND I'LL DEAL WITH HIM.
HAVE A SAFE TRIP HOME.
OH, ONE LAST THING: YOU LOOK EVEN LOVELIER FULLY CLOTHED.
SMEK
I RESPECTFULLY DISAGREE, VAMPIRELLA!
WAY TO RUIN A SWEET MOMENT, GUYS.

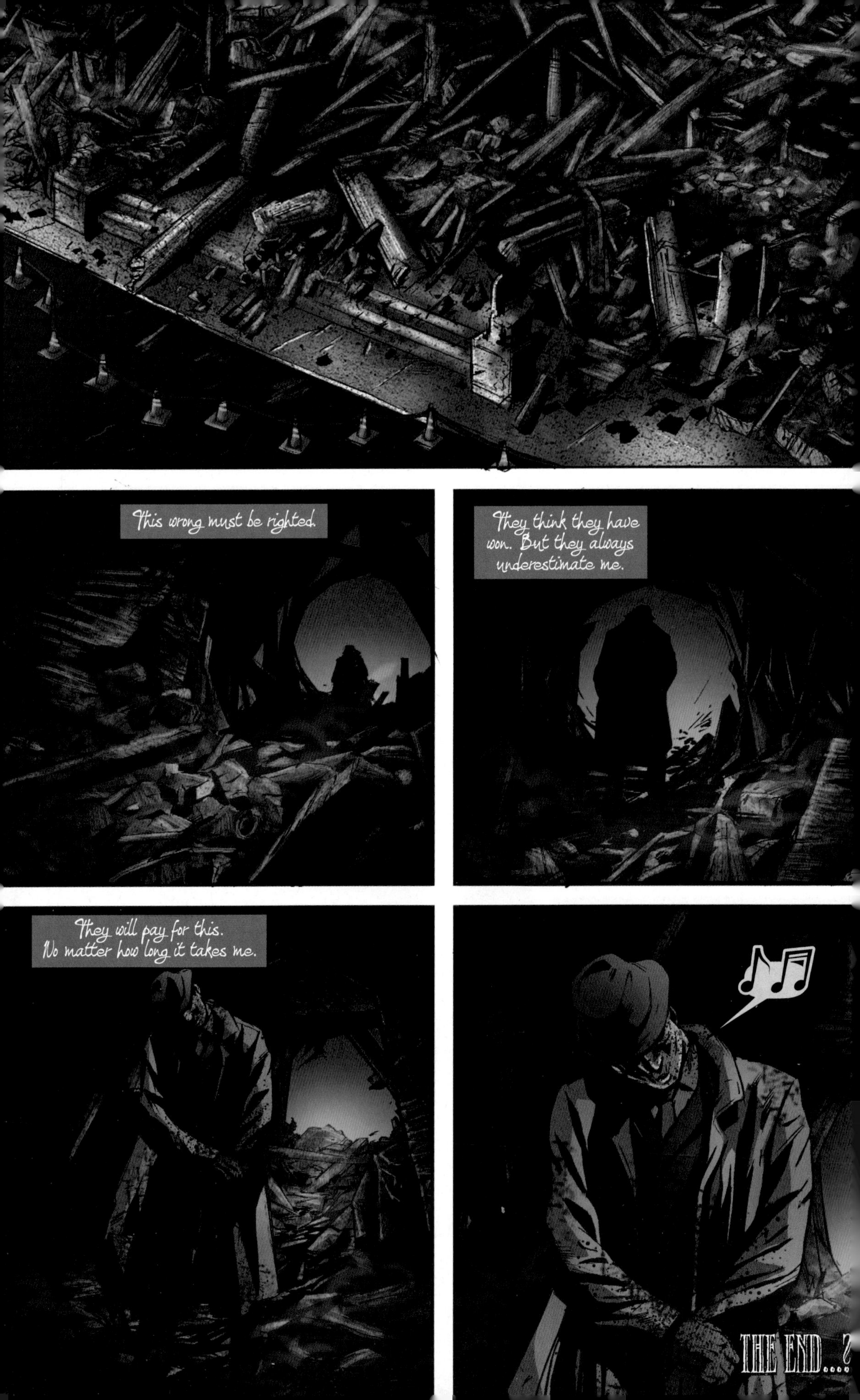
This wrong must be righted.
They think they have won. But they always underestimate me.
They will pay for this. No matter how long it takes me.
THE END...?